Dreams, Vampires and Ghosts

Also Available from Bloomsbury

Bollywood Horrors, Edited by Ellen Goldberg, Aditi Sen and Brian Collins
The Construction of the Supernatural in Euro-American Cultures, Benson Saler
Spiritual Sensations, Sarah K. Balstrup

Dreams, Vampires and Ghosts

*Anthropological Perspectives on the Sacred
and Psychology in Film and Television*

Louise Child

BLOOMSBURY ACADEMIC
LONDON • NEW YORK • OXFORD • NEW DELHI • SYDNEY

BLOOMSBURY ACADEMIC
Bloomsbury Publishing Plc
50 Bedford Square, London, WC1B 3DP, UK
1385 Broadway, New York, NY 10018, USA
29 Earlsfort Terrace, Dublin 2, Ireland

BLOOMSBURY, BLOOMSBURY ACADEMIC and the Diana logo are trademarks of
Bloomsbury Publishing Plc

First published in Great Britain 2023
This paperback edition published 2025

Cover design by Rebecca Heselton
Cover image: Leonora Carrington, The Q Symphony, 2002 © Estate of Leonora
Carrington / ARS, NY and DACS, London 2023

A catalogue record for this book is available from the British Library.

A catalog record for this book is available from the Library of Congress.

ISBN: HB: 978-1-3500-8710-1
PB: 978-1-3504-0248-5
ePDF: 978-1-3500-8711-8
eBook: 978-1-3500-8712-5

Typeset by Newgen KnowledgeWorks Pvt. Ltd., Chennai, India

To find out more about our authors and books visit.bloomsbury.com
and sign up for our newsletters.

Contents

Acknowledgements

This book has been germinating for a number of years and has been nourished along the way by many people. At the University of Leeds I was given kind and inspiring supervision by Professor Philip Mellor who got me excited about social theory and the concept of collective consciousness. Professor Hugh Pyper gave me my first opportunity to lead a university module and encouraged my enthusiasm for using film to teach the anthropology of religion. At Cardiff University I was given opportunities to build on this further with an undergraduate module on Myth and the Movies and an MA programme on Myth, Narrative and Theory. I want to thank all the students who participated in these modules and helped me to develop many of the ideas in this book with their questions and different ways of seeing the material. In particular I want to thank Dr Gina Bevan for the exciting discussions we had during her PhD supervision and Professor Laurence Totelin for her guidance as the senior supervisor. Cardiff University also gave me research leave in 2021–2 that was invaluable in completing this book. Anonymous reviews offered important insights and I also want to thank all of the team at Bloomsbury for their kind assistance and in particular Lalle Pursglove and Lily McMahon.

Professor Graham Harvey sparked my interest in contemporary animism which I was able to nourish through his numerous monographs and edited collections, and I also want to thank Professor Mary Keller whose work on spirit possession has been an inspiration. I was given opportunities to present papers at the British Association for the Study of Religion annual conferences, the New Interpretations of Spirit Possession conference convened by Professor Bettina Schmidt, GANZA (the Gothic Association of Australia and New Zealand), the Gothic Feminism project and Buffy + Studies. The opening up of online conferences and other activities has been instrumental in my thinking about popular film and television. The *Open Graves Open Minds* project run by Dr Sam George and Dr Bill Hughes is a wonderful example as is the Contemporary Gothic reading group run by the Department of English, Manchester Metropolitan University. I wanted to thank all the staff and students for their lively and stimulating conversations at these events. The website and YouTube channel *Romancing the Gothic* run by Dr Sam Hirst is something for which

I reserve a special mention. This entirely voluntary initiative has been a warm and welcoming online environment that has sustained many of us in difficult times and has opened up a wealth of new ideas and questions around equality and diversity issues and how to approach them.

On a more personal note I want to thank my family and especially Bob, Olive, Denise, Susan, Marion, Lesley, Rebecca and Louisa for all their kind help and support. I am also very lucky to have a wonderful chosen family who have kept the laughter and music flowing as well as numerous stimulating conversations about film and television. Thank you Martina, Nick, Sarah, Michael and Cecile. Lucilla, Darren and Helen kept me dancing and laughing in equal measure. I would like to conclude these acknowledgements with one of my earliest sources of inspiration. Thank you Mark, for introducing me to seeing films differently.

1

Dreaming: Anthropology, Psychology and the Study of Film and Television

Can popular films and television programs with ghosts tell us anything about religion in the societies in which they are made and watched? To what extent are the pleasures of modern gothic vampires related to emotions about blood, kinship, death and magic? Do depictions of dreams and dreaming on big and small screens always conform to Freudian theories' structures and meaning? These are some of the questions that are explored in this book, and they are questions that are informed by my engagement with the anthropology of religion. The aim here is to demonstrate that this sub-discipline has much to offer the study of film and television and that the inverse is also true, that film and television are important cultural artefacts deserving of the attention of anthropologists seeking to understand religion in the modern world.

My understandings of both religion and the visual narratives are broad in scope, and I suggest that this expansion of the field is heralded by some of the innovative work that precedes my own. While the study of religion and film was initially developed by reflections from the perspectives of world religions and thematic studies (see Blizek, 2009; Miles, 1996; Mitchell and Plate, 2007), scholars have also used concepts originating in the anthropology of religion in exciting ways to think about visual culture. Examples include using the sacred (as understood by Eliade, 1961) as a potential analytical concept for studying film (Bird, 1982); explorations of audience behaviour, including rituals and myths inspired by films and television, such as *Matrix* or *Star Trek* weddings (Plate, 2007: 428–31, 2008: 78–91); and even the suggestion that the practice of film viewing can be understood as a religion and that therefore 'the dialogue between religion and film is really just another form of interreligious dialogue' (Lyden, 2007: 416). The field has continued to expand and diversify with growing interests in wide-ranging visual and digital cultural phenomena, including the study of music videos (Bevan, 2021), innovations in visual ethnography

(Vecchi and Odorico, 2019) and gaming (Dudeck, 2019). Recent studies have demonstrated how developments in visual cultures have pushed the boundaries of what constitutes participant observation by including online forums on magic and shamanism (Puca, 2019 and 2020) and using online ethnography to demonstrate how processes that begin as creative writing online can also be regarded as mythmaking, challenging anthropologists of religion to re-examine their debates about the nature and definitions of belief (Asimos, 2020 and 2021).

Although I utilize some of the studies that anthropologists have made of fandom, unlike Clark's (2003) work, this book is focused on narrative, visual techniques and editing within film and television and is not the product of a participant observation study or series of interviews with fans. It is closer in approach to the work of Sutton and Wogan (2009: 3) who explain that their book 'provides a textual reading of Hollywood movies, rather than an ethnographic analysis of their production or reception by specific audiences'. In so doing I aim to offer a contribution from the perspective of the anthropology of religion to the study of popular cultures and the societies that enjoy them, albeit tentatively, given that even though I limit myself to English-language products of America and Europe, the communities receiving these visual narratives are large, diverse and multifaceted. Nonetheless, I suggest that the emphasis on the social offered by anthropology can offer the study of film and television a perspective that challenges, nuances and enters into interesting forms of dialogue with studies of visual media that have traditionally been more influenced by psychoanalytic perspectives.

On one level, this perspective takes the form of an 'ethnographic eye' over media content. This phrase forms part of the title of an excellent examination of anthropological documentary cinema (Grimshaw, 2001) that pays attention to this media in the context of debates about the role of sight in modernity (Grimshaw, 2001: 6–8, see also Child, 2020: 69–86). Grimshaw (2001: 16–31) also explores the rise of anthropology as a discipline and developments in the history of cinema more broadly, and given that the period between the late 1800s and the 1920s is also key to the early history of psychoanalysis, there are some interesting parallels to be drawn. However, in this context, I want to use the phrase 'ethnographic eye' to suggest potential contrasts between seeing and reading fictional films using methods influenced by psychoanalysis and methods informed by an immersion in anthropological texts. One example is the emphasis on a (usually male) protagonist whose viewpoint is often aligned with that of the camera (and thereby the audience of the film) and who drives the narrative action towards the attainment of passive females who are framed and gazed upon as objects of desire, as so famously critiqued by Mulvey (1999 [1975]) and De Laurentis (1984). These works provide fascinating insights into the ways in which Oedipal narratives were not only used by Freud to theorize the sources of psychological conflicts within individuals; they are also potentially so deeply embedded within the cultures that produced and consumed classical Hollywood film narratives that they can be regarded as part of the ideological hegemonies that reinforce gender as well as class dichotomies in society. However, I will suggest that anthropology offers alternative modes of reading films that can be combined in exciting ways with the insights of later film and television theorists to study the wider field of characters and how they form sub-groups and interact with one another as a society.

Secondly, this book pays special attention to themes and motifs in film and television that are also often found in ethnographic accounts of indigenous societies. These include ghosts, spirits and possession; alternate dimensions and the beings that inhabit them; and communicative dreaming. What many of these motifs have in common are examples of communicative, permeable personhood that recognizes and respects a wider range of persons than is common in Western modernity (including animal and spirit persons) and I will suggest that, although there are significant differences between indigenous ritual contexts and the depiction of these motifs in English-language film and television, there are enough points in common to suggest a rich engagement with notions of permeable personhood in cinema and television that potentially challenges the idea that secular individualism has superseded more religious and social understandings of what it means to be a person in the late twentieth and early twenty-first-century Europe and America. Instead, visual narratives often explore creative tensions between collective, religious perspectives and popular ideas about science, individualism and psychology. Despite the apparent predominance of psychological models of the individual in modern Western culture, there is a wealth of evidence to suggest that collective emotions and symbols are a source of vitality and hope, as well as anxiety and distrust.

One way of illustrating these points is to take a particular example – dreaming. Dreaming has long been a key theme in psychoanalytic approaches to the study of cinema (Lebeau, 2001: 32–60; Marcus, 2007), and several chapters in this book explore dreams and dream-like states in film and television and compare these depictions with psychological theories, such as those of Freud, as well as numerous accounts of indigenous societies recorded by ethnographers. Of particular interest is the ways in which theories about dreaming derived from Freud focus on the interior state of the dreamer, whereas anthropologists often uncover indigenous theories of dreaming that include ideas about an aspect of the person (often translated as soul) that can travel in dreams to visit humans, animals and spirits in this world and other dimensions, or alternatively other persons can visit the dreamer. Although these ideas are recorded in a range of anthropological accounts, a branch of anthropology called contemporary animism is of particular interest because it places emphasis on indigenous notions of permeable, communicative, personhood. However, the story of animism in anthropology does not begin with these theorists but with Tylor, a figure writing at the turn of the nineteenth and twentieth centuries, a period that I have already identified as key to the foundations of film, anthropology and psychology.

Dreaming and Animism: Tylor and Hallowell

Tylor famously espoused a theory of religion that took as a minimum definition 'the belief in Spiritual Beings' (Tylor, 2010 [1871], vol. 2: 383) and gives the term 'Animism' to describe doctrines related to a range of terms that are translated as soul by the anthropologists of his day that Tylor was using. He suggests that Animism is found almost universally in societies that he terms primitive but is also a bedrock (in diluted form) in religions of societies that he calls 'high modern culture'. The nature of the material he was exploring could have been classified under the term 'Spiritualism', but Tylor explains that this would be confusing as Spiritualism was a religious tradition in its own right that was popular in his time (Tylor, 2010 [1871]: 385). Thus, although Tylor did assert that all societies have religions, he nonetheless espoused a problematic evolutionary theory based on a questionable and under-theorized assumption that science had overtaken religion in industrially developed countries and that other societies are therefore examples of a past way of thinking and acting that is destined to disappear. This idea ignores the possibility that non-industrial societies have been subject to their own forms of change and have futures that include both participation in new technologies and indigenous religions, and Tylor's theories are therefore closely bound up with the colonial project and its assaults upon nations and ethnic groups. Moreover, indigenous religions have not disappeared in the wake of science and technological innovation. There is a wealth of scholarship that demonstrates the vibrancy of indigenous cultures and religions within modernity (e.g. Olupona, 2004) and one of the aims of this book is to argue that, on the contrary, film and television technologies have enabled creative projects that explore and highlight animist orientations to the world as well as ideas more commonly associated with psychology.

There are, nonetheless, aspects of Tylor's work that remain of interest and have been examined by recent scholarship (Tremlett, Sutherland and Harvey, 2017). Harvey, for example, explores the diversity of ways in which scholars use the word animism (2013: 1). Pointing to contrasts between different contemporary Pagan views that he wrote about in more detail in an article (Harvey, 1993), and later in a book (Harvey, 2006), he suggests that some Pagans describe encounters with tree, river or ancestor spirits, an animism that Harvey describes as metaphysical and one which would have been recognized by Tylor (Harvey, 2013: 2). However, 'other Pagans seemed to use "animism" as a shorthand reference to their efforts to re-imagine and redirect human participation in the larger-than-human, multi-species community. This animism was relational, embodied, eco-activist and often "naturalist" rather than metaphysical' (Harvey, 2013: 2).

Although the spirits and souls in Tylor's (2010 [1871]: 384) theories suggest a spiritual rather than material emphasis, they are nonetheless described as often having a subtle essence that can survive the death of the body in an apparitional or ghost soul. It resembles 'a vapor, film or shadow'. It is

> the cause of life and thought in the individual it animates; independently possessing the personal consciousness and volition of its corporeal owner, past or present; capable of leaving the body far behind to flash swiftly from place to place; mostly impalpable and invisible, yet also manifesting physical power, and especially appearing to men waking or asleep as a phantasm separate from the body of which it bears the likeness; able to enter into, possess, and act in the bodies of other men, of animals, and even of things. (Tylor, 2010 [1871]: 387)

According to Tylor (2010 [1871]: 387) this conception is used to explore questions about what animates the living body and distinguishes it from a dead one, and also what are the human shapes that appear in dreams and visions. This touches on numerous themes of interest in the context of this book, including dreams, possession trance, vampires (if conceived as a form of demonic possession) and communications with ghosts and spirits. For example, he cites ethnographic accounts in which the soul can temporarily exit the body and go out hunting, dancing and visiting with other humans, animals and spirits, including those in the land of the dead (2010 [1871]: 397–8). Moreover, the inverse is also possible so that 'human souls can come from without to visit the dreamer who sees them as dreams' (Tylor, 2010 [1871]: 399).

Although the wealth of examples that Tylor offers is interesting, his theorizing is more problematic, suggesting that indigenous peoples have 'excessive superstitiousness. Their imaginations become so lively that they can scarcely distinguish between their dreams and their waking thoughts, between the real and ideal, and they consequently utter falsehood without intending, and profess to see things which never existed' (Tylor, 2010 [1871]: 400). This is connected to an evolutionary train of thought where he suggests that 'dream-apparitions may be traced in progress of gradual determination, from the earlier conviction that a disembodied soul really comes into the presence of the sleeper, toward the later opinion that such a phantasm is produced in the dreamer's mind without the perception of any external objective figure' (Tylor, 2010 [1871]: 402). This idea, that the origin of dream images is within the dreamer, precedes Freud's (2001 [1900]) *Interpretation of Dreams* by about thirty years, but nonetheless has much in common with it and suggests something about the intellectual milieux in which Freud was working.

However, there is also a conviction here that indigenous peoples, even when awake have 'never learnt to make that rigid distinction between subjective and objective, between imagination and reality, to enforce which is one of the main results of scientific education' (Tylor, 2010 [1871]: 402). Many later scholars who are interested in animism take issue with this assumption, which, together with Tylor's dismissal of indigenous beliefs in souls of 'lower animals' (Tylor, 2010 [1871]: 422–3) impoverishes his work.

Bird-David (2002 [1999]: 73–5), for example, reviews how numerous scholars have continued to use the term animism in ways reminiscent of Tylor's writings and argues for a rethinking of the concept in the light of a wealth of more detailed and culturally sensitive ethnography. Calling for a critical revision of the term, she highlights Tylor's approach as grounded in a cultural landscape of Euro-American modernism that took certain conceptions of personhood for granted, including ideas that limit personhood to humans, and dualisms between matter and spirit (Bird-David, 2002 [1999]: 75). When he encountered different models of personhood in the ethnographies he was reading, as well as in Spiritualist séances in Europe that he was able to investigate firsthand in London (Kalvig, 2017; Stocking, 1971), Tylor explained these differences in terms of evolution, so that although the ethnographies of indigenous peoples he was reading, as well as his observation of Spiritualism, were based on observations in his era, he nonetheless dismissed both as based on 'primitive' delusions (Bird-David, 2002 [1999]: 78). Bird-David suggests a very different strategy; namely, adjusting the theoretical tools to better understand the material gleaned from ethnographic studies, and the key concept she advocates re-evaluating is that of personhood. Drawing from both Strathern (1988) and Hallowell (2002 [1960]), she suggests utilizing more rigorously the indigenous modes of thinking about personhood, including the relational emphasis of many social groups who understand self in terms of actions in social and natural environments, rather than focusing on modernist conceptions of ontology and belief (Bird-David, 2002 [1999]: 76–7).

Hallowell, whose work is often cited as a key inspiration for contemporary animist studies (Harvey, 2005: 20), was an anthropologist who worked in the early to mid-twentieth century in southern central Canada engaging with the Ojibwa peoples located east of Lake Winnipeg along the Berens River in the eastern part of the province of Manitoba and western Ontario (Hallowell, 1976 [1966]: 453–4). He noticed that Ojibwa languages have nouns that are designated animate or inanimate. While this could be a purely linguistic designation (much as, e.g. the gendering of nouns in French is), Hallowell was intrigued and wanted to know if there were more profound links with Ojibwa world views. Study of the subject, including conversations with his informants, suggested that the animate/inanimate dichotomy commonly found in modernist Western conceptions of the world did not hold true for the Ojibwa, and by extension dichotomies between natural and supernatural did not apply either (Hallowell, 2002 [1960]: 22–3). Instead, the significant category is the designation of persons, who are not defined by being human but by their participation in webs of relationships that include reciprocity, mutual obligations, and responsibility. He includes a range of examples, such as the response of one man to his question about whether stones were alive (because they are grammatically animate) to which the man responded 'No! But *some* are' (Hallowell, 2002 [1960]: 24). Similarly thunder and lightning are personified, and the Thunder Bird is an example of a powerful person (Hallowell, 2002 [1960]: 30–3). He also explores metamorphosis, a phenomenon that is common in Ojibwa stories and is underpinned by the idea that appearances can be deceptive. What is important is the vital part or soul, so that a human soul may be clothed temporarily in an animal's body, for example, or the soul may travel and appear to another person in the form of an animal (Hallowell, 2002 [1960]: 37). Powerful *ätíso'kanak* (a particular kind of other-than-human person) can also visit human persons in dreams and offer gifts derived from their power, but the social rules of sharing, reciprocity, balance and fairness that govern the Ojibwa social world include social interactions with other-than-human beings (Hallowell, 2002 [1960]: 39–42). Dreams are therefore understood as actual experiences of a self that participates within wider social and cultural contexts including other-than-human persons such as animals, thunder and powerful soul/spirit entities (Hallowell, 1976 [1966]: 453).

In a key essay on the subject, he suggests that the Ojibwa culture does not have the same kind of dichotomy between dreaming and waking experience that prevails in the anthropologist's own mainstream American culture and that the 'reality' of dream figures and events is more present for the Ojibwa (Hallowell, 1976 [1966]: 452). The examples he gives demonstrate contrasting perspectives to those shaped by conventional Freudian psychology. In one dream, figures were identified as symbolic of the analyst, but the patient still asked the analyst where he went after he disappeared from the patient's dream (Hallowell, 1976 [1966]: 452, Devereaux, 1951: 86). In another example, he explores indigenous Papuan people who had apparently been converted to Christianity and expressed that they were aware that they were not responsible for their dream content, but nonetheless confessed adultery that had only occurred in their dreams (Hallowell, 1976 [1966]: 452–3, Deveraux, 1951: 86).

Work by Tuzin (1975), an anthropologist working with the Ilahita Arapesh people of Papua New Guinea, notes a similar phenomenon among them, whereby a female member of the group interprets adulterous dreams as being the result of deliberate sorcery on the part of her co-dream-adulterer. Tuzin weaves some interesting blends of psychoanalytic and social anthropological interpretation into his analysis of the phenomena, but the key point is the assumption on the part of the indigenous dreamers that dreams are not merely internal projections, but that they may contain elements that originate outside the dreamer, including communications with other persons (Tuzin, 1975: 564). Moreover, it is of interest that Tuzin (1975: 1–2) begins his article with a discussion of Tylor's (2010 [1871]) work.

Hallowell (1976 [1966]: 454–5) is careful to distinguish his own analysis from that of Tylor, arguing that attributing an objective reality to key dream persons and happenings does not equal an inability to make distinctions between imagination and reality. On the contrary, some of these distinctions are essential for physical survival and rather than making assumptions about peoples as primitive and using unhelpful, oversimplified, linear subject/object dichotomies, he suggests instead a much more nuanced and subtle approach that accounts for how differences in cultural environment can produce different understandings of self and orientations of self to social worlds. Further to this, he suggests that the orientation between self and other in Ojibwa society

> is elaborated with particular emphasis upon the interaction of 'persons' in a 'society' that is cosmic in scope … but they are unified by traditionally

established rights and obligations. There are two categories of the 'person' class which can be differentiated: human beings and other than human persons. While animals, plants, and inanimate objects constitute other classes of being in the Ojibwa world, 'persons' are the focal point of their ontology and the key to the psychological unity and dynamics of their outlook. (Hallowell, 1976 [1966]: 455–6)

Much of the social interaction with other-than–human persons happens in dreams, and these experiences are understood in social terms rather than as messages from one aspect of the self to another (Hallowell, 1976 [1966]: 456). Hallowell (1976 [1966]: 456–7) is careful not to use the term 'supernatural' when describing interaction with dream entities because a dichotomy between natural and supernatural is an inappropriate distinction in the context of Ojibwa culture. Similarly, the outward appearance of beings is not always thought to tell the whole story. Hallowell explores the example of the Thunderbird, who is usually avian in form but who can metamorphose and become human in appearance (Hallowell, 1976 [1966]: 458–9). Although some of his evidence comes from storytelling traditions that might be labelled as myth in a Western academic context, Hallowell explains that for the Ojibwa, myths are not fiction. Not only do they relate the past adventures of other-than-human persons, but their telling also evokes these persons. Myths themselves are personified as they are collectively referred to as 'our grandfathers' (Hallowell, 1976 [1966]: 460). Moreover, when an other-than-human person appears to someone in a dream, he addresses them as 'my grandchild', suggesting, according to Hallowell, 'the unity of thought which prevails in anecdote, myth, and dream (Hallowell, 1976 [1966]: 457–8). Although there are some specialists who can communicate with other-than-human persons in a 'conjuring performance' (Hallowell, 1976 [1966]: 459), the appearance of other-than-human persons in dreams is relatively commonplace and the interactions with these 'dream visitors', far from being metaphorical, form an important part of Ojibwa social relations as well as personal well-being (Hallowell, 1976 [1966]: 461). This approach to dreaming that emphasizes its capacity for communication with other beings contrasts starkly with Freudian approaches.

Psychology and dreaming: Freud and Jung

For Freud, the key to dream interpretation lies in a process of analysis that people can do for themselves, but which is often most productive when they are speaking to a psychoanalyst. In this process the person tries to remember the dream itself as clearly as possible, documenting what Freud terms the manifest contents of the dream. Secondly, the dreamer searches for associations between the dream and thoughts and events in their lives, the latent content (Freud, 2001 [1901]: 635–41). Freud argues that the dream has taken the latent content and 'worked' it in various ways, so that, for example, multiple ideas and emotions are condensed into a few symbols or happenings in the dream (Freud, 2001 [1901]: 642–53; Ewing, 2003: 46). The principal aim of this work is to both express and partially disguise the wishes of the dreamer, which in Freud's view are most often sexual in nature (Freud, 2001 [1901]: 671–5). The more the wish is forbidden from the perspective of the conscious mind, the more distorted and obscure the dream material, but its meaning is nonetheless accessible through analysis.

Key to Freud's method of dream analysis is that it is focused on the individual. The precise nature of the disguised wish in the dream is related to the particularities of an individual's life. This is one of the reasons why, early in *The Interpretation of Dreams*, Freud dismisses oracular means of interpreting dreams and in particular dream divination through books that suggest a very limited number of interpretations for each dream symbol (Freud, 2001 [1900]: 1–5). For Freud, it is not gods, ancestors or spirits who communicate with us through dreams, but our personal unconscious that indicates repressed wishes and desires. Although he suggests these desires have broadly similar structures, such as the Oedipus complex, the associations and significance of dream symbols are unique to the individual and the specific circumstances in their lives.

Freud's exploration of the Classical Greek legend of Oedipus Rex and the play by Sophocles of the same name is significant here because a number of film theorists explore the Oedipal dynamics of film plots. Freud explains that Oedipus is abandoned and left to die at the behest of his father, King Laius of Thebes, because of an oracle that predicted that the child would murder his father and marry his mother. The child survives and is adopted, but he is unaware of this, and when, as a young man, he also hears an oracle predicting the same fate, he tries to escape it by running away, unwittingly killing his real father in a fight in the road and marrying his widow, Jocasta. Although Freud mentions the significance of the oracle to the ancient Greeks and the tension in the play between the will of the gods and the attempts of people to escape their destiny, he argues that the play's real significance is not oracular but in the repressed wishes in all of us that the play explores (Freud, 2001 [1900]: 261–4).

The Freudian emphasis on wish fulfilment as an explanation for dreaming is thus very different to explanations explored by anthropologists, particularly those studying indigenous societies practising traditional religions. Ewing (2003: 45) explores differences between indigenous dream practices and theories and Freudian approaches, arguing that 'Freud thus clearly distinguished his scientific search for causes from traditional forms of dream interpretation, which often claimed to be oracular or predictive. Suggesting that dreams could predict the future was, in his opinion, necessarily unscientific.'

Jung (2002 [1948]: 65) utilizes many aspects of Freudian dream analysis but argues that Freud's emphasis on wish fulfilment and sexuality as the sole roots of the interpretation of dreams is too narrow and that the whole psyche with its multiplicity of instincts and needs should be taken into account. Instead, he compares dream motifs with mythological ones arguing that both are expressions of archaic modes of thought (Jung, 2002 [1948]: 35–6) and suggesting that the dream is 'a spontaneous self-portrayal, in symbolic form, of the actual situation of the unconscious' (Jung, 2002 [1948]: 51). Jung explains that images in dreams (what he terms *imago*), including those of people the dreamer knows, should not necessarily be understood as relating directly to those people, but rather carry symbolic weight, often pointing to aspects of the dreamer's own personality (Jung, 2002 [1948]: 54). This process, of projecting parts of oneself onto other people (Jung, 2002 [1948]: 52–3), can cloud people's judgements, but, if recognized, can provide vital clues to processes of healing and wholeness (Jung, 2002 [1948]: 47).

Further to this, Jung explains how projected elements may be from the unconscious personal experiences and emotions of a person, but he suggests an additional source of projected contents, 'the manifestations of a deeper layer of the unconscious where the primordial images common to humanity lie sleeping' the *collective unconscious* (1966 [1943]: 65–6). Common motifs that arise from this layer include wizards, demons and goddesses that populate religions and mythologies and he terms these images 'archetypes' (Jung, 1966 [1943]: 64, 77). He explains that, 'the primordial images are the most ancient and the most universal "thought-forms" of humanity. They are as much feelings as thoughts; indeed, they lead their own independent life rather in the manner of part souls' (Jung, 1966 [1943]: 66). While their emergence can be a sign that the person is undergoing a positive spiritual transformation, their appearance also has its dangers, partly because the images are of evil as well as good beings, but also because, 'owing to their specific energy – for they behave like highly charged autonomous centres of power – they exert a fascinating and possessive influence upon the conscious mind' (Jung, 1966 [1943]: 70).

The argument in brief

Key, therefore, to these different approaches to the study of dreaming are different ideas about personhood. Ewing (2003: 48) suggests that 'psychoanalytic theory has removed the social dimension of dreaming except in the highly circumscribed setting of the private psychotherapy session – because it is an approach that is itself intellectually shaped by our cultural understandings, social pressures, and scientific perspective, all of which presume and constitute individuals with private interiors'. Where Freudian psychology regards people as comparatively hermetically sealed, animist world views tend to focus more on the web of relations that not only *surround* the person, but actually constitute personhood. Dreams in these societies may enable 'soul' or 'spirit' travel for the dreamer who can experience alternate dimensions, dream worlds or their own environment from a different perspective (such as an animal's). Alternatively, the dreamer may be visited by animal, deity or ancestor beings or spirits who offer advice or lend the dreamer powers. Whereas both Freud and his contemporary Tylor dismissed animism as primitive, a mistaken attribution of life and soul to natural phenomena where in their opinion there was none (Harvey, 2005: 5–11), there are a growing number of scholars analysing religion who observe the dynamism of animistic religions in the late twentieth and early twenty-first centuries (Harvey, 2005). Although the emphasis of these developments has been in the study of indigenous religions, there are examples of animist studies of European religious practices (Whitehead, 2013), literature (Curry, 2013; Germaine, 2013) and Japanese animated film (Brienza, 2013).

The aim of this book is both to offer anthropological and in particular animist insights into the study of film and television and to explore ways in which these insights offer a contrast to models of film analysis informed by Freudian psychology. In doing so, it is important to note that while this contrast is useful for the purposes of analysis, there are in fact many good anthropological texts that combine ethnographic techniques and theory with the insights of psychology (Heelas and Lock, 1981; Stephen, 1995). Moreover, the book will also explore Jungian approaches to film analysis, arguing that in some ways Jung's conception of the *collective unconscious* places his work at a midway point between the Freudian emphasis on the individual and the social focus of indigenous traditions that regard the individual as comparatively porous. Moreover, although Jung's theories contain some evolutionary elements, including an interest in Tylor that carries with it unhelpful dismissals of animism in indigenous contexts (Jung,

2002 [1948]: 60; Stephenson, 2009: 44), there are also features that have more in common with later twentieth-century anthropological thinking, particularly in his openness to considering spirits and possession (Stephenson, 2009: 66–7).

Chapter 2 begins with a more detailed analysis of how Freud has been used in film, starting with examples of classical Hollywood Cinema through the works of the director Alfred Hitchcock. Although his films have many unique qualities, they were also shaped by the Hollywood studio system and he, in turn, helped to shape many of the features we tend to associate with classical Hollywood (1935–60). In contrast with later television productions, where large writing teams with different people working on different episodes are common, Hitchcock is known for his control over relatively formal narrative and technical styles, such as his use of storyboarding to represent each scene visually in considerable detail prior to filming (Moral, 2005: 67–72). The chapter focuses on two films, *Spellbound* (1945), produced by David O. Selznick, and *Marnie* (1964) with Universal Pictures, both of which demonstrate Hitchcock's considerable interest in psychology, including traumatic experiences and Freudian interpretations of dreaming. I argue that although several elements in these films utilize a genuine engagement with psychology (one which helped to shape how future films and television treated the subject), they also raise important questions about the power dynamics of the therapeutic process, in particular by conflating the roles of doctor and lover in both films.

The films also exemplify the idea that dreams are private, and rarely shared beyond descriptions to one other person (most often a therapist). However, anthropological studies suggest that many societies regard dream sharing as a cultural event that can involve whole groups of people (Tedlock, 2001; Vishvajit, 2004). This kind of sharing activity can serve social purposes, such as success in hunting. Dreaming can also be social in the sense that it can enable communications with the dead, spirits and deities (Stewart and Strathern, 2003), a quality that has given dreams an important role in many religious traditions (Bulkeley, 1999, 2008; O' Flaherty, 2015; Pick and Roper, 2004; Shulman and Stroumsa, 1999).

Hitchcock's films such as *Vertigo* (1958), *Marnie* (1964) and *Rear Window* (1954) are also among the examples used in a key feminist study of classical Hollywood film by Laura Mulvey (1999 [1975]: 66). The control that Hitchcock exercised over plot direction, composing of scenes and the images of women on screen make his work an excellent example of the alignment of the director, the camera and thus the spectator of films with the male gaze which Mulvey associates with sadistic drives. Mulvey's work has been both utilized and critiqued by feminist film theorists, but it also provokes questions about ways of seeing and gender when the mode of telling visual stories changes. For example, what happens in serial television when the single director is replaced with large directorial and writing teams, and in which multiple characters are given development and viewpoint. An article by Modleski (1979) highlights specific features of serial soap operas, for example. In contrast to the single controlling figure driving the narrative in many films, soap operas tend to have more open-ended plots, and 'insist on the insignificance of the individual life. A viewer might at one moment be asked to identify with a woman finally reunited with her lover, only to have that identification broken in a moment of intensity and attention focused on the sufferings of the woman's rival' (Modleski, 1979: 14). This constant switching of attention between individual characters and assessing their place in a larger web of relationships, is, I suggest, more like an anthropologist's way of seeing, and I therefore go on to explore its possibilities in two groundbreaking serial dramas, *Twin Peaks* (1990–1) and *Buffy the Vampire Slayer* (1997–2003).

Chapter 3 focuses on *Twin Peaks*, which, as Jowett and Abbott (2013: 159) note, has been heralded as a particularly innovative example of Quality Television. One of its defining features is the way it combines multiple genres using melodrama as a base that is melded at different times with the detective show, the gothic and horror (Jowett and Abbott, 2013: 160–5). Key to their analysis is *Twin Peaks'* use of surrealism and dream worlds, which they argue undermine the conventions of linear narrative and 'unravel the boundaries between dream and reality', creating a space in which 'the barriers that restrain emotion are broken down' (Jowett and Abbott, 2013: 163, 165).

These characteristics, together with its myriad of characters make *Twin Peaks* a good example to explore using an anthropological analysis. In addition, there are ways in which personhood is attributed to animals and the Log Lady's Log in the series that suggest animist perspectives. Moreover, other-worldly beings appear to Agent Cooper in dreams and visions, and he is thought to have had a telepathic dream with the murder victim, Laura Palmer, that defies the confines of narrower Freudian interpretations of the significance and nature of dream phenomena.

However, aspects of the series such as BOB the demon fit less well with animist interpretations, and the chapter therefore utilizes the analytical psychology of Jung to examine them. Ideas about archetypes such as the shadow and the anima help to explore the relationship between Leland Palmer and BOB the demon who possesses him and commits crimes against his daughter,

Laura. Scholars such as Izod propose Jungian analyses of films, in part because of Jung's interest in emotion (termed often by Jung as *affect*) and mythology, interests easily transferred to mythological storytelling in visual media and potentially amplified by comparative analysis of stories, characters and plots across a range of cultural settings (Izod, 2001: 7). Jung's analysis of emotion is also highly relevant to this study because of his suggestion that emotions can possess the individual, rather than the other way around (Izod, 2001: 7). This use of the analogy of possession makes Jung an apt theorist to utilize in examining storylines that include spiritual or demonic possession.

Moreover, Jung is a potentially very useful theorist for film noir storylines, as the villain can be seen as a shadow figure and key heroines, particularly the femme fatale, act like anima archetypes. However, when characters are read as aspects of a single person's psyche (see, e.g. Hockley, 2001: 114–20) it can lead to a focus on a single male protagonist, who, instead of relating to those around him as fully fledged social individuals, is thought to be relating only to other parts of themselves. This imbalance can lead to female characters being subsumed as aspects of men. This tendency can be seen in *Twin Peaks*, in which Laura is the most obvious anima figure, but all the female characters are idealized figures and often the objects of violence. I therefore examine a series in the following chapter in which the central protagonist is a heroine and where many of the other characters have more sophisticated narrative arcs and emotional development, *Buffy the Vampire Slayer*.

Chapter 4 continues with a focus on television media, but instead of a film noir/soap opera it explores an episodic gothic melodrama, *Buffy the Vampire Slayer*. The gender balance in this series is different to that in *Twin Peaks* because the central protagonist is a young woman and many of the characters around her are developed with fully fledged storylines and backstories that give them emotional depth and development. Wilcox and Lavery's (2002: xxii, xxiii) analysis of what makes 'Quality TV' points to a large ensemble cast and a 'memory' in which characters and relationships develop and refer back to significant incidents. In the context of the television series that they explore, *Buffy the Vampire Slayer*, the audience is given an opportunity to see interactions between different characters that other characters are not privy to, offering a vantage point not unlike that of an anthropologist who observes a multiplicity of perspectives. This chapter explores in some depth interactions within the *Buffyverse* (the show's social and cosmological world) considering how social groups such as Buffy's school friends, the grown-ups and the vampires engage with one another through the lens of gender and with particular reference to the *Bluebeard* fairy tale.

While excellent histories of the vampire such as Groom (2018) explore the vampire's roots in folklore and medieval Christianity, I suggest that *Buffy the Vampire Slayer* has more in common with its gothic literary and cinematic heritage. Morrison and Baldick's (1998: ix) introduction to Polidari's (1998 [1819]) book, *The Vampyre*, explores its place within romantic writing circles that included Byron. Its central aristocratic vampiric character, Lord Ruthven, is in stark contrast to the vampires of folklore. Myths in Serbia and Hungary, for example, depicted the monsters as 'bloated, shaggy, foul-smelling corpses' of peasants', while Polidori's work was innovative in its depiction of the aristocratic vampire and his seductive charm, and this innovation would influence the majority of film and literary portraits that followed (Morrison and Baldick, 1998: xii).

Williamson (2005: 36–8) also points to the influence of Byron and the romantic creative circle in the development of the literary and film vampire. She explains that this goes beyond Byron and Polidori's writings and extends to the ways in which Byron and his exploits had captured the popular imagination and created the figure of the artistic bohemian, so that the vampire also took on characteristics of a flawed, rebellious hero, including 'glamorous outsiderdom, morose fatalism, social and artistic rebellion' (Williamson, 2005: 36–7). From this evolved the sympathetic vampire in gothic melodramas such as *Interview with a Vampire* (1994) and *Buffy the Vampire Slayer* (Williamson, 2005: 40) who embodies more sophisticated explorations of good and evil that are particularly suited to the serial drama format and its 'shifting perspectives and extended middles that, as many feminists have noted in relation to soap opera, contribute to the moral complications that surround characters' (Williamson, 2005: 48).

In *Buffy the Vampire Slayer*, these moral complications are explored through a combination of psychological metaphors and a mythology in which vampires have had their souls displaced by demonic entities. The vampire Angel embodies dilemmas associated with the sympathetic vampire. Re-ensouled by a curse, he fights vampires with the heroine Buffy and becomes her boyfriend, but the curse is lifted when they consummate their relationship, and Angel's soul is once again replaced with a demon, turning him into his evil Angelus persona, one of her most dangerous enemies. The show thus explores the shadow but offers the perspective of a woman torn between loyalty to her lover and her duty to fight his shadow-side counterpart. Moreover, it explores ways in which she is the object of his projections and her responses to this dilemma, a plotline that evokes *Bluebeard* fairy tales and their incarnations in gothic literature and film. By using an ethnographic eye, the chapter's analysis extends to the cast of characters surrounding the heroine, many of whom also explore shadow sides to their personalities. This wider observation of Buffy's social circle facilitates a deeper exploration of how patriarchy works to transmit mechanisms of projection across generations.

While both *Buffy the Vampire Slayer* and *Twin Peaks* use the fictional trope of demonic possession to explore the nature of evil and human personhood, Chapter 5 offers anthropological analyses of possession rituals from fieldwork observations that often have much more positive connotations because the possessing agent is a spirit, deity or ancestor who offers help and advice to the community. Rather than an affliction, possession can be a ritual skill and mediums are valued by their communities (Brown, 2001 [1991]). Because the most common instances of positive communications with spirits in English-language film and television are found in the ghostly romance genre, this chapter examines films such as *Ghost* (1990), and how they depict suspensions of disbelief when loved ones encounter ghosts and only gradually accept their reality. This ambivalence may reflect mixed attitudes to ghosts and the afterlife in European and American audiences, given that within these societies Spiritualist churches thrive and philosophical speculation about the afterlife is not uncommon, although that speculation may have mixed degrees of religious roots and may itself be partly shaped by modern media and fiction, including film (Deacy, 2012). These tensions can also be found in ghost films that simultaneously appear anti-Spiritualist but also 'attest to the fascination of the cinematic supernatural' (Leeder, 2017: 353).

A different approach is taken by scholars such as Bronfen (2017) who draw from Freud's psychological theories to examine how characters' engagement with ghosts and ghost stories are bound up with complex notions of seeing, revealing and trauma. One of the most famous of Freud's (2001 [1919]) essays, *The Uncanny*, has been particularly useful for scholars exploring ghosts on film, but this chapter critiques the assumption within this essay that engagements with spirits are incompatible with modernity and are therefore receding (with the exception of unusual personal crises in individuals). On the contrary, modernity and modern media have merely become new vehicles of dissemination and exploration of a range of spirit traditions globally (Behrend, Dreschke and Zillenger, 2015).

Moreover, although many global spirit traditions include deities as well as spirits of the deceased, both kinds of possession or spirit encounter are rooted in social communication. This chapter therefore examines examples of deity possession traditions, with particular reference to African and the

African diaspora, examining debates about the relationship between deities and their mediums, and exploring how racial prejudice has influenced the misrepresentation of them in popular film. Moreover, it argues that anxieties in ghost films and anxieties around African religion have common roots because they are both forms of porous social behaviour and personhood that challenge conceptions of the hermetically sealed individual that is idealized as part of the ideologies of Western late capitalism and colonialism.

Chapter 6 explores this ambivalence from another angle. Examining the past life backstory of *Bram Stoker's Dracula* (1992) and depictions of thrall and mesmerism in *Dracula* (1931) and *Dracula's Daughter* (1936), it suggests that part of the attraction of the vampiric fiends in these films is their capacity for forms of *collective consciousness* with the film's heroines. This idea is a development of Durkheim's thesis in *The Elementary Forms of Religious Life* (1995 [1912]) in which he argued that the vitality of social life is charged by social energies that uplift and transcend individuals who participate in a collective consciousness that is in tension with individual identity. While recognizing the dangers of the volatility of social energies, so that, for example, he used the term contagion to describe the way in which these energies can sweep through a society and potentially result in chaotic and barbaric collective behaviour, Durkheim (1995 [1912]: 321–9) also saw them as the foundation of social life, held in check, but not eradicated by mechanisms of social order.

Scholars have built on Durkheim's ideas to suggest ways in which the romantic couple can be thought of as part of this broader social dynamic and as also having a mini collective consciousness in itself. Mellor (2002) has examined this idea in relation to marriage and mad love (as understood by the surrealist movement) while Child (2007) has utilized it to examine the consort relationship in tantric Buddhism.

This chapter examines the depictions of mad love on film, and its one-sided role in homicide and vampire narratives, arguing that while the dangers of the irrational energies between the couple are highlighted, the pleasures of shared social vitality are only alluded to as illicit because they are shaped by discourses around desire and relationships that are founded upon structures of patriarchy and heteronormativity. The fact that lesbianism was so often linked to crime and vampirism in twentieth-century cinema while healthy and loving lesbian relationships were largely absent from the screen is one example (Wilts, 2009: 54). Nonetheless, the attractions of boundary-breaking passions are glimpsed even when the heroine is restored to the loving arms of patriarchy in the form of a conventional male suitor at the end of the film because, as

Weinstock (2012: 34) drawing from Benshoff (1997) suggests, once introduced to the delights of transgression, they can remain with audiences long after the monster has been staked. 'Mad love', even when it is depicted between persons of opposite sexes, such as in *Bram Stoker's Dracula* (1992) offers assertions of past life connections and shared dreams that are a source of disquiet in these films but are also compelling because of their roots in social phenomena.

Moreover, shared dreams and visions can participate in the fabric of social life in some indigenous societies who regard them as part of their system of gifts and obligations that order their social world, because these govern both humans' behaviours towards one another and exchanges with animal, nature and spirit persons. This point is related to Saler's (1977) observation that the 'supernatural' is a Western category that should not be clumsily applied in indigenous contexts where other-than-human persons are understood to be part of the natural world.

While I explore ghosts and spirits in indigenous films elsewhere (Child, 2020), my aim in this book is to suggest that tensions expressed in popular films about passionate relationships and shared visions are indicative of anxieties about porous, boundary-breaking energies that are actually part of the social fabric itself. Different societies shape and reflect upon that fabric in different ways, but the creative works of film and television are often the best clues, in modern Western societies, to the continued attractions of connections and communications that are part of social being, and that cannot be fully explained by psychoanalytic theories of the individual.

Bibliography

Asimos, V. (2020) 'Everything is true here even if it isn't: The performance of belief online', *JBASR: The Journal of the British Association for the Study of Religion*, vol. 22, pp. 44–54.

Asimos, V. (2021) *Digital Mythology and the Internet's Monster: The Slender Man*. London: Bloomsbury Academic.

Behrend, H., Dreschke, A., and Zillinger, M. (eds) (2015) *Trance Mediums and New Media: Spirit Possession in the Age of Technical Production*. New York: Fordham University Press.

Benshoff, H. (1997) *Monsters in the Closet: Homosexuality and the Horror Film*. Manchester: Manchester University Press.

Bevan, G. (2021) 'Pop! Medusa: The reappropriation of the Gorgon in pop music'. Thesis Submitted for Doctor of Philosophy (Religious and Theological Studies). Cardiff: Cardiff University.

Bird, M. (1982) 'Film as hierophany', in J. R. May and M. Bird (eds), *Religion in Film*. Knoxville: University of Tennessee Press, pp. 3–22.

Bird-David (2002 [1999]) ' "Animism" revisited: Personhood, environment and relational epistemology', in G. Harvey (ed.), *Readings in Indigenous Religions*. London: Continuum, pp. 72–105.

Blizek, W. L. (ed.) (2009) *The Continuum Companion to Religion and Film*. London: Continuum.

Brienza, C. (2013) 'Objects of *otaku* affection: Animism, *anime* fandom, and the gods of … consumerism?', in G. Harvey (ed.), *The Handbook of Contemporary Animism*. Durham: Acumen, pp. 479–90.

Briggs, J. L. (1970) *Never in Anger: Portrait of an Eskimo Family*. Cambridge, MA: Harvard University Press.

Bronfen, E. (2017) 'Enchanted visions: Ghostly media from E.T.A. Hoffman to Alfred Hitchcock', in S. Brewster and L. Thurston (eds), *The Routledge Handbook to the Ghost Story*. London: Routledge, pp. 361–9.

Brown, K. M. (2001 [1991]) *Mama Lola: A Vodou Priestess in Brooklyn*. Berkeley: University of California Press.

Bulkeley, K. (1999) *Visions of the Night: Dreams, Religion and Psychology*. Albany: State University of New York Press.

Bulkeley, K. (2008) *Dreaming in the World's Religions: A Comparative History*. New York: New York University Press.

Charet, F. X. (1993) *Spiritualism and the Foundations of C. G. Jung's Psychology*. Albany: State University of New York Press.

Child, L. (2007) *Tantric Buddhism and Altered States of Consciousness: Durkheim, Emotional Energy and Visions of the Consort*. Aldershot: Ashgate.

Child, L., and Rosen, A. (eds) (2020) *Religion and Sight*. Sheffield: Equinox.

Child, L. (2020) 'Sensing reelism: Portals to multiple realities and relationships in world, indigenous and documentary cinema', in L. Child and A. Rosen (eds), *Religion and Sight*. Sheffield: Equinox, pp. 69–86.

Clark, L. S. (2003) *From Angels to Aliens: Teenagers, the Media, and the Supernatural*. New York: Oxford University Press.

Creed, B. (1993) *The Monstrous Feminine: Film, Feminism, Psychoanalysis*. London: Routledge.

Creed, B. (2005) *Phallic Panic: Film, Horror and the Primal Uncanny*. Melbourne: Melbourne University Press.

Curry, P. (2013) 'The third road: Faërie in hypermodernity', in G. Harvey (ed.), *The Handbook of Contemporary Animism*. Durham: Acumen, pp. 468–78.

Deacy, C. (2012) *Screening the Afterlife: Theology, Eschatology and Film*. London: Routledge.

De Laurentis, T. (1984) *Alice Doesn't: Feminism, Semiotics, Cinema*. London: Macmillan.

Descola, P. (1989) 'Head-shrinkers vs shrinks: Jivaroan dream analysis', *Man*, vol. 24, no. 3, pp. 439–50.

Devereux, G. (1951) *Reality and Dream*. New York: International Universities Press.

Dudeck, M. (2019) 'The temple of artifice: Constructing a digital religion' (conference paper), *Visualising Cultures: Media, Technology and Religion*, Leeds: Leeds Trinity University, 2–4 September.

Durkheim, E. (1995 [1912]) *The Elementary Forms of Religious Life* (trans. Karen E. Fields). New York: Free Press.

Eliade, M. (1961) *The Sacred and the Profane*. New York: Harper.

Ewing, K. P. (2003) 'Diasporic dreaming, identity, and self-constitution', in J. M. Mageo (ed.), *Dreaming and the Self: New Perspectives on Subjectivity, Identity and Emotion*. New York: State University of New York Press, pp. 43–60.

Freud, S. (2001 [1900]) 'The Interpretation of Dreams', in J. Strachey (trans.), *The Standard Edition of the Complete Psychological Works of Sigmund Freud*, vol. 4 (1900), pp. 1–338, and vol. 5 (1900–1), pp. 339–630. London: Vintage.

Freud, S. (2001 [1901]) 'On Dreams', in J. Strachey (trans.), *The Standard Edition of the Complete Psychological Works of Sigmund Freud*, vol. 5. (1900–1). London: Vintage, pp. 631–86.

Freud, S. (2001 [1919]) 'The Uncanny', in J. Strachey (trans.), *The Standard Edition of the Complete Psychological Works of Sigmund Freud*, vol. 17 (1917–19). London: Vintage, pp. 217–56.

Freud, S. (2001 [1921]) 'Psychoanalysis and telepathy', in J. Strachey (trans.), *The Standard Edition of the Complete Psychological Works of Sigmund Freud*, vol. 18 (1920–2). London: Vintage, pp. 175–94.

Freud, S. (2001 [1922]) 'Dreams and telepathy', in J. Strachey (trans.), *The Standard Edition of the Complete Psychological Works of Sigmund Freud*, vol. 18 (1920–2). London: Vintage, pp. 195–220.

Gabbard, G. O., and Gabbard, K. (1999) *Psychiatry and the Cinema* (2nd edn). Washington, DC: American Psychiatric Press.

Germaine, C. (2023) *The Dark Matter of Children's Fantastika: Speculative Entanglements*. London: Bloomsbury.

Gregor, T. (1981) '"Far, far away my shadow wandered ...": The dream symbolism and dream theories of the Mehinaku Indians of Brazil', *American Ethnologist*, vol. 8, no. 4, pp. 709–20.

Grimshaw, A. (2001) *The Ethnographer's Eye: Ways of Seeing in Modern Anthropology*. Cambridge: Cambridge University Press.

Groom, N. (2018) *The Vampire: A New History*. New Haven, CT: Yale University Press.

Hallab, M. Y. (2009) *Vampire God: The Allure of the Undead in Western Culture*. Albany: State University of New York Press.

Hallowell, I. (2002 [1960]) 'Ojibwa ontology, behavior, and world view', in G. Harvey (ed.), *Readings in Indigenous Religions*. London: Continuum, pp. 17–49.

Hallowell, I. (1976 [1966]) 'The role of dreams in Ojibwa culture', in A. I. Hallowell and R. D. Fogelson (eds), *Contributions to Anthropology: Selected Papers of A. Irving Hallowell*. Chicago: University of Chicago Press, pp. 449–74.

Hanson, H. (2007) *Hollywood Heroines: Women in Film Noir and the Female Gothic Film*. London: I.B. Tauris.

Harvey, G. (1993) 'Gods and hedges in the Greenwood: The cosmology of contemporary Paganism', *Cosmos*, vol. 9, pp. 89–94.

Harvey, G. (2005) *Animism: Respecting the Living World*. London: Hurst.

Harvey, G. (2006) *Listening People, Speaking Earth: Contemporary Paganism* (2nd edn). London: Hurst.

Harvey, G. (2013) 'Introduction', in G. Harvey (ed.), *The Handbook of Contemporary Animism*. Durham, NC: Acumen, pp. 1–16.

Harvey, G. (ed.) (2013) *The Handbook of Contemporary Animism*. Durham, NC: Acumen.

Heelas, P., and Lock, A. (eds) (1981) *Indigenous Psychologies: The Anthropology of the Self*. London: Academic Press.

Hewitt, M. A. (2014) *Freud on Religion*. Durham, NC: Acumen.

Hewitt, M. A. (2020) *Legacies of the Occult: Psychoanalysis, Religion, and Unconscious Communication*. Sheffield: Equinox.

Hockley, L. (2001) *Cinematic Projections: The Analytical Psychology of C.G. Jung and Film Theory*. Luton: University of Luton Press.

Ingold, T. (2000) *The Perception of the Environment: Essays on Livelihood, Dwelling and Skill*. London: Routledge.

Izod, J. (2001) *Myth, Mind and the Screen: Understanding the Heroes of Our Time*. Cambridge: Cambridge University Press.

Jowett, L., and Abbott, S. (2013) *TV Horror: Investigating the Dark Side of the Small Screen*. London: I.B. Tauris.

Jung, C. G. (1966 [1943]) 'The personal and the collective unconscious', in R. F. C. Hull (trans.), *Two Essays on Analytical Psychology*, vol. 7 of *The Collected Works of C.G. Jung*, Bollingen Series xx. Princeton, NJ: Princeton University Press, pp. 64–79.

Jung, C. G. (2002 [1948]) 'General aspects of dream psychology', in *Dreams*. London: Routledge, pp. 25–68.

Kalvig, A. (2017) 'Necromancy is a religion: Tylor's discussion of Spiritualism in *Primitive Culture* and in his diary', in P. Tremlett, L. T. Sutherland and G. Harvey (eds), *Edward Burnett Tylor, Religion and Culture*. London: Bloomsbury, pp. 123–40.

Lebeau, V. (2001) *Psychoanalysis and Cinema: The Play of Shadows*. London: Wallflower.

Leeder, M. (2017) 'Screening the spectre: Ghosts on film', in S. Brewster and L. Thurston (eds), *The Routledge Handbook to the Ghost Story*. London: Routledge, pp. 351–60.

Lyden, J. C. (2003) *Film as Religion: Myths, Morals and Rituals*. New York: New York University Press.

Lynch, G. (ed.) (2007) *Between Sacred and Profane: Researching Religion and Popular Culture*. London: I.B. Tauris.

Marcus, L. (2007) 'Dreaming and the cinematographic unconscious', in C. Liu, J. Mowitt, T. Pepper and J. Spicer (eds), *The Dreams of Interpretation: A Century Down the Royal Road*. Minneapolis: University of Minnesota Press, pp. 197–214.

May, J. R., and Bird, M. (eds) (1982) *Religion in Film*. Knoxville: University of Tennessee Press.

Mellor, P. A. (2002) 'Sacred love: Religion, marriage, and l'amour fou', in A. Thatcher (ed.), *Celebrating Christian Marriage: New Hopes, New Agendas*. London: T&T Clark, pp. 119–41.

Mellor, P. A., and Shilling, C. (1997) *Re-forming the Body: Religion, Community and Modernity*. London: Sage.

Miles, M. R. (1996) *Seeing and Believing: Religion and Values in the Movies*. Boston: Beacon Press.

Mitchell, J., and Plate, S. B. (eds) (2007) *The Religion and Film Reader*. New York: Routledge.

Modleski, T. (1979) 'The search for tomorrow in today's soap operas: Notes on a feminine narrative form', *Film Quarterly*, vol. 33, no. 1, pp. 12–21.

Modleski, T. (2008 [1982]) *Loving with a Vengeance: Mass Produced Fantasies Produced for Women*. London: Routledge.

Moral, T. L. (2005) *Hitchcock and the Making of Marnie*. Lanham, MD: Scarecrow Press.

Moretti, F. (2005 [1978]) 'Dialectic of fear', in F. Moretti (ed.), *Signs Taken for Wonders: On the Sociology of Literary Forms*. London: Verso, pp. 83–108.

Morrison, R., and Baldick, C. (1998) 'Introduction', in R. Morrison and C. Baldick (eds), *The Vampyre and Other Tales of the Macabre*. Oxford: Oxford University Press, pp. vii–xxii.

Mulvey, L. (1999 [1975]) 'Visual pleasure and narrative cinema', in S. Thornham (ed.), *Feminist Film Theory: A Reader*. Edinburgh: Edinburgh University Press, pp. 58–69.

Mulvey, L. (1999 [1981]) 'Afterthoughts on "visual pleasure and narrative cinema" inspired by King Vidor's *Dual in the Sun* (1946)', in S. Thornham (ed.), *Feminist Film Theory: A Reader*. Edinburgh: Edinburgh University Press, pp. 122–30.

O'Flaherty, W. D. (2015) *Dreams, Illusion, and Other Realities*. Chicago: University of Chicago Press.

Olupona, J. K. (2004) *Beyond Primitivism: Indigenous Religious Traditions and Modernity*. New York: Routledge.

Pick, D., and Roper, L. (eds) (2004) *Dreams and History: The Interpretation of Dreams from Ancient Greece to Modern Psychoanalysis*. New York: Routledge.

Plate, S. B. (2007) 'The footprints of film: After images of religion in American space and time', in J. Mitchell and S. B. Plate (eds), *The Religion and Film Reader*. New York: Routledge, pp. 427–37.

Plate, S. B. (2008) *Religion and Film: Cinema and the Re-creation of the World*. London: Wallflower.

Polidori, J. W. (1998 [1819]) 'The Vampyre', in R. Morrison and C. Baldick (eds), *The Vampyre and Other Tales of the Macabre*. Oxford: Oxford University Press, pp. 1–24.

Puca, A. (2019) 'The tradition of segnature: Underground indigenous practices in Italy', _Journal of the Irish Society for the Academic Study of Religions_, no. 7, pp. 104–23.

Puca, A. (2020) 'The impact of social media on Italian shamanism and folk magic', _JBASR: Journal of the British Association for the Study of Religion_, vol. 22, pp. 55–70.

Rowland, S. (2002) _Jung: A Feminist Revision_. Cambridge: Polity.

Rueschmann, E. (2000) _Sisters on Screen: Siblings in Contemporary Cinema_. Philadelphia: Temple University Press.

Sabbadini. A. (2014) _Moving Images: Psychoanalytic Reflections on Film_. New York: Routledge.

Saler, B. (1977) 'Supernatural as a western category', _Ethos_, vol. 5, no. 1, pp. 31–53.

Shulman, D., and Stroumsa, G. G. (eds) (1999) _Dream Cultures: Explorations in the Comparative History of Dreaming_. New York: Oxford University Press.

Stephen, M. (1995) _A'aisa's Gifts: A Study of Magic and the Self_. Berkeley: University of California Press.

Stephen, M. (1996) 'Dreams and self-knowledge among the Mekeo of Papua New Guinea', _Ethos_, vol. 24, no. 3, pp. 465–90.

Stephenson, C. E. (2009) _Possession: Jung's Comparative Anatomy of the Psyche_. London: Routledge.

Stewart, P. J., and Strathern, A. J. (2003) 'Dreaming and ghosts among the Hagen and Duna of the Southern Highlands, Papua New Guinea', in I. Lohmann (ed.), _Dream Travellers: Sleep Experiences and Culture in the Western Pacific_. New York: Palgrave Macmillan, pp. 43–59.

Stocking, C. W. (1971) 'Animism in theory and practice: E. B. Tylor's unpublished "Notes on spiritualism"', _Man_, vol. 6, pp. 88–104.

Strathern, M. (1988) _The Gender of the Gift: Problems with Women and Problems with Society in Melanesia_. Berkeley: University of California Press.

Sutton, D., and Wogan, P. (2009) _Hollywood Blockbusters: The Anthropology of Popular Movies_. Oxford: Berg.

Tacey, D. J. (1997) _Remaking Men: Jung, Spirituality and Social Change_. London: Routledge.

Tedlock, B. (2001) 'The new anthropology of dreaming', in K. Bulkeley (ed.), _Dreams: A Reader on the Religious, Cultural, and Psychological Dimensions of Dreaming_. New York: Palgrave, pp. 249–64.

Tremlett, P., Sutherland, L. T., and Harvey, G. (eds) (2017) _Edward Burnett Tylor, Religion and Culture_. London: Bloomsbury.

Turner, V. (1967) _The Forest of Symbols: Aspects of Ndembu Ritual_. Ithaca, NY: Cornell University Press.

Tuzin, D. (1975) 'The breath of a ghost: Dreams and fear of the dead', _Ethos_, vol. 3, no. 4, pp. 555–78.

Tylor, E. B. (2010 [1871]) _Primitive Culture: Researches into the Development of Mythology, Philosophy, Religion, Art, and Custom_, vols. 1 and 2. Cambridge: Cambridge University Press.

Vecchi, I., and Odorico, S. (2019) 'Digital methods in visual anthropology' (conference paper and workshop), *Visualising Cultures: Media, Technology and Religion.* Leeds: Leeds Trinity University, 2–4 September.

Vishvajit, P. (2004) 'Forest smells and spider webs: Ritualized dream interpretation among Andaman Islanders', *Dreaming*, vol. 14, nos. 2–3, pp. 136–50.

Weinstock, J. (2012) *The Vampire Film: Undead Cinema.* London: Wallflower.

Whitehead, A. (2013) 'The new fetishism: Western statue devotion and a matter of power', in G. Harvey (ed.), *The Handbook of Contemporary Animism.* Durham: Acumen, pp. 260–70.

Wilcox, R. V., and Lavery, D. (2002) 'Introduction', in R. V. Wilcox and D. Lavery (eds), *Fighting the Forces: What's at Stake in Buffy the Vampire Slayer.* Lanham: Roman & Littlefield, pp. xvii–xxix.

Williamson, M. (2005) *The Lure of the Vampire: Gender, Fiction and Fandom from Bram Stoker to Buffy.* London: Wallflower Press.

Wilts, A. (2009) 'Evil, skanky, and kinda gay: Lesbian images and issues', in L. Y. Edwards, E. L. Rambo and J. B. South (eds), *Buffy Goes Dark: Essays on the Final Two Seasons of Buffy the Vampire Slayer on Television.* Jefferson, NC: McFarland, pp. 41–56.

Filmography

Bram Stoker's Dracula (1992) Directed by Francis Ford Coppola: Columbia Pictures.

Buffy the Vampire Slayer (1997–2003) Created by Joss Whedon: Mutant Enemy Productions and 20th Century Fox Television. Seasons 1–5, Warner Bros, Seasons 6 & 7, United Paramount Network: 10 March.

Dracula (1931) Directed by Tod Browning: Universal Pictures.

Dracula's Daughter (1936) Directed by Hillyer Lambert: Universal Pictures.

Ghost (1990) Directed by Jerry Zucker: Paramount Pictures.

Interview with a Vampire (1994) Directed by Neil Jordan: Warner Bros.

Marnie (1964) Directed by Alfred Hitchcock: Universal Pictures.

Rear Window (1954) Directed by Alfred Hitchcock: Paramount Pictures.

Spellbound (1945) Directed by Alfred Hitchcock: United Artists.

Twin Peaks (1990–1) (Seasons 1 and 2) Created by Mark Frost and David Lynch: CBS Television, ABC: 8 April.

Vertigo (1958) Directed by Alfred Hitchcock: Paramount Pictures.

2

Dreams as Detection: Trauma and Psychology in the Films of Alfred Hitchcock

This chapter begins an exploration of dreams, trauma and Freudian psychology in film using examples from the work of the director Alfred Hitchcock. Hitchcock's films are often a starting point for film theorists for a number of reasons. His work spans from the early 1920s through to the mid-1970s, including silent pictures and talkies, black-and-white films and films in colour. Perhaps most famously, he experimented liberally with visual and sound devices in order to elicit a range of emotional responses in his audiences and in order to create and release tension, making him a 'Master of Suspense' (Knight and McKnight, 1999; Moral, 2005: 3; Smith, 2000: 16–48). Of particular interest in the context of this book is his engagement with and visual representations of psychological ideas and motifs such as hysterical amnesia and dream analysis. Because of Hitchcock's interest in emotion these themes can arguably be detected in most of his cannon, but three films in particular are noteworthy for their depictions of psychoanalysis or their use of psychoanalytic tropes, namely, *Spellbound* (1946), *Psycho* (1960) and *Marnie* (1964), and this chapter will explore in some detail *Spellbound* and *Marnie*, in part because these films offer the most detailed treatments of relationships that have a psychoanalytic dimension. However, Hitchcock problematizes these relationships by giving them a sexual and personal component in both cases, and in *Marnie*, Mark's role of psychoanalyst has no professional context, he is an amateur analysing his wife.

Solving external and internal mysteries simultaneously, many of Hitchcock's films exemplify movies depicting psychoanalysis in which the resolution of trauma is linked to a detective story. Gabbard and Gabbard (1999: 56) identify this trend more broadly in the film noir movies of the late 1940s and early 1950s, suggesting that they 'reflect the less optimistic vision of American life that was emerging in this period as well as a growing fascination with psychiatry' that was in part fuelled by accounts of the psychiatric treatment of servicemen returning from the Second World War (Gabbard and Gabbard, 1999: 57; see also Biesen, 2014). They suggest that the depictions of psychoanalysis in crime melodramas are somewhat problematic because it is 'regularly confused with or relegated to detective work, partially because its methodologies require gathering clues and following through on hypotheses, but also because crime detection provides a neatly simplified version of psychiatry – problems can be thoroughly solved and forgotten once a culprit has been identified' (Gabbard and Gabbard, 1999: 58–9).

In *Spellbound* this link is strengthened even further because a dream of one of the central characters is closely described, depicted and ultimately 'analysed' to solve a murder. The film does explore in places the role of the wish in Freudian theory, such as when a man who is suffering from an unfounded belief that he has killed his father is reassured by a psychiatrist that this is a 'guilt complex' based on momentary wishes in childhood. This idea, also called the *omnipotence of thoughts* is outlined in an essay by Freud called *The Uncanny* (2001 [1919]) and is explored further in Chapter 5 of this book. However, crucially, the dream in *Spellbound* does not really explore the dreamer's wishes. Instead, it acts like a puzzle, which, once solved, identifies a murderer by putting together events that the dreamer has witnessed, but subsequently forgotten, due to traumatic amnesia. Set in a psychiatric facility, called Green Manors, *Spellbound* focuses on Constance Peterson, a young doctor working there who is apparently uninterested in romance until Anthony Edwardes arrives, a psychiatrist who has written about the guilt complex and who is replacing the chief in charge of Green Manors, Dr Murchison. Constance and Anthony fall quickly in love but their romance is interrupted by Anthony having an episode in an operating theatre where he rambles incoherently and faints in a way that looks like a depiction of a panic attack or hysteria. Once he has come to his senses Anthony reveals to Constance that he is suffering from amnesia, but he knows he is not Anthony and believes that he must have replaced the latter because he killed him. Initials on a cigarette case reveal his true name only to the extent of J. B. and he runs away from Green Manors leaving Constance a note just before the police are made aware of the murder of Anthony Edwardes and begin to pursue the impostor, believing him to be the murderer. Constance follows J. B. and takes on the triple role of lover, psychiatrist and detective, in an attempt to uncover and explore J. B.'s identity and solve the murder.

In *Marnie*, there is also a key dream that helps the central characters solve a mystery. The film does not show this dream in full, but only the female protagonist, Marnie, having a nightmare in which she hears taps on a window and feels cold. In this case, the mystery surrounding Marnie concerns her kleptomania and the fact that she does not want to have sex with men. Unlike J. B., who communicates with Constance about his amnesia and fears about what he might have done, Marnie does not initiate a psychoanalytic investigation. It is Mark Rutland, a wealthy man who owns one of the companies that Marnie robs, who captures her, blackmails her into marriage and 'diagnoses' her with problems rooted in childhood when she refuses to have sex with him and explains that she has strong feelings against having sex with men. In the climactic final scenes of the film, Marnie shoots a beloved horse after an accident during a hunt injures him, and in what appears to be a trance-like state of shock, she is taken back to her mother by Mark, who gets Marnie's mother to recount some significant facts from Marnie's childhood. In order to fill in the missing pieces, Mark initiates a recall of the dream by tapping three times on a wall, and Marnie re-lives a terrifying night that she has apparently repressed, after which she asks Mark if she can go home, implying that this cathartic recall has resolved her issues with theft and reconciled her with heterosexual relations and marriage.

Although both films draw from Freudian psychology to some extent for their plot content, the therapist and patient dynamic is seriously compromised by the relationships between them in both cases. In *Marnie* this dynamic is rendered even more disturbing as Mark is not a therapist at all but someone who blackmails and rapes Marnie, and uses pop psychology to investigate her and convince her that she has problems and is unable to take responsibility for herself. One explanation for the filming of this plot is that Hitchcock was a misogynist who delighted in subjecting his female leads to unpleasant storylines, but scholars such as Modleski (2016 [1988]) offer a more sophisticated feminist approach that explores in some depth the complex nature of gender dynamics in his films. She argues that Hitchcock is neither 'utterly misogynistic *nor* … largely sympathetic to women and their plight in patriarchy, but that his work is characterised by a thoroughgoing ambivalence about femininity', and she explains why 'it has been possible for critics to argue with some plausibility on either side of the issue' not least because although female characters are often subjected to violence in Hitchcock's films, they nonetheless remain 'resistant to patriarchal assimilation' (Modleski, 2019 [1988]: 3). Part of the problem, according to Modleski, is an emphasis on auteur theories of cinema that pay insufficient attention to the broader cultural and social milieux in which films are made. In contrast she asserts that feminist critics of cinema, including her own work, 'use Hitchcock's works as a means to elucidate issues and problems relevant to women in patriarchy. In so doing, these critics implicitly challenge and decentre directorial authority by considering Hitchcock's work as an expression of cultural attitudes and practices existing to some extent outside the artist's control' (Modleski, 2019 [1988]: 3).

In the case of the films *Spellbound* and *Marnie* I want to suggest that Hitchcock *both* reflects *and* highlights patriarchy and power dynamics between the genders. Moreover, he both reflects and highlights issues of power inherent within the therapeutic relationship as conceived by Freud. By conflating the roles of investigator, therapist and lover, these films provoke uncomfortable questions about psychology at the same time as they make some of its basic principles accessible to the wider public.

Dreams and trauma in Freud's psychoanalysis

Both *Spellbound* and *Marnie* hinge on significant dreams. However, the clues in these dreams are used to piece together significant events that have been forgotten by the protagonists, rather than uncovering repressed wishes and desires. Arguably, the latter process is more evident through the way that the films explore the actions of Marnie and John while awake, because for both characters, there is a quality of sleep walking, daydreaming or trance in the way they are depicted and their amnesia is related to violence, murderous wishes and their guilt about them. While on the one hand Marnie is an excellent thief, carefully planning and executing her crimes, on the other the film suggests that there is a compulsion behind her crimes, and the last time we see her try to rob a safe she is in an altered mental state after having to kill her horse. When Mark finds her, he reminds her that the money is hers, as she is his wife at this point, and that she can take the money but the camerawork suggests that she is in a trance and her eyes stare blankly. Moreover, there are several scenes in the film that suggest triggers for Marnie's painful repressed memories as she has strong emotional reactions to seeing the colour red and an unusually strong fear of storms. *Spellbound* similarly uses the narrative device of triggers that evoke painful repressed memories. J. B. has strong negative reactions to white lines on Constance's robe and on a bed cover and is shown getting up in the middle of the night, starting to shave and walking down the stairs in a trance-like or sleepwalking state with a razor in his hand. He and Constance, posing as newlyweds, are staying at this time with the psychiatrist who was her mentor and analyst, Dr Alexander Brulov, and he, intuiting that something may be wrong, is waiting downstairs for J. B., offering him some milk with bromide in it to make him sleep as the doctor is afraid that J. B. might be dangerous in this state. J. B. also has fainting fits associated with getting close to recalling repressed memories. Taken together, this range of symptoms are suggestive of hysteria, although this point needs to be made with the caveat that it is tricky to diagnose fictional characters at the best of times and that while hysteria as a diagnosis is an interesting part of the history of psychoanalysis, it is highly controversial and is explored here in the context of its impact on cultural studies, including the study of film.

Bernheimer's (1990) exploration of hysteria explicitly links both its history and cultural receptions with gender relations. Deriving from the Greek word for uterus, he suggests that hysteria in the context of ancient Greek medicine was understood to be a female illness that had a physical origin, but that ideas about the illness and its symptoms have always been shaped by society's ideas about what constituted normal female behaviour and what deviated from that. For example, sexual abstinence was regarded as a symptom and marriage and pregnancy the treatment so that, 'thus was established a diagnosis of female sexual disturbance, and a cure by submission to the yoke of patriarchy (the reproduction of mothering), both of which remained basic to the medical concept of hysteria for centuries to come' (Bernheimer, 1990: 3). Turning to the Victorian age, he locates the origin of hysterical symptoms, as well as their diagnosis, in patriarchal European societies and their contradictory expectations of women to be

> gentle, submissive, naive, and good … [and] perfectly controlled in her decorous conduct. Faced with this conflict, numerous Victorian women developed unconscious defensive strategies whereby they disavowed the intense anger and aggressive impulses for which the culture gave them no outlet. … Thus were generated the conversion reactions … whereby women transformed their repressed hostility and desire into physical symptoms that simultaneously acknowledged and disowned those feelings. (Bernheimer, 1990: 5–6)

Unlike Charcot, who used hypnotism to try to cure his patients, Freud applied a technique of carefully listening to them, and noted their resistance to certain things in their verbal behaviour, famously linking this observation to his theories of repression and the unconscious (Bernheimer, 1990: 8). This linking of resistance and repression is talked about in *Spellbound*, when one of the doctors explains to a patient that their subconscious is putting up a fight and does not want the patient to get well, but both *Marnie* and *Spellbound* also have scenes that suggest that things are not so simple and that when a 'therapist' diagnoses a patient and insists on the rightness of their conclusions, even when the patient denies the interpretation, there may also be a power dynamic in the situation that needs further examination. One of the most famous examples of this happening in Freud's own work is found in a case history of a young woman that he calls Dora (Bernheimer and Kahane, 1990; Freud, 2001 [1901]a; Mahony, 1996). This case is interesting for several reasons. It is one of the earliest analyses of dreams after the publication of *The Interpretation of Dreams* (Freud, 2001 [1900]); it outlines many of Freud's early theories of hysteria; and it is an example of a case where the patient abruptly terminated the therapeutic relationship because she did not agree with his assessment of her illness.

As recounted by Kahane (1990: 20), Dora, aged eighteen years, was brought to Freud by her father (Philip Bauer), suffering from recurring loss of voice, coughing fits and depression. She had also threatened to commit suicide. These symptoms had begun two years before after an incident at a vacation home in the Alps where Dora's parents had joined their friends Mr and Mrs K. Dora accused Herr K. of sexually propositioning her, whereupon she slapped his face and fled. Herr K. denied the incident ever took place and Dora's father, in bringing her to Freud, was suggesting that the incident was a mere fantasy and part of her illness. However, the situation turns out to be more complex, because Philip Bauer was having an affair with Frau K. and 'hands Dora over to Herr K. in return for his complicity' (Kahane, 1990: 21). Although Bauer appeared to want Freud to make Dora more compliant, 'Freud, recognizing his motives, seems to refuse a complicit part and, instead, confirms Dora's perceptions' (Kahane, 1990: 21).

Nonetheless, Freud insisted that Dora had repressed a love for Herr K. and this idea is core to Freud's interpretation of her key dreams, despite Dora's resisting this interpretation and abandoning analysis, a decision that Freud had trouble accepting (Ramas, 1990: 167). In one key dream, Dora is rescued from a burning house by her father, who refuses to wait for her mother to rescue her jewel case (Freud, 2001 [1901]: 64–93; Mahony, 1996: 77). Freud's interpretation reads the jewel case as a sexual metaphor and suggests that Dora wanted to give her jewel case to Herr K but was afraid of these feelings and puts up as a defence her childhood attachments to her father (Mahony, 1996: 80–2). Moreover, Mahony (1996: 81) suggests that Freud was 'symptomatically directive' in his analysis, rather than allowing Dora to pursue her own train of thought. Ramas (1990) explores the complex dynamics of Dora's case from a feminist perspective that examines the heteronormative implications of Freud's contentions on female sexual development and Dora's possible sexual feelings for Frau K., but key to this chapter's analysis of *Marnie* is the way that Dora's frigidity is understood as *in itself* a symptom of hysteria (Ramas, 1990: 150). In making this comparison between Dora and Marnie, I am not suggesting that Hitchcock was aware of specific details of Freudian texts, but the exaggerated premises of the film do arouse a level of discomfort with the power dynamics of therapy and of patriarchy in combination that highlights the workings of both.

It is interesting in this context to note paradoxes in relation to male hysteria, the symptoms of which became lines of inquiry in consideration of illnesses presented by veterans of the First and Second World Wars. Although Freud took an interest in these in the context of his research into hysteria, Mitchell (2000: 110–11 and 126–7) argues that the term had been steadily declining in use and that, as male sufferers came to the fore, the term 'hysteria' was eschewed in favour of theories of trauma. Nonetheless, key features of the illness, such as bodily symptoms that did not originate from bodily sources, paralyses, amnesia, catatonia and mutism, continued to be reported by people who had been in combat (Mitchell, 2000: 127) and Hitchcock employs some of these symptoms to depict J. B.'s illness in *Spellbound*.

Hysteria and trauma in *Spellbound*

Kaplan (2005: 24–41) in her detailed analysis of developments and uses of trauma theory also makes links between Freud's initial investigations into hysteria and its implications for understanding trauma in war veterans. She suggests that rather than trying to write a theory of trauma, the concept emerges from collaborative work with Breuer on hysteria early in Freud's career (Breuer and Freud (2001 [1893]) where hysteria and memory are linked and traumatic hysteria is distinguished from other kinds by the elusiveness of the causative memories that act like a foreign body in the psyche (Kaplan, 2005: 26). While noting a potential conflict between the identification of an external event in war neuroses and the importance of unconscious fantasy in hysteria in Freud's work from Dora's case history onwards, Kaplan does not regard this conflict as impossible to reconcile because, 'the traumatic event may trigger early traumatic happenings, already perhaps mingled with fantasy, and shape how the current event is experienced. There may, for instance, in the case of battle trauma, be unconscious guilt at surviving an attack; or events in battle may unconsciously recall childhood violence where the victim wished for a sibling's death' (Kaplan, 2005: 32). (See also Mitchell, 2000: 318–20 for the role of sibling rivalry in hysteria).

It is precisely this kind of multiple triggering and combination of external events and unconscious processes that is found is *Spellbound*. After J. B. has awoken from his bromide-induced sleep at the home of Brulov, Constance and Brulov analyse together J. B.'s dream and shortly afterwards J. B. suffers another panic attack that Constance attributes to lines made in the show outside the window. Deducing that Dr Anthony Edwardes (as was his somewhat eccentric habit with patients) may have taken J. B. to a ski resort, she and J. B. go there in order to try to recreate the fateful events that led to Edwardes's death in the hope that this re-enactment will revive J. B.'s memory. On one level, this plan works. J. B. remembers a fatal accident that happened when J. B. was a child playing with his brother on balustrades and the young J. B. watches while his brother falls and is impaled on a fence. Having recovered this memory (presumably mixed up in his unconscious with guilt arising from childhood wishes stemming from sibling rivalry) J. B. also begins to recover from other parts of his amnesia and remembers his name, John Ballantine, but before his recovery can progress the police find the body of Dr Edwardes on the slope and Ballantine is arrested for murder.

Kaplan, however, notices a second trauma that brought John Ballantine into treatment with Dr Edwardes. Initially, this appears in the film when Constance and J. B. are in the New York hotel, reunited after he had fled from Green Manors. Constance sees that he has been badly burned and asks him about it and he relives the pain of an accident he was in but nothing about where or how this might have happened (Kaplan, 2005: 78). Kaplan (2005: 79) explains that this introduces the Second World War 'sideways', because Constance does not focus on John's war trauma, although the audience is given further clues when the couple leave New York by train and she asks him to try to name the place he was going with Dr Edwardes. John says Rome, and once on the train (heading to her mentor's home) Constance deciphers that John must be talking about Rome in Italy. When she asks about it the railway tracks trigger another attack and, 'we hear gunshots and the roar of planes on the soundtrack, while Edwardes in a trance says, "Fighter planes spotted us." Peterson interjects, "You were flying?" He responds: "Transport, Medical Corps; flying over Rome they hit us. Bailed out."' (Kaplan, 2005: 78). Constance asks him if he left the army, but J. B. cannot remember any more, only that he hated the killing.

Kaplan argues, therefore, that the lines are also linked to war trauma, as well as the skiing accident and the childhood accident, but the war trauma is not investigated further in the film. One reason for this, Kaplan suggests, is that war trauma is related to society as a whole as well as to individuals, and societies may also have symptoms of dissociation and forgetting. However, it is important to remember that national politics, and the interests of perpetrators, may also play a part in this process (Kaplan, 2005: 66-7, 74). Her analysis takes a particular interest in melodrama (see also Haeffner, 2005: 17-18, 56-8 for a discussion of melodrama and Hitchcock's films), because, she suggests that this genre may serve the function of 'registering *while negotiating* the cultural traumas of modernity, including those of war, race, and gender, through the mirror of what I am calling "quiet" or "common" trauma' (Kaplan, 2005: 69). On one level, therefore, melodrama explores difficult societal questions, but rather than confronting them head on, they are to an extent, displaced and made easier to relate to by the focus of melodrama on the emotions of individuals and their interplay in intimate social worlds (Kaplan, 2005: 72). Furthermore, she expresses an interest in the things in common 'between the visuality common to traumatic symptoms (flashbacks, hallucinations, dreams) and the ways in which visual media like cinema become the mechanisms through which a culture can unconsciously address its traumatic hauntings' (Kaplan, 2005: 69).

She suggests that *Spellbound* is a good example of films that indirectly consider the Second World War trauma and place the mechanisms of remembering and forgetting in the context of an individual character, while simultaneously performing ambivalent remembering and forgetting of the shocks of collective trauma. It is of note that Selznick, the film's producer, sought psychoanalytic help with May Romm, who became an accredited consultant to the film, and the orientation of *Spellbound* towards helping the wider public understand psychoanalysis better was arguably driven by Selznick (Kaplan, 2005: 75-6). However, she suggests that he both knew and did not know what the film was about because, Selznick 'wanted a film that would educate Americans about psychoanalysis, but not directly about their most urgent problem, namely post war trauma illnesses in veterans. How self-conscious he was of his own "amnesia" about his project is a question that cannot be answered' (Kaplan, 2005: 75).

In contrast, Kaplan (2005: 76) suggests that Hitchcock never warmed to Freud, but he had the rights to the novel *The House of Dr. Edwardes* (Beeding, 1927) and was interested in making a picture about psychoanalysis. She contrasts the visual treatment of John's panic attacks with the rendering of the dream and its analysis, arguing that 'the visuality of trauma attacks and their emotional suffering emerge in the representation of Edwardes' classic trauma symptoms of flashbacks and hallucinations rather than in the reductive pseudo-Freudian dream analysis of Dr Brulov (standing in for Freud). Hitchcock seems more at ease in cinematic rendering of these episodes than in the dream images'

(Kaplan, 2005: 77). This is because while the panic attack scenes appear to be related to strong emotional responses and unconscious wishes (such as sibling rivalry and guilt), the decoding of the dream is used in the film to uncover an objective event that John Ballantine witnessed and subsequently forgot as part of his traumatic amnesia.

The dream in *Spellbound*

Although Dr Brulov appears to give a good summary of Freud's (2001 [1901] b: 648–66) theories about processes such as condensation and displacement in dreams when he explains to J. B. that dreams present what people are trying to hide from themselves. 'But they tell it to you all mixed up, like pieces of a puzzle that don't fit. The problem of the analyst is to examine this puzzle and put the pieces together in the right place, and find out what the devil you are trying to say to yourself.' However, the analysis of John's dream does not really happen during the session with Constance and Dr Brulov, but right at the end of the film, after John Ballantine has been wrongly convicted of the murder of Dr Edwardes. Constance has returned to Green Manors and is briefly consoled by Dr Murchison, the doctor who is in charge of Green Manors and who Dr Edwardes was going to replace. In this conversation Dr Murchison lets slip that he had met Edwardes previously and Constance's mind starts to race as she re-reads her notebook where she had recorded the details of John Ballantine's dream. Going back in to Dr Murchison's office, Constance asks for a second opinion on her revised interpretation of John's dream.

The dream begins in a gambling house with no walls but only curtains with eyes, a place that Constance now identifies as Green Manors. J. B. is playing cards with a bearded man and turns over the seven of clubs and the bearded man says that that makes twenty-one. Then the proprietor of the club comes over and has an argument with the bearded man, asserting that it was his club and not the bearded man's. Constance and Murchison deduce that J. B. is thinking of the Twenty One Club in New York and that the bearded man is Dr Edwardes and the proprietor is Dr Murchison himself (referring to being in charge of Green Manors). In the second segment of the dream the bearded man falls off a sloping roof, while another man stands behind a chimney and drops a small wheel, which Constance deduces to be a revolver. Having been discovered as the murderer, Dr Murchison threatens Constance with a gun, before finally turning the gun on himself and committing suicide.

While this handling of dreams makes for an excellent climatic solving of a murder at the end of the film, its relationship to Freudian analysis is tenuous, as it is the decoding of a memory, rather than a wish. While elements do echo Freud, such as the wordplay of dreams that translates the word revolver into a small wheel (Freud, 2001 [1900]: 406–7, 421–5), in Freud's accounts there is much more discussion of this in the context of the dreamer's emotions and wishes, as deduced from an analysis of their associations between the dream material and incidents that they recall.

Nonetheless, the dream sequence, as imaginatively depicted by Dalí, is famous as one of the first of its kind, and because of Dalí's associations with the surrealist movement, a group of artists and writers who were fascinated by Freud's writings on the unconscious. Dalí had also collaborated with the film director Buñuel to make what has been lauded as 'the quintessential Surrealist motion picture', *Un Chien Andalou* (1929) (King, 2007: 17). This film did not have a conventional narrative plot, but put together scenes and images in ways that resembled the jumbled contents of dreams.

Hitchcock asserted in a BBC interview (1966) with Philip Jenkinson, that his reasons for involving Dalí were not simply about publicity, but primarily because Dalí's work was solid and sharp. Hitchcock wanted to better represent the experience of dreaming and avoid the technique of blurring dream sequences in films that was, in his opinion, an inaccurate representation (King, 2007: 79). However, partly because of the film running over budget and partly to clarify the dream sequence and its role in the plot, Hitchcock's idea of filming it outside in bright light was dropped, as were several scenes imbued with Dalí's ideas. According to King (2007: 86), by taking out several of Dalí's ideas, the dream sequence was impoverished, with less of a dream-like quality and fewer references to Freudian concepts.

The dream sequence in *Spellbound*, therefore, is arguably much less in line with Freudian ideas than the panic attack sequences and the ways that they are explained in the film. Chaotic sequences envisaged by Dalí that had little to do with the plot's denouement were removed, and Constance solves the dream, and therefore the murder that John Ballantine had witnessed, by decoding the dream without John being there at all. Rather, it is the murderer, Dr Murchison, that she consults to verify the facts hidden in John's dream.

In addition to the ways in which psychoanalysis was shaped to suit the structured detective story in *Spellbound*, it was also shaped, and to some extent superseded, by other themes that interested the director, including class, power, gender and romantic love. Brill (1988: xiv) suggests that Hitchcock's films are deeply concerned with romantic love and notes how love challenges the cold professionalism of the psychiatric storyline because Constance trusts her love for J. B. and potentially puts herself in danger to help him, against the advice of Dr Brulov (Brill, 1988: 239–40). In this sense Constance is a very active partner in the relationship, first following J. B. to New York, and then leading him to her mentor's home and to the ski resort in order to try to uncover the memories that J. B. has lost. Nonetheless, audiences are reminded that she is a woman. There is an awkward scene early in the film in which a male colleague chides her for being too cold and involved in her work (because he wants to date her and she is not interested in him). Later in the film, Dr Brulov suggests that women are the best psychiatrists, until they fall in love and lose all perspective and J. B. also reminds us of Constance's gender when he tries to resist her persistent questioning by telling her he hates smug women. On one level, this resistance can be read in Freudian terms as a patient resisting analysis because the unconscious is trying to protect its buried memories. However, as explored in the case of Dora, the dismissal of a person's own feelings and explanations raises questions about the power dynamics between therapists and patients and *Spellbound* also appears to raise these questions.

Pomerance (2004: 79–82) suggests a reading of the scene between policemen as they wait to question Dr Brulov in his home and discuss a demanding mother and a boss unwilling to promote one of them as indicative of wider power relations, including those engendered by post-war capitalism that Hitchcock quietly exposes in the film. Moreover, Pomerance (2004: 88) also suggests that mental powers are explored in *Spellbound*, and that it identifies the doctor–patient relation itself as a power relation in which patients defer to 'the analytic powers and language of the discipline, as embodied by the person of the analyst'. The potentially problematic nature of this submission is illustrated in the scene in Dr Brulov's home, the morning after he has given J. B. bromide to make him sleep, when Constance and Dr Brulov analyse J. B.'s dream. Pomerance (2004: 89) explains that it is easy to forget that

> this particular patient enters the extremely vulnerable therapeutic relation with two analysts, not one – hence, outnumbered – and under the residual influence of drugs. This culminating scene is thus a brutal portrait of a therapeutic assault by an artist whose intense sensitivity to the language and intellectual modelling of Freud did not extend to a fondness for the institutionalisation of his ideas in the psychoanalytic establishment.

Hitchcock's ambivalence towards psychoanalysis and its potential brutality are even more highlighted in the second film discussed in this chapter, *Marnie*, because the gender dynamic is reversed, with a man analysing a woman, and because this takes place not because she has asked for analysis, but because she has been blackmailed into marriage with a man who sets himself up as an amateur psychiatrist in order to solve the 'mystery' of her frigidity under these circumstances.

Marnie

Marnie (1964) was made nearly twenty years after *Spellbound* (1946). While there are a number of features in common with the earlier film, including the theme of traumatic amnesia and the use of triggers to illustrate the protagonist's mental state and its causes, *Marnie* is also influenced by the fact that in this period film-makers were able to explore and depict darker themes. Famously Hitchcock had made *Psycho* (1960), a film that secured his reputation as an influencer of later horror films, in addition to gothic thrillers (Boyd and Palmer, 2006). The process of making *Psycho* (1960) as well as Hitchcock's groundbreaking use of publicity for the film is explored in the film *Hitchcock* (2012), based on the book by Rebello (1990). The film and the book both highlight the importance of Hitchcock's wife, Alma Reville, as a partner in his film-making career, but also touch upon controversies in his private life and fantasies that impacted his treatment of female actors. A second film that came out in 2012, *The Girl*, gave even more emphasis on an interpretation of Hitchcock's own psychology. Based on Spoto's (1999 [1983]) book, which in turn includes a lot of information from Tippi Hedren, the actor who played the female protagonist in both *The Birds* (1963) and *Marnie* (1964), *The Girl* depicts, for example, the filming of a scene in *The Birds* in which Tippi Hedren's character is attacked by the birds. In order to create the scene Hitchcock ordered handlers to throw live birds at Hedren. The two-minute scene was meant to be finished in two takes, but in fact Hitchcock insisted on repeating the process over five days, leaving Hedren injured and traumatized. One can argue that this kind of cruelty was due to a callous determination to depict terror as realistically as possible, but *The Girl* suggests a degree of sadistic pleasure in Hitchcock's actions that may in part have been fuelled by Hedren's rejection of his sexual advances. Both *Psycho* and *The Birds* have been analysed in some detail by Žižek in the series *The Pervert's Guide to Cinema* (2006, see also Žižek, 1992) using Freudian theories, but debates continue about both the quality of Hitchcock's depictions of psychoanalysis and his own psychological motivations with regard to his female cast that are also relevant to the film *Marnie*.

The plot of *Marnie* centres on solving the mysteries surrounding its female protagonist, Marnie, and this is made clear at the start of the film where we see a smartly dressed female figure from behind walking along a train station, putting a suitcase in a station locker and throwing away the key. The film does not show her face until a scene where she is shown standing back from a sink after dyeing her hair blond. Intercut with these scenes are shots in which an angry business man (Mr Strutt) shouts to the police about his company safe having been robbed by a pretty employee with no references. A rich client of the company, Mark Rutland, overhears the conversation with some amusement and guesses, when Marnie is interviewed for a position at his firm, that it is the same woman. Intrigued, he instructs the interviewer to hire Marnie, and starts to pursue her, firstly by asking her to work for him alone on a Saturday and subsequently on dates to horse races and a visit to his home to meet his father. When Marnie steals from his company's safe, Mark secretly replaces the stolen money and tracks Marnie down, using his knowledge about her love of horses, to a riding stable. Rather than letting her go or calling the police Mark declares that he is in love with Marnie and insists that she marry him, but is disappointed when, on their honeymoon cruise she is terrified of him and explains that she is repelled by the thought of sex with men. Mark's response is to reluctantly agree to not try to have sex with her, but he thinks that she needs help, probably from a psychiatrist, and as he tries to engage her in conversations, he also starts to educate himself with books such as 'Sexual Aberrations of the Criminal Female'. However, the tensions between them come to a head when Mark rapes Marnie and she tries to commit suicide, after which they return home in an uneasy truce punctuated by Mark's continued attempts to psychoanalyse Marnie and find out more about her past.

The rape scene has been a point of considerable critical debate about *Marnie*. For example, Brill (1998) doubts whether intercourse is implied in this scene, because being stripped would be enough to incite Marnie to try to commit suicide and he suggests that, 'critics often assume that Mark rapes Marnie and that his violation of her leads to her suicide attempt. This assumption strikes me as unwarranted and unnecessary ... Mark, moreover, has given her his word earlier that he "wouldn't", a promise that it would be out of character for him to break' (Brill, 1998: 251). Wood is more ambivalent, trying to describe the scene from both Marnie's and Mark's points of view, he suggests that because Mark makes tender gestures, the terror on Marnie's face only makes this 'virtually' a rape, and later describes the scene as one 'where Mark sleeps with (or rapes?) Marnie' (Wood, 2002 [1989]: 189, 192).

However, a closer analysis of the processes that went into the making of *Marnie* clearly suggests that a rape scene was Hitchcock's intention. Moral

(2005) offers such an analysis, including a step-by-step depiction of Hitchcock's engagement with three screen writers, Joseph Stefano, Evan Hunter and Jay Presson Allen. He suggests that Hunter was dropped from the project precisely because of the doubts he expressed about this scene. Evan Hunter was worried about how audiences would receive Sean Connery in a role where he is a rapist of a woman who is terrified, but Hitchcock was explicit in his response to Hunter's objections (Moral, 2005: 28, 36). Nonetheless, Moral (2005: xiv) affirms that the film, following the book (Graham, 1997 [1961]), has feminist agendas and exposes issues related to patriarchal capitalism in the workplace, suggesting that, 'Marnie's rape becomes a literal metaphor for female repression at the hands of social patriarchy'. However, of particular interest to this chapter is the way in which Wood characterizes the scene and its place within the film, as part of a cure for Marnie's mental disturbances. For example, he explores a scene set once the couple have returned home in which Marnie has what appears to be a recurring nightmare. Mark and Lil wake her up and when Lil has gone Mark suggests to Marnie that the dream might be something that really happened to her, and advises that she read some books about psychology to help herself. In a still half-awake state Marnie says that her mother asks her to get up in the dream and she does not want to because then she would feel cold and hear strange noises. As Mark questions her further, she wakes up properly and jokes, 'You Freud. Me Jane?'. She resists his suggestion that she read psychology books but taunts that he is 'just dying to play doctor' and suggests the free association game. While on one level this scene appears to be about resistance of patients to psychotherapy, Wood (2002 [1989]: 195) argues that on another level Marnie is encouraging Mark to help her, and that 'every sequence of *Marnie* is constructed as a necessary stage in the breaking down of Marnie's defensive barriers, all that prevents her being fully alive' (Wood, 2002 [1989]: 191) including her inability, until the end of the film, to effect a transference of her emotional needs from her mother to Mark (Wood, 2002 [1989]: 183). Although this understanding of the film fits in well with a Freudian analysis, Modleski's (2019 [1988]: 5) emphasis suggests that perhaps her attachment to her mother is not so much a problem for Marnie as it is for a patriarchal social order, and this kind of critique reveals an alliance between Freudian perspectives and the power dynamics of gender relations in the era in which Freud worked and wrote.

Marnie appears to give more attention than *Spellbound* to Oedipal theories or the 'family romance' as these issues are sometimes described. One example is through the character of Marnie herself, who visits her mother, Bernice Edgar, early in the film. We learn that Bernice brought up Marnie alone. A working-class

Baptist living in Baltimore, Bernice babysits for a neighbour's child, Jessie, and seems more at ease with this child than with Marnie, who financially supports Bernice and lavishes her with gifts. Bernice is unaware of Marnie's compulsive thefts, but Marnie expresses a connection between them and her love for her mother, which she feels is not reciprocated, partly because Bernice recoils from her touch. One of the film's themes, therefore, is the transfer of love and thirst for affection from a dysfunctional attachment to her mother, to a 'normal' heterosexual relationship with Mark. The normality of this relationship is highly questionable, however, as Mark sexually harasses a woman who declares her hatred for touching men, and frequently asserts that Marnie neither understands her own problems or what she needs. Whether the film reflects (and is therefore a part of) or highlights and questions patriarchal power structures is debatable, but the ways in which those power structures are linked with psychoanalytic practice and theory is interesting. Marnie frequently asks Mark to let her go or leave her alone when he interrogates her, and responds to his first declaration of love with the assertion that he does not love her, she is just something that he caught and that the marriage proposal is simply a matter of taking legal possession, a point that he does not dispute. Moreover, Piso (2009: 281) explores in some depth the gift economy of the film, arguing that people themselves are commodified and their exchanges robbed of the personal, social and community significances of the gift that exist in pre-industrial societies and are imbued instead with the lifeless exchanges of corporate capitalism. This analysis re-examines Marnie's thefts as a (somewhat futile) defence against the soulless power of the money-driven economy and emphasizes Marnie's mother as not just a rival for her affection in a psychological plot, but as a working class woman and exploited prostitute pitted against Mark's easy wealth and the power that this gives him, 'and we must ask ourselves why we think it is healthy that Marnie abandon her' (Piso, 2009: 283).

A second family romance dynamic is set up with the character of Lil. Mark is a widower and Lil is the sister of his first wife, who lived with them when she was young. The film suggests that Lil is in love with Mark, setting up a clear Oedipal conflict with her dead sister who had played the role of mother to her when she was alive (see also Modleski, 2016 [1988]: 41–53 for a discussion of Oedipal theory and rivalry between women in Hitchcock's *Rebecca* (1940)). This rivalry is transferred to Marnie, and is partly a plot device to set Lil up as someone who spies on Marnie, overhearing her talk to Bernice on the telephone and informing Mark that Marnie's mother is alive (and thus enabling him to further investigate Marnie's childhood). Lil also finds out that Mark has paid off Strutt (although she does not know what for) and invites Strutt to a house party where he recognizes Marnie, so that she has to admit to Mark that she has committed several other robberies.

In addition to Oedipal themes and compulsive behaviour, *Marnie*, also refers to trauma and its symptoms, as Bellour (2007) discusses in some depth. Bellour suggests that trauma is a prominent theme in many of Hitchcock's films, and that 'in order to be clarified, and, ultimately, resolved, the original trauma has to be conveyed through the whole film by its actual clinical symptoms, and finally to be shown in itself, as a sort of final primal scene' (Bellour, 2007: 255). While this method inevitably leads to some crude oversimplifications, it also raises some fascinating questions about the depiction of psychoanalytic theory and practice on the screen, including 'how can the image, through its figurative and figural choices, express the abstractions with which Freud is concerned; but also, how can the image qualify and carry more fundamentally something of the economic dimension Freud consistently attached to trauma?' (Bellour, 2007: 255).

In the case of the film *Marnie*, this is most often achieved through the film's use of the colour red, which Bellour (2007: 254) argues emblematizes the 'coming back' effect of the initial trauma. There are several scenes in which Marnie is profoundly affected by the colour red, including some red gladioli in her mother's house, when she spills some red ink on her blouse and when she sees red on a jockey's clothing, but it is not explained until the end of the film, when Marnie relives a traumatic childhood event, why red is a trigger for her. According to Bellour, therefore, this cinematic device enables Hitchcock to 'recreate figuratively the appearances of the symptoms and the final explosion of the primal traumatic scene itself' (Bellour, 2007: 255). In these scenes in which red is a cause of distress for Marnie, her emotional reactions are not the only clues. Instead the red object appears to pulse, growing larger and smaller again, and then the screen is taken over by red, in order to depict Marnie's state of mind, expressing 'through the sudden irruption of a color the intensity of an interior state, further than the actor's performance can bear, further than words can say' (Bellour, 2007: 256, see also Wood, 2002 [1989]: 175–6). Marnie also expresses her trauma through a terror of storms (because there was also a storm on the night of the traumatic incident). We see this reaction on the day that Marnie is working for Mark alone in his office, as she struggles to reach a light switch and, frozen with terror, says that she wants the colours to stop. Bellour (2007: 257) explains that different gradations of colour are linked in this scene, including red, mauve and blue 'to the total whiteness of the lightning out of which the colors seem to stream'.

While critics looking for realism in the film might argue that red is found almost everywhere in ordinary life, it should be borne in mind that the colour symbolism is a cinematic device intended to express the process of Marnie's trauma surfacing, rather than a precise reading of a case history. Moreover, there are several indicators to suggest that other factors, as well as seeing red, have contributed to Marnie's reactions. The gladioli are in her mother's house, the home of some very uncomfortable emotions for her, and when she sees the red on the jockey's clothing at the races, she has just been questioned by a private detective who appears to recognize her as the perpetrator of a previous robbery. In a later scene in the film Marnie is affected by the red on the jacket of one of the riders in the hunt. This scene takes place just after sequences where Strutt recognizes her at the party and she has had to explain to Mark about her other crimes. Moreover, it occurs just after the killing of a fox, which may also have contributed to her response. Normally an excellent rider, Marnie is overwhelmed by the red in this scene and loses control of her beloved horse, Forio, who trips over a wall and lies mortally wounded. Marnie knocks on the door of a nearby cottage and begs for a pistol so that she can shoot the horse and end its suffering. She leaves in an altered state and tries to steal money from the Rutland safe, and the film depicts her conflicted state of mind by showing the money in the safe appear to get larger and smaller, until Mark finds her and takes her back to her mother's house in order to help her to remember the childhood incident that originally traumatized her.

Already in a vulnerable state of mind, Marnie's memories are compelled to resurface through a number of reminders in this scene. She and Mark arrive at her mother's house in the midst of a raging storm that so terrifies Marnie that she has to be dragged out of the car by Mark, and once inside Mark explains to Bernice that he is Marnie's husband and that she is unwell and needs to remember the night of her mother's accident, a night that Bernice asserts only she knows the whole truth about. Mark confronts her with the revelation that she was a prostitute and a scuffle breaks out between them that Marnie responds to in a child's voice and we learn that this reminds her of a fateful night when a sailor comes out to Marnie as a child to try to comfort her from the terrors of a storm and Bernice, fearing for the child's safety, starts to hit him. A confused fight leads to him falling on Bernice (hurting her leg) and the child, rushing to defend her mother, hits him over the head with a stick (a poker), accidentally killing him. We see the rush of blood from his head fill the screen and hear the mother and child scream, understanding at last the traumatic incident that has caused the reactions of Marnie to red throughout the film.

There are thus remarkable similarities between *Spellbound* and *Marnie* in relation to the way that the dream is scripted as a hidden memory of a real incident, rather than a wish. Both films, as well as depicting psychology, suggest its questionable power dynamics. In *Spellbound*, there is some nod to the idea of resistance, as J. B. irritably fends off questions from Constance and tells Dr Brulov that he thinks Freud is 'huey', but the main tension in this film is actually between different aspects of Constance's selfhood, her professional self that fends off the advances of her colleagues, and the woman in love, who listens to her heart and believes in J. B.'s innocence even when the evidence goes against him. In this film the two come together when she applies cold logic to an analysis of his dream that solves the murder he has been accused of and sets him free.

In *Marnie* the theme of resistance is much more pronounced. Not only are the genders of 'patient' and 'therapist' reversed, but Marnie does not want help from Mark and it is he who insists on analysing her, as well as marrying her, against her will. It is as if Freud and Herr. K. have been rolled into one person in this film and the result has a terrifying undercurrent of psychoanalysis as itself a kind of violation. Critics have questioned the marriage as cure theme that Wood (2002 [1989]) espouses in the film and I suggest here that Hitchcock presents this theme with both irony and ambivalence. However, I suggest that it is not just Freud that is being questioned here, but a much broader set of assumptions that underlie fairy tales and melodramas. When Mark first catches Marnie, she tries to suggest that she chose to steal from Rutland's because they were getting too close and she might get hurt. She appears to be referring to a fear that a women of her background would eventually be discarded, and in this light, Mark, through his declaration of love and offer of marriage, appears to be giving Marnie the fairy-tale ending of women's dreams. Mark uses both his wealth and upper-class confidence to try to erase Marnie's crimes and her rejection of his displays of power and generosity shed light not just on the dangers of psychoanalysis, but on the assumptions about love and marriage that disguise patriarchy in numerous storytelling genres. In so doing, as Modleski (2016 [1988]: 4) suggests about Hitchcock's films more broadly, the way that women are oppressed in patriarchy is revealed and the female spectator is allowed to feel an anger that is very different from the 'masochistic response imputed to her by some feminist critics'. Moreover, just as Freud tried to expose the disguised powerful drives that, because hidden so well in his society, were making people sick, Hitchcock tries to explore and expose difficult but interesting aspects of human nature. It is notable in this regard that both J. B. and Marnie are traumatized by killing; J. B. in the accident that killed his brother and during his service in the Second

World War, and Marnie in the 'accidental' killing of the sailor. While the killing of the sailor is done by Marnie as a young child in defence of her mother, she hits the sailor on the head with the poker multiple times and it is therefore plausible that the explosion of this scene is partly about anger and Marnie's own power to kill (and its inherent pleasures), that is repressed and that leads to her rejection of sexuality. Moreover, this sheds light on the emphasis of Mark's interests in animals and instinctual behaviour. Unlike her mother, who recoils at Marnie's touch because of witnessing what she is capable of, Mark's love for Marnie includes her animal nature.

The recollection of this killing is closely related to the key dream in *Marnie*, which is characterized as a partial surfacing of the memory of it. In both *Marnie* and *Spellbound*, therefore, dreams have more to do with resolving the amnesia of the central characters than dreams in Freudian case studies, but they are nonetheless integrated into many Freudian themes. Most notably, dreams are about the interior life of the individual in these films, and this approach can be usefully contrasted with many dreams reported to anthropologists in societies where dream theory includes the possibility of dreams being a vehicle of communication with others as well as the self.

Anthropological work on dreaming

Key to many of Hitchcock's works, and in particular the two films that have been the main subjects of this chapter, *Marnie* and *Spellbound*, is the way that the central action is focused on the dynamics between two people. In both of these films the central characters are both romantically and therapeutically involved, a combination which suggests a critique of, as well as an interest in, Freudian psychology. However, this also highlights a broader set of cultural assumptions within which Hitchcock was working, namely ideas about the proper context for dream conversation and analysis. While it appears almost taken for granted in his films that people tend to discuss dreams with very few other people, and most often in a clinical setting with one other person, anthropological studies of dreaming in a range of global settings suggest that there are numerous ways in which the dreaming can play a part in social life and the contexts in which they are spoken about. For example, Robbins (2003: 19) suggests that in parts of Melanesia dream reports can have political significance, albeit limited and short-lived. Among the Urapmin of Papua New Guinea, he observed a combination of Christian and traditional attitudes to dreaming and explains that, according to the Urapmin, when a person dreams their spirit leaves the body and can have contact with spirits of other people, nature spirits, spirits of the dead, evil spirits and the Christian God or Holy Spirit. These spirits can show, through the dream, events that are currently happening but are hidden or reveal future happenings, 'often, the supernatural who gives the dream will also appear in the dream and offer an interpretation of the meaning of what the dreamer is seeing' (Robbins, 2003: 25). Such dreams can provoke people who are not normally thought of as politically influential in their group to speak out and potentially change a course of events. It is as if the spirits have temporarily lent their power and charisma to the dreamer (Robbins, 2003: 29–35). Vishvajit's (2004) study of the Ongee of the Andaman Islands examines in some depth the processes through which dreams are talked about. In this context, dreams and events of the previous and following days are discussed together by everyone just prior to falling asleep, a habit that aims to create a shared group memory and also to engender dreams that can aid people to accomplish their goals, aims that are often deeply connected to the forest and the changing practical necessities of life in response to the weather (Vishvajit, 2004: 3–5). A key analogy used by the Ongee to refer to this process is the spider's web, and this works on a number of levels, referring to the weaving together of dreams and dream discourse, the way that animals and humans leave and collect smells that map the forest in waking and dreaming activities, and individual webs as connected to bigger community webs (Vishvajit, 2004: 7–9).

Ewing (2003) explores differences between indigenous dream practices and theories and Freudian approaches. She suggests that for many indigenous peoples, dreams are a social phenomenon that are part of folk healing and are often used to predict the future. In contrast, drawing from Basso (1992) she notes Freud's emphasis on the dreamer's 'idiosyncratic personal history', arguing that although Freud's search for meaning in dreams was revolutionary, its focus was on understanding the personal past of the dreamer in order to identify their ongoing conflicts and traumas (Ewing, 2003: 44). Bourguignon (2003: 133) explains that her anthropological approach to dreaming has points in common with that of Hallowell (1976 [1966]) in that she explores how dreams help individuals communicate their inner life to others and aid group life. She emphasizes the difference between dreams as dreamt and dreams as narrated, because memories of dreams are often fragmentary and appear as puzzles to be solved (Bourguignon, 2003: 135–6). She argues that dreams are not just interpreted differently in different cultures but that their content is also different. In other words, the context of talking about dreams helps to shape what is actually dreamt (Bourguignon, 2003: 134). She contrasts religious contexts in which 'the message may be thought to come from divinities or deceased ancestors' with psychoanalytically informed practices where 'the message is understood as one from the self to the self, or, perhaps, to the therapist, that is, the audience of the dream narration' (Bourguignon, 2003: 136).

These anthropological examples occur during fieldwork, where scholars are listening to social accounts of dreams or interviewing dreamers, and the contrast between social and psychological explanations of dreams is striking. Moreover, they beg questions about depictions of dreams in American and European contexts in which psychoanalytic theory has seeped into popular understandings of personhood and the role of the dream. This chapter has suggested ways in which Hitchcock's films both drew from ideas rooted in psychoanalysis and in turn helped to shape the cinematic reception of psychology and his innovative approach to dream narratives is key to that process. On the one hand, Dr Brulov in *Spellbound* suggests that the secrets of who we are and what has made us run away from ourselves are to be found in our dreams, if only (with the help of a psychiatrist) we can sort through the confused pieces of the puzzle and decode them. On the other hand, this decoding in the film is less about uncovering of wishes and desires, and more about finding out who committed a murder that the protagonist witnessed. The secrets of who John Ballantine really is are much more effectively explored through Constance's analysis of his panic attacks and what triggers them, although Gabbard and Gabbard (1999: 55) are sceptical about the degree to which the talking cure actually appears in the film, asserting Hitchcock's own assessment of it as 'just another manhunt story wrapped up in pseudo-psychoanalysis' (Truffaut, 1984: 165) is correct. There are certainly critiques of psychoanalysis in both *Spellbound* and *Marnie* as the characters being analysed voice their resistance to the process and the audience are left wondering whether their illnesses are resisting the analyst or whether there is something in the therapeutic power dynamic that should be resisted, or at least questioned. Moreover, emphasis on the recall of actual events, rather than the complex emotional responses of the characters, is moulded to reshape psychoanalytic theory to suit the conventions of suspense, catharsis and resolution in melodramatic detective stories.

Models of dream narration and explanation found by anthropologists studying numerous indigenous contexts, however, find alternative modes of telling and decoding dreams. Recounting dreams can happen in much larger social groups than the one-on-one model familiar to therapeutic accounts, and the dreams can have much wider social significance than the interior conflicts of the individual. Moreover, many of these dreams are social in the sense that a dream self/soul/double/spirit is thought to visit or be visited by spiritual beings who offer information or powers that are potentially useful to the dreamer and their community. To break the code of these dreams is to simultaneously explore and reaffirm social relationships that have religious and spiritual dimensions. The following chapter therefore turns to a different example of visual storytelling that explores dreams, the television series *Twin Peaks*. While this series includes psychoanalytic dimensions to its plot and storytelling modes, there are also numerous examples of dreams and visions that resonate with anthropological accounts of dreams, including characters that are spirit beings from other worlds.

Bibliography

Allen, R., and Ishii-Gonzales, S. (eds) (1999) *Alfred Hitchcock: Centenary Essays.* London: British Film Institute.

Beeding, F. (1927) *The House of Dr. Edwardes.* London: Hodder & Stoughton.

Bellour, R. (2007) 'The *Marnie* colour', in C. Liu, J. Mowitt, T. Pepper and J. Spicer (eds), *The Dreams of Interpretation: A Century Down the Royal Road.* Minneapolis: University of Minnesota Press, pp. 253–62.

Basso, F. (1992) 'The implications of a progressive theory of dreaming', in B. Tedlock (ed.), *Dreaming: Anthropological and Psychological Interpretations.* Santa Fe, NM: School of American Research Press, pp. 86–104.

Bernheimer, C. (1990) 'Introduction: Part One', in C. Bernheimer and C. Kahane (eds), *In Dora's Case: Freud-Hysteria-Feminism* (2nd edn). New York: Columbia University Press, pp. 1–18.

Bernheimer, C., and Kahane, C. (eds) (1990) *In Dora's Case: Freud-Hysteria-Feminism* (2nd edn). New York: Columbia University Press.

Biesen, S. C. (2014) 'Psychology in American film noir and Hitchcock's gothic thrillers', *Americana: The Journal of American Popular Culture*, vol. 13, no. 1, pp. 1–8.

Bourguignon, E. (2003) 'Dreams that speak: Experience and interpretation', in M. Mageo (ed.), *Dreaming and the Self: New Perspectives on Subjectivity, Identity, and Emotion.* Albany: State University of New York Press, pp. 133–53.

Boyd, D., and Palmer, R. B. (eds) (2006) *After Hitchcock: Influence, Imitation, and Intertextuality.* Austin: Texas University Press.

Breuer, J., and Freud, S. (2001 [1893]) 'On the psychical mechanism of hysterical phenomena: Preliminary communication', in J. Strachey (trans.), *The Standard Edition of the Complete Psychological Works of Sigmund Freud*, vol. 2 (1893–5). London: Vintage, The Hogarth Press and the Institute of Psychoanalysis, pp. 1–17.

Brill, L. (1988) *The Hitchcock Romance: Love and Irony in Hitchcock's Films.* Princeton, NJ: Princeton University Press.

Bronfen, E. (1998) *The Knotted Subject: Hysteria and Its Discontents*. Princeton, NJ: Princeton University Press.

Creed, B. (2007) 'The untamed eye and the dark side of surrealism: Hitchcock, Lynch, and Cronenberg', in G. Harper and R. Stone (eds), *The Unsilvered Screen: Surrealism on Film*. London: Wallflower Press, pp. 115–33.

Deutelbaum, M., and Poague, L. (eds) (2009 [1986]) *A Hitchcock Reader*. Oxford: Wiley-Blackwell.

Ewing, K. P. (2003) 'Diasporic dreaming, identity, and self-constitution', in J. M. Mageo (ed.), *Dreaming and the Self: New Perspectives on Subjectivity, Identity and Emotion*. New York: State University of New York Press, pp. 43–60.

Freedman, J. (ed.) (2015) *The Cambridge Companion to Hitchcock*. Cambridge: Cambridge University Press.

Freud, S. (2001 [1900]) 'The Interpretation of Dreams', in J. Strachey (trans.), *The Standard Edition of the Complete Psychological Works of Sigmund Freud*, vol. 4 (1900), pp. 1–338, and vol. 5 (1900–1), pp. 339–630. London: Vintage.

Freud, S. (2001 [1901]a) 'Fragment of a case of hysteria', in J. Strachey (trans.), *The Standard Edition of the Complete Psychological Works of Sigmund Freud*, vol. 7 (1901–5). London: Vintage, pp. 1–122.

Freud, S. (2001 [1901]b) 'On dreams', in J. Strachey (trans.), *The Standard Edition of the Complete Psychological Works of Sigmund Freud*, vol. 5 (1900–1). London: Vintage, pp. 631–86.

Freud, S. (2001 [1919]) 'The Uncanny', in J. Strachey (trans.), *The Standard Edition of the Complete Psychological Works of Sigmund Freud*, vol. 17 (1917–19). London: Vintage, The Hogarth Press and the Institute of Psychoanalysis, pp. 217–56.

Gabbard, G. O., and Gabbard, K. (1999) *Psychiatry and the Cinema* (2nd edn). Washington, DC: American Psychiatric Press.

Graham, W. (1997 [1961]) *Marnie*. London: Pan Books.

Haeffner, N. (2005) *Alfred Hitchcock*. Essex: Pearson Education.

Hallowell, A. I. (1976 [1966]) 'The role of dreams in Ojibwa culture', in A. I. Hallowell (ed.), *Contributions to Anthropology: Selected Papers of A. Irving Hallowell*. Chicago: University of Chicago Press, pp. 449–74.

Kahane, C. (1990) 'Introduction: Part Two', in C. Bernheimer and C. Kahane (eds), *In Dora's Case: Freud-Hysteria-Feminism* (2nd edn). New York: Columbia University Press, pp. 19–32.

Kaplan, E. A. (2005) *Trauma Culture: The Politics of Terror and Loss in Media and Literature*. New Brunswick, NJ: Rutgers University Press.

Knight, D., and McKnight, G. (1999) 'Suspense and its master', in R. Allen and S. I. Gonzalès (eds), *Alfred Hitchcock: Centenary Essays*. London: British Film Institute, pp. 107–21.

King, E. H. (2007) *Dalí, Surrealism and Cinema*. Harpenden, Hertfordshire: Kamera Books.

Mahony, P. J. (1996) *Freud's Dora: A Psychoanalytic, Historical, and Textual Study*. New Haven, CT: Yale University Press.

McElhaney, J. (1999) 'Touching the surface: *Marnie*, melodrama, modernism', in R. Allen and S. Ishii-Gonzales (eds), *Alfred Hitchcock: Centenary Essays*. London: British Film Institute, pp. 87–105.

Mitchell, J. (2000) *Mad Men and Medusas: Reclaiming Hysteria*. New York: Basic Books.

Modleski, T. (2016 [1988]) *The Women Who Knew Too Much: Hitchcock and Feminist Theory* (3rd edn). London: Routledge.

Moral, T. L. (2005) *Hitchcock and the Making of Marnie*. Lanham, MD: Scarecrow Press.

Piso, M. (2009) 'Mark's *Marnie*', in M. Deutelbaum and L. Poague (eds), *A Hitchcock Reader*. Oxford: Wiley-Blackwell, pp. 280–94.

Pomerance, M. (2004) *An Eye for Hitchcock*. New Brunswick, NJ: Rutgers University Press.

Ramas, M. (1990) 'Freud's Dora, Dora's hysteria', in C. Bernheimer and C. Kahane (eds), *In Dora's Case: Freud-Hysteria-Feminism* (2nd edn). New York: Columbia University Press, pp. 149–80.

Rebello, S. (1990) *Alfred Hitchcock and the Making of Psycho*. London: Boyars.

Romer, E., and Chabrol, E. (1992 [1979]) *Hitchcock: The First Forty-Four Films* (trans. Stanley Hochman). Oxford: Roundhouse Publishing.

Robbins, J. (2003) 'Dreaming and the defeat of charisma: Disconnecting dreams from leadership among the Urapmin of Papua New Guinea', in R. I. Lohmann (ed.), *Dream Travellers: Sleep Experiences and Culture in the Western Pacific*. New York: Palgrave Macmillan, pp. 19–41.

Smith, S. (2000) *Hitchcock: Suspense, Humour and Tone*. London: British Film Institute.

Spoto, D. (1999 [1983]) *The Dark Side of Genius*. New York: Da Capo Press.

Trotter, D. (2010) *The Uses of Phobia: Essays on Literature and Film*. Oxford: Blackwell.

Truffaut, F. (1984) *Hitchcock* (revised edn). New York: Simon & Schuster.

Vishvajit, P. (2004) 'Forest smells and spider webs: Ritualized dream interpretation among Andaman Islanders', *Dreaming*, vol. 15, nos. 2–3, pp. 136–50.

Wood, R. (2002 [1989]) *Hitchcock's Films Revisited*. New York: Columbia University Press.

Žižek, S. (ed.) (1992) *Everything You Wanted to Know about Lacan but Were Afraid to Ask Hitchcock*. London: Verso.

Filmography

'A film profile: Alfred Hitchcock' (1966) (interview with P. Jenkinson) Directed by Christopher Doll, Episode 29 (series 1) in the TV series *Film Preview*, BBC: 12 September.

The Birds (1963) Directed by Alfred Hitchcock: Universal-International Pictures.

The Girl (2012) Directed by Julian Jarrold: BBC and HBO Films.

Hitchcock (2012) Directed by Sacha Gervasi: Fox, Searchlight Pictures.

Marnie (1964) Directed by Alfred Hitchcock: Universal Pictures.

Notorious (1946) Directed by Alfred Hitchcock: RKO Pictures.

The Pervert's Guide to Cinema (2006) Directed by Sophie Fiennes, scripted and presented by Slavoj Žižek: P. Guide Ltd, ICA Projects.

Psycho (1960) Directed by Alfred Hitchcock: Paramount Pictures

Rebecca (1940) Directed by Alfred Hitchcock: United Artists.

Spellbound (1946) Directed by Alfred Hitchcock: United Artists.

Un Chien Andalou (1929) Directed by Luis Buñuel: Les Grandes Films Classiques.

3

Animism, Anima and the Shadow in
Twin Peaks

In the previous chapter I explored Freud's approaches to dreams and to relationships between therapists and patients, and suggested ways in which the films of Hitchcock both utilize and ask difficult questions about Freudian psychology. In addition, I juxtaposed these approaches with examples from societies studied by anthropologists in which dreams are thought to have social and communicative significance beyond that of personal psychology. I outlined a broad contrast between psychological approaches derived from Freud that analyse dreams in terms of an individual's inner life and personal experience and approaches to dreaming recorded by anthropologists that suggest that dreaming is a social experience during which information can be communicated by ancestors, deities and spirits. This social aspect of dreaming in many indigenous contexts suggests key points in common with the branch of anthropology known as contemporary animism.

Although Hitchcock's film-making has been recognized as distinctive by many scholars and critics, there are also many aspects of his work, especially from the late 1940s onwards, that ally his films with classical Hollywood styles. His feature-length pictures, intended to be shown in the cinema, had clear structures and storylines (often inspired by books) and were influenced by, and helped to shape, genres such as film noir and melodrama. In this chapter, I aim to offer some contrast between cinema and television by exploring the serial drama *Twin Peaks* (Frost and Lynch). This series, which ran for two seasons between 1990 and 1991, and was then revived for a third season in 2017, is considered by many to be a marker of innovation in television and a precursor to the category 'Quality TV' (Booy, 2010: 28–30). Although both Frost and Lynch already had significant film-making experience when they worked on *Twin Peaks*, they also embraced the episodic format of television and there was a large directorial team with different episodes directed by different people (for a full list see Lavery,

1995: 196–7). In addition to innovations associated with developments in serial drama, *Twin Peaks* is also known for its experiments with genre. While there are in fact points in common with Hitchcock's films that I reflect on later in the chapter, there are also, nonetheless, clear differences that are important for this book's broader argument, because the style as well as the content of *Twin Peaks* can be illuminated by analysis through the lens of contemporary animism.

At first glance viewers tuning into the show may have expected a more traditional television police procedural drama. Its central tenet is a murder mystery surrounding the death of an adolescent girl, Laura Palmer, whose life is revealed to be deeply interwoven into the fabric of the small (fictional) Pacific North-Western town of Twin Peaks. An apparently related incident involving another girl, Ronette Pulaski, who, traumatized and assaulted, is found walking across a bridge that crosses state lines, brings into the town the FBI Agent, Dale Cooper, and he works with the local Sheriff's office to try to solve Laura's murder and the assault. It is not long, however, before the illusion of a simple police procedural programme breaks down, as the show continually dissolves the boundaries of its genre (Matthees, 2005: 102–5). It explores the complex relationships and lives of multiple members of the town like a soap opera, while simultaneously using plot devices and techniques from surrealism, comedy, film noir and horror genres to suggest that the mystery extends far beyond a who-done-it, and into more religious and esoteric themes. Unusual evidence and witnesses are brought to bear. Dreams and visions that include figures from alternate dimensions such as the Man from Another Place and the Giant guide Agent Cooper and witnesses include a Log, carried around by the Log Lady, otherwise known as Margaret Lanterman, who calmly asserts the Log's communicative powers and wisdom, and Waldo the Bird, who is shot at the Sheriff's office before he can repeat the voices and sounds that he overheard on the night of Laura's murder (1006: 'Cooper's Dreams' and 1007: 'Realization Time'). Arguably most mysteriously of all, the identity of the murderer is 'discovered' in the show but is at the same time palpably unclear. On the one hand, Laura's father, Leland Palmer, is discovered to have committed serial rape and assault upon his daughter and finally to have killed her. On another, he is thought to have been possessed by a demon called BOB, who actually committed the crimes and Leland's true culpability is left in question in a way that has led to some piercing questions from feminist academic critics of the series.

The idea that the true mystery of a film noir can go beyond the secular concerns of the who-done-it is not totally new. Hirsch (1981: 78) distinguishes film noir from other kinds of detective stories, suggesting that noir's preoccupation with alienation and entrapment is developed through styles and devices such as fractured time frames, shifting points of view and 'maze-like storylines'. These features also open film noir to theological analysis. Deacy (2001), for example, examines film noir from the 1940s and 1950s and the cinema of Martin Scorsese (1970s–1990s) using concepts rooted in Christian theology with a particular emphasis on notions of redemption. However, *Twin Peaks* has particularly animist features, including its explicit emphasis on dreams and visions in the detection process, the suggestion that the town contains portals to other worlds and their visionary inhabitants, and the way in which interaction with these beings, as well as The Log and Waldo the Bird, highlights their personhood. Care needs to be taken with this approach, however. There is no evidence that indigenous religions or films were researched by the team making the series. On the contrary, scholars such as Nochimson (2016: 48, 66) have explored the series in the light of Lynch's interest in Hindu religion and mythology which he expressed to her in interviews conducted in 2010, and Wilson (2007) notes Lynch's practice of transcendental meditation, suggesting that a 'transcendental irony' pervades his work. Moreover, some of the relationships with spirit beings express the reciprocity and personhood that are key to animism better than others. Particularly problematic is the demon BOB, who although personified, represents a generalized evil rather than a rounded person with individual subjectivity or motivations in his own right. For these reasons, I utilize an additional lens to examine *Twin Peaks* – that of Jungian analytical psychology. Jung's work on the *collective unconscious* adds an interesting social dimension to his analysis of dreams. Moreover, his work on archetypes opens up a potential analysis of BOB as a shadow figure. Further to this, the film noir genre has been of particular interest to Jungian scholars of film, who map key archetypes onto staple characters in the film noir plot, such as the detective (protagonist), the villain (shadow) and the femme fatale (anima). In light of this mapping, I structure this chapter with a focus on Agent Cooper, the demon BOB and Laura.

Agent Cooper as detective, anthropologist and dreamer

The character of Agent Cooper is intimately bound up with his relationship with the town of Twin Peaks, a town that is in many ways also a character in the show. Although fictional, Twin Peaks has multiple features that are associated with small towns in the Pacific Northwest, including landscape and environmental features such as the woods and the Douglas fir trees and its iconic waterfall, and its network of social relationships. It is therefore significant that Agent Cooper, an outsider and a representative of an external organization, the F.B.I., is brought into the town by crimes that cross state lines, is gradually drawn into an 'other' world which increasingly yields wonderous happenings and other-than-human persons. Weinstock (2016: 32, 36) uses the term 'animated with spirits' to describe the town and especially the woods within it. His suggestion that the trees are both animate and possess a kind of sentience is evocative of worldviews explored by contemporary animism. In addition, the use of the episodic soap opera format offers multiple plot lines and highlights the relationships and perspectives of many of its characters, suggesting a break from the emphasis in classical Hollywood films on a single protagonist.

These factors suggest that one way of understanding Agent Cooper's engagement with Twin Peaks is analogous to that of an anthropologist exploring the multiple viewpoints offered through participation in a chosen place for fieldwork. He displays wide-eyed curiosity about the town and its inhabitants, for example, when he asks Sheriff Truman what the local trees are called (1001: 'Pilot episode'). Moreover, he is gradually drawn into the perspective of Twin Peaks, defending the need of its inhabitants to hold a prompt funeral for Laura Palmer against the more scientific view of fellow F.B.I. Agent Albert Rosenfeld, who wants to conduct further tests to gather forensic evidence (1004: 'Rest in Pain') and donning local apparel when he is temporarily suspended from the F.B.I. (2011: 'Masked Ball'). He is even introduced to Twin Peak's secret society, an all-male group that defends the townspeople against the more malevolent aspects of the local woods. As Sheriff Harry Truman explains to Cooper, the differences between Twin Peaks and other places make it a wonderful place to live, but it also has a dark side, a 'back end' to this difference, 'something very very strange in these old woods' (1004).

Discussions about the complex role that Agent Cooper plays in the series abound, with Lavery (1995: 13) suggesting, for example, that it encompasses both private eye and ethnographer. While the latter designation is useful for illustrating the animist aspects of the programme, it should also raise a note of caution. The degree to which a good ethnographer should be immersed in the culture and religion of the society that they study is a question of debate in anthropology (Bowie, 2000) and there are some interesting accounts of situations where this can go wrong, including Stoller's exploration of his initiation into magical practices leading to magical attacks by his teacher's rivals (Stoller and Olkes, 1989). Moreover, while Agent Cooper engages with both human and spiritual persons in the town, he also brings with him an openness to engagement with methods of detection that are more like shamanic divination than they are reminiscent of observation by either ethnographers or detectives.

For example, he explains to the staff of the Sheriff's office about his interest in Tibetan Buddhism and that three years before he had woken from a dream from which he had subconsciously gained knowledge of a deductive technique that combined mind-body coordination and the deepest level of intuition. In an attempt to find out if the letter 'J' written in Laura's diary might indicate a meeting with a potential suspect, Cooper has the name of each person with a first initial 'J' read aloud, together with their connection to Laura. Simultaneously, he throws a rock at a bottle perched on a log, declaring that if the stone breaks the bottle, the name is significant. That night, Cooper has a dream in which Laura whispers the name of her killer to him (1003: 'Zen or the Skill to Catch a Killer'). Although for many episodes he forgets the name, he nonetheless focuses on trying to interpret this dream as a key deductive method of analysis, declaring to the investigative team that his dream is a code waiting to be broken: 'Break the code, solve the crime' (1004: 'Rest in Pain').

Although Nickerson (1993: 272) uses this phrase to suggests that 'even when the investigative methods get weird – interpretation of dreams and mind-body coordination – the guiding principle Cooper declares allegiance to is … one that has been fundamental to detective fiction since Poe'. However, Cooper's communication with human and spirit persons in dreams and visions points to a complex character who 'walks between two worlds' in various ways, not least by embodying the rationality of the detective genre (as exemplified by Hitchcock) and then expanding and subverting it. Riches, for example, argues that

> Freud's work on dream interpretation reveals how dreams might be understood as providing us with knowledge about ourselves, but this is not the central issue in *Twin Peaks*. Rather, what makes Cooper such an interesting character, and his method of detection so compelling, is the fact that dreams appear to provide him with knowledge of the world outside of his mind. (Riches, 2011: 29)

Hague (1995: 130) also refers to the 'derationalization of detection in *Twin Peaks*', suggesting that 'both classical and hardboiled fiction detection posits that rational solutions can be found to human crimes, that mysteries are physically-based and accessible to the powers of the logical intellect' (Hague, 1995: 130). In contrast, Dale Cooper uses his intuition and other 'unorthodox crime-solving techniques, which include clairvoyance, precognitive and "shared" dreams, visions, and an obsession with Tibetan Buddhism' which 'violate ratiocinative detection' (Hague, 1995: 136). She therefore utilizes Jungian analyses of the unconscious, intuition and synchronicity, to explore what she suggests are broader methods of enquiry and detection in the series.

This hybrid characterization of Agent Cooper can be explored as part of Lynch's well-known engagement with surrealist ideas and techniques, including the use of mixing, dissolving and editing images to express a fascination with the juxtaposition of waking and unconscious states (Creeber, 2004: 51) and its use of dreams and visions (Jowett and Abbott, 2013: 163). Creed (2007) explores this in relation to a number of Lynch's films, in an article that also highlights surrealist influences on Hitchcock's work. This article is a useful reminder that although *Twin Peaks* pays more attention to multiple characters and plots than the more formal style of Hitchcock's film narratives, they nonetheless have common factors and themes. For Creed, Hitchcock's surrealism can be found in his 'style, *mise-en-scène*, imagery, motifs, symbolism, jokes and his own persona which – like Dalí– he manufactured or staged as a surreal event' and his themes of 'murder, transgressive sexual desires, voyeurism, sadism, cannibalism, necrophilia, the compulsion to repeat, death and the uncanny' (Creed, 2007: 122, 123). Using 'the aesthetics of shock', Hitchcock aimed 'to challenge complacency and liberate the darker side of the imagination' (Creed, 2007: 121). While the dream sequence in *Spellbound* that was visually designed by Dalí is the most obvious and famous use of surrealism in Hitchcock's work, Creed provokes a deeper analysis of this influence, suggesting ways in which the films are guided by a 'hallucinatory logic' in which the states of dream and reality are hard to distinguish (Creed, 2007: 121–3). Nonetheless, while Hitchcock's surrealism is 'embedded ... more formally and unobtrusively, into the *mise-en-scène* ... as a means of intensifying his characters and his audience' Lynch's films explore the dark side of the human psyche with less of a foothold in linear narrative. His dream logic splices stories and images in disturbing ways (Creed, 2007: 129). What is clear in both directors is their fascination with dreams and the unique ways in which cinematic arts can tap into and explore their imagery in motion and their powerful links to human emotion. This potential for cinema not only to depict but also to evoke imaginative and dream states was noted by early surrealists such as Goudal (2000 [1925]) who suggested that 'watching a film unfolding in a darkened cinema embodied the closest thing to a dream' because of the way that experience shuts out distractions and also because the images unfold according to their own logic, sometimes moving the narrative between past and present at speed or lingering on stray images and ideas like a dream (Creed, 2007: 119).

As explored in the previous chapter, Hitchcock's interest in exploring the human psyche and its expressions in dream content was influenced by psychoanalysis, including that outlined by early proponents of the discipline such as Freud. However, although Hitchcock and various members of his production teams were informed about psychoanalysis and used ideas derived from its theory and practice for inspiration, Hitchcock films were not intended as documentaries, but as fictional entertainment pictures and this aim meant that psychoanalysis and its tropes were often both critiqued and transformed in his films. Gabbard and Gabbard (1999: 28) have, for example, pointed out that a number of films depicting psychoanalysis use the narrative trope of the 'cathartic cure, the sudden and dramatic recovery from mental illness' and suggested that while this 'formula lends itself well to the building of dramatic tension and its climatic release' it is rare in real life clinical experience. In these instances, the boundaries between psychological drama and detective film become blurred so that the aim of the protagonist in the film becomes to unlock the mysteries of another person. In Hitchcock's *Marnie*, the climactic scene is one in which Marnie is able to unblock and re-live a painful memory that acts as the key to all her symptoms and presumably cures her of them. *Spellbound* is more complex, however, in that there are at least two revelations. The first is a childhood memory that effects a cure on the hero, but he remains accused of a murder he did not commit and is jailed. It remains for the therapist to clear him of that murder and by extension to find the real killer and this occurs in the scene towards the end of the film in which she re-analyses his dream as a coded memory of events that had actually taken place, but which remained obscured in amnesia for her patient. While this scene can be analysed from a number of different angles, the significance here is that it captures the ways in which classical Hollywood cinema in its fusing of depictions of psychoanalysis with detective genres can distort dream analysis away from its roots in Freudian theories. In particular, while Freud did work to uncover repressed memories, his emphasis was not a mundane piecing together of events but was more orientated to the complex emotions that patients had surrounding those events. For him, the significance of the dream was the wish that had been repressed into unconsciousness and that had resurfaced in coded form to be given limited expression and release in dream symbolism.

While Lynch has also been influenced by psychoanalysis in his choices of themes and 'passions of the unconscious' in his films, his use of dreams in his film and television productions have been multifaceted and cannot always be aligned with specific theories (Bulkeley, 2003: 49). Bulkeley examines Cooper's dream at the end of episode 1003 where Cooper is transformed into a man twenty-five years older, sitting in a Red Room. He speaks with the Man from

Another Place and his cousin, a woman who looks just like Laura Palmer. Bulkeley (2003: 54) suggests that this dream is analogous with the Dalí-designed dream in *Spellbound*, because it is a 'seemingly nonsensical dream that turns out to be the key to solving ... a mysterious death'. Not only does the figure who Cooper identifies as Laura whisper the name of the killer in Cooper's ear (although he forgets the name of the murderer on waking), but various features in the dream are also regarded as clues by Cooper in a way that suggests that this dream contains fragments of Laura's memory, in much the same way that John's dream is also a memory. For example, Albert Rosenfeld's examination of forensic evidence suggests that Laura was tied up twice on the night of the murder, on one occasion with her hands behind her, a finding that Cooper links to dream Laura's words 'sometimes my arms bend back' (1004). A search of the home of one of the suspects, Jacques Renault, turns up a picture of a cabin in the woods with red drapes that Cooper connects with the red drapes in the room of his dream (1006: 'Cooper's Dreams'). Nonetheless, the clues and the ways in which Cooper follows them extend beyond psychoanalysis or memories of this-worldly events. The search for the cabin leads to the investigators coming across the home of the Log Lady, creating an opportunity for them to listen in detail to the testimony of her Log (1006). Moreover, at the beginning of the dream Cooper sees the two spirit entities, BOB and MIKE. Concerned that he is a strong telepathic sender, he therefore avoids being in the same room as Laura's mother, Sarah, when she gives a detailed description of BOB to a sketch artist, based on her vision of a man in Laura's bedroom. Upon seeing the sketch, Cooper confirms that it is the same man (1005: 'The One-Armed Man'). The final resolution of the dream only come when Cooper decides to use magic to find Laura's killer (2009: 'Arbitrary Law'). Gathering a group of key characters at the Roadhouse, he instructs them to make a space at the centre of the room. The old waiter enters and offers Cooper some gum, saying 'that gum you like is going to come back in style', a comment that echoes one made by the Man from Another Place in the dream. Suddenly the characters are frozen and bathed in light, the Man from Another Place appears and is dancing and in the dream room Cooper finally hears what Laura whispers: 'My father killed me.' In a previous vision, a Giant offered Cooper some advice and set him on a spiritual path like those of protagonists in fairy tales, declaring that when Cooper realizes that the things that the Giant has told him are true, he will return the ring (2001: 'May the Giant be With You'). This Giant reappears and signifies that Cooper has understood his clues by giving him back the ring, which appears in the Roadhouse and clatters to the floor (2009). While these visionary figures could be interpreted as manifestations from Cooper's own unconscious mind, as he processes subtle clues, the location of the dream in the social world, rather than solely as a manifestation of an individual's internal mental processes, is implied by the discovery that this same dream is also recorded by Laura in her secret diary, but Laura had the dream at a different time (22 February, a few days before she died) (2009) and Cooper thereafter refers to it as 'our dream'. This feature raises the issue of mutual or telepathic dreaming, a phenomenon that is harder to place clearly within or outside the boundaries of Freudian dream theory, because while he dismissed outright the idea that occult beings such as spirits existed independently of human mental processes, he was intrigued enough by telepathy to consider accounts in more depth (Hewitt, 2014: 61–83).

In a prominent example, Freud (2001 [1922]) examines accounts of dreams and telepathy in patients and correspondents. He suggests that his position is neutral with regard to telepathy, not least because of a lack of personal experience, but argues that in spite of the common association in the popular imagination between telepathy and dreams, the undetermined possibility of telepathic content in dreams should not alter the tenets of dream analysis that he has set out elsewhere (2001 [1922]: 197). In the first example, a man writes to Freud about a dream in which his wife gives birth to twins then hears that his daughter gave birth that same night (several months early) and also had twins (something that was not known before the birth) (Freud, 2001 [1922]: 200–1). Freud requested more information from his correspondent and concludes that whether or not the dream contains material transmitted telepathically, it does express an unconscious wish (the root of dream material in Freud's opinion), in this case that of a father who wishes his daughter was his wife (Freud, 2001 [1922]: 206). While acknowledging the possibility that a telepathic message from his daughter may have been transmitted to the dreamer, he suggests that this should only be considered as one among many stimuli that dreams utilize, and that unconscious wishes remain the key to the formation and analysis of dreams (Freud, 2001 [1922]: 207). Later in the paper, Freud makes this a circular argument by suggesting that, 'a dream without condensation, distortion, dramatization, above all, without wish-fulfillment, surely does not deserve the name' and that therefore a purely telepathic dream cannot exist but should instead be called 'a telepathic experience in a state of sleep' (Freud, 2001 [1922]: 208). Freud's position on the phenomena of spirits was even more strongly sceptical, in that while he was interested in the psychoanalytic implications of some accounts of belief in demons (e.g. cases in seventeenth-century Europe that he diagnoses as neurosis) (Freud, 2001 [1923]: 69–105), he was anxious to protect the fledgling science of psychoanalysis as a discipline and to avoid it falling into disrepute by association with 'the murky world of fraudulent mediums, séances, table-rapping and the conjuring of spirits that so powerfully captivated the popular imagination in *fin-de-siècle* Europe and America' (Hewitt, 2014: 85). There is therefore an incompatibility between contemporary animist readings of Cooper's dream and visions and Freudian perspectives that is difficult to reconcile, as anthropological accounts from numerous indigenous peoples suggest that at least some spirit beings are external to the dreamer or visionary, while Freud, despite his nod to the possibility of telepathy between human beings, keeps his focus on the internal workings of the individual mind.

An alternative psychological framework of analysis is the analytical psychology of Jung. Jung's engagement with religious symbolism and mythology suggested that spiritual transformation could be a goal of the analytical process. Moreover, his positing of the *collective unconscious*, residing below the unconscious and acting as a repository for collective emotions and energies is significant, in that these contents can manifest in an individual's dreams and creative materials such as artworks. While interpretations of Jung's *collective unconscious* vary, the positing of a collective dynamic to this subterranean layer of consciousness opens up more possibilities for analysing consciousness as permeable to external forces and persons and a much more developed and sophisticated exploration of the mind's potential for unconscious communication.

In one example, he explores this potential in his analysis of the phenomenon of synchronicity (Jung, 2008 [1955]). Reflecting on a range of materials, including ESP (extrasensory perception) studies, Jung suggests that space and time are primarily organizing principles of the psyche, and that therefore synchronicity is 'a psychically conditioned relativity of space and time' (Jung, 2008 [1955]: 28). Such a definition would furnish an explanation for the dream that Cooper and Laura seem to share, despite experiencing it at different times. Further to this, he connects the phenomena to the archetypes, which he suggests structure the *collective unconscious*, and which can be perceived in dream images and individual behaviour patterns when they become charged with emotional energy (Jung, 2008 [1955]: 29). Because the *collective unconscious* is a level of consciousness that connects human beings with each other and also with the outside world in subtle ways, the 'simultaneous occurrence of two meaningfully but not causally connected events' suggests reflections between certain psychic states and happenings in the external world (Jung, 2008 [1955]: 36). Another way of saying this is that an event remote in space and time can produce a corresponding psychic image because 'there is in the unconscious something like an *a priori* knowledge or immediate presence of events which lacks any causal basis' (Jung, 2008 [1955]: 43–4). This idea, that the structures of the *collective unconscious* can facilitate both telepathy and clairvoyance, is an important point of contrast with Freud, who acknowledges the possibility of unconscious communication, but maintains a theoretical focus on the inner life and wishes of the patient as the primary topic of investigation in psychology and who was keen to distinguish the emerging discipline from the investigations and aspirations of people interested in researching the occult.

Jung's theories of the *collective unconscious* and the *archetypes* also lend themselves to different ways of interpreting mythology, folklore and other kinds of storytelling that have led to some interesting developments in the study of cinema (Bassil-Morozow and Hockley, 2017; Hauke and Alister, 2001; Hauke and Hockley, 2011; Hockley, 2001; Izod, 2001; Waddell, 2006). On one level, this is because the *archetypes* are closely related to figures commonly found in storytelling, for example the Old Man/Woman who acts as a mentor or spiritual guide, or the helper who often takes animal form. Moreover, because Jung's theory is naturally imbued with dynamism, with different archetypes becoming animated with emotional energy at different times, they are not conceived as fixed entities, but manifestations on a spiritual journey to wholeness (individuation) and therefore lend themselves very well as tools to explore stories as journeys of the hero/heroine.

This approach is exemplified particularly well by Hockley (2001: 103–22), who suggests Jungian analyses of films in which the protagonist (often a detective) is taken on a journey by the story where they are pitted against the villain (their shadow) and have complicated dealings with characters of the opposite sex such as the femme fatale that signify engagements with the anima (for women these engagements would be with a male *animus* figure). This kind of interpretation is potentially interesting in the case of *Twin Peaks*, because BOB, as a possessing force behind the evil deeds of Leland, lends himself well to the role of the shadow, and is, moreover, a figure that signifies the *collective consciousness* of the town, being seen by and referred to by several inhabitants. Similarly, Laura, whose identity is notoriously elusive, appears to be a repository for the projections of most of the other characters in *Twin Peaks*, at times a figure of deep sympathy and at others a femme fatale, Laura is arguably a personification of the *anima*. I therefore explore both of these hypotheses below, while at the same time suggesting ways in which both Jungian interpretations in general and analyses of the femme fatale in particular raise difficult questions for cinema and television studies.

The trouble with BOB

In the previous section I have argued that the world of *Twin Peaks* appears to have many features in common with animist perspectives as noted by modern anthropologists, but that the extent to which this is intended by Lynch and Frost is uncertain. The totem poles and other artwork that resembles Native American designs, for example, were already on location where the pilot episode was filmed. While the Giant and the Man from Another Place (dwarf) play roles of visionary beings, they are figures more commonly found in European folklore. Rather than suggesting that the animism in *Twin* Peaks is consistent or intentional, I have suggested that it is a product of the hybrid nature of the series and the ways that it borrows from multiple genres and motifs. Film noir is certainly a key element but romantic comedy, surrealism, space exploration, science fiction, the gothic and horror are also found (Nickerson, 1993: 275). By placing all of these generic expressions under the umbrella of melodrama and soap opera, the series offers multiple storylines and the perspectives of various characters, a move that I have suggested lends itself well to anthropological in addition to psychological analysis. Moreover, I have explored additional persons in the series such as the Log Lady's Log and the Giant that suggest an expanded view of personhood that lends itself well to examination through the lens of the work of contemporary animists.

Nonetheless, while some features in the series appear to be imbued with animism, it is certainly not a perfect fit. Particularly problematic is the hybrid figure of the character of BOB, an evil inhabiting spirit who possesses Leland when he murders his daughter and her cousin Maddy. BOB tantalizingly introduces a motif of spirit possession into the programme, but the character does not neatly conform to either medieval Christian theologies of evil or possessions in indigenous societies which are often conceived as by either positive or neutral spirits, ancestors or deities (see Chapter 5 for more exploration of indigenous possession phenomena). Christianity seems to be a point of reference in Cooper's dream when a reformed spirit called Mike describes BOB as his former companion and a 'devilish one', while Mike's transformation and renunciation of evil is triggered by seeing the 'face of god' (1003). However, there is no sustained exploration of Christian theology in the series and no consultation with priests or exorcists in the search for BOB or in discussions between the characters trying to understand who or what he is. The analysis of animist understandings of evil is a subject that needs further research beyond the scope of this book, but I note here that although BOB is a separate entity that appears to Cooper and Sarah in dreams and visions and who stares back from the mirror when he possesses Leland and later Agent Cooper, BOB is more a generalized personification of evil than a motivated entity in his own right. Most animist customs, mythological stories and practices for 'living well' emphasize processes of negotiation with other persons. Animal persons, for example, may become troublesome if their natural habitat is disturbed and they need to forage for food in places humans frequently use (Harvey, 2005: 99–106). Similarly, there are important behaviours and rites of exchange needed with spirit persons, and if these are ignored, potential helpers can become dangerous. In each of these examples, animals and spirits are not primarily orientated to humans, they are 'doing their own thing' but can help or hinder humans, depending on the effectiveness of humans' abilities to offer co-operation, understanding, respect, and exchange. BOB does not conform to this model. We do not know him except as a representation of forces that incite evil doing in humans and although he can be described as evil personified, the lack of depth and nuance to his character makes him a poor example for personhood in the sense used by contemporary animists. I therefore explore a different framework as a lens through which BOB can be understood, namely Jungian Analytical Psychology, and suggest that both BOB and the alternate dimensions of the White and Black lodges are best explored through analysis of Jung's work on the *shadow*.

According to Jung (1981 [1951]: 8) 'the shadow is a moral problem that challenges the whole ego-personality'. Defining the shadow as one of the archetypes, Jung thereby suggests its roots in the *collective unconscious*. However, compared to other archetypes, the shadow is relatively accessible and easy to experience because many other archetypes are more closely associated with the depths of the *collective unconscious* and therefore more obscure. Being closer to the personal unconscious (which Jung locates as midway point between consciousness and the *collective unconscious*) the shadow's 'nature can in large measure be inferred from the contents of the personal unconscious' although it is still challenging for people because 'no one can become conscious of the shadow without considerable moral effort' (Jung, 1981 [1951]: 8). This effort relates in part to the fact that recognizing the shadow side entails an examination of one's own darker characteristics and inferior qualities, but it is also because these qualities are emotional in nature, they have a 'kind of autonomy, and accordingly an obsessive or, better, possessive quality' (Jung, 1981 [1951]: 8). Moreover, the shadow can be very resistant to recognition 'because the cause of the emotion appears to lie, beyond all possibility of doubt, in the *other person* ... it is not the conscious subject but the unconscious which does the projecting. Hence one meets with projections, one does not make them ... projections change the world into the replica of one's own unknown face' (Jung, 1981 [1951]: 9).

The reference to possession is interesting in the context of *Twin Peaks*, because BOB possesses people in order to commit crimes. Moreover, Jung does not use this term lightly, as there were significant episodes in his life and career that fostered a lifelong interest in spirits and mediums. After his break with Freud in 1913, Jung 'resolved to take the decisive step and drop deep into a world of fantasy, visions, and dreams ... several of these experiences were of an undeniably spiritualistic nature. Visions and ghostly figures populate these years' (Charet, 1993: 61). Charet (1993: 59) points to a 'certain tension in Jung ... in his attempt to understand and interpret Spiritualism. This tension first manifests itself in Jung's early experience of the conflict between his parents and their families. The result was to cause a split in him that it was the burden of his life to try to heal'. His father was a Protestant clergyman while various members of his mother's side of the family spoke of visions and encounters with spirits (Charet, 1993: 67–9) and his medical dissertation drew from observations of a medium, Helene Preiswerk, who was also a cousin on the maternal side (Charet, 1993: 151–5). This dissertation is interesting for several reasons. Firstly, although his analysis is a psychological one, he does not exclude the possibility of the paranormal (Charet, 1993: 150). Secondly, it is an important early step in Jung's formulation of theories of archetypes and the process of individuation (Charet, 1993: 154). Thirdly, Jung suggests that the 'spirits' that Helene manifests can be understood as 'subconscious personality complexes' that are relatively independent of the conscious mind', and Charet's chapter on Jung's dissertation is called 'multiple personality and spiritualism' (Charet, 1993: 159). This latter point is something that Jung later develops into the idea that people may be seized by autonomous complexes in ways that resemble them falling subject to possession by a spirit.

Surface resemblances between the manifestations of multiple personality in American psychiatry and behaviours of possessing spirits observed by anthropologists have been explored by Bourguignon (1989). Using a couple of case studies, she argues that while there are apparent similarities the very distinct sociocultural contexts for the phenomena mean that there are radical differences and that 'for the two cases discussed here there is only analogy, not substantial identity of phenomena' (1989: 383). This needs to be borne in mind because although Jung's theories were informed by anthropological accounts of possession, and he uses the analogy in subtle ways that do not exclude the possible reality of spirits and spiritual influences, it is important to be aware that a television show such as *Twin Peaks* is more likely to be influenced by film and television depictions of demonic possession or multiple personality than by an in-depth reading of Jung's work. The fact that, whether understood as a demon or an alternate, BOB engages in criminal activity taps into important precedents in cinema.

One of the most foundational depictions of alternate personality appears in Hitchcock's film *Psycho* (1960). Although the phenomenon was used to create suspense and shock in the film, the explanation towards the end given by the psychiatrist who takes Norman's confession conforms in many ways to Oedipal conflict dramas. He explains that he got the confession from Norman's mother, or rather the 'mother' half of Norman's mind. When asked if Norman committed the murders, he responds 'yes and no', but this ambivalence does not raise questions in the film about Norman's legal fate, it is merely a matter of interest to those gathered to hear the story. It transpires that Norman killed his mother and her lover out of sexual jealousy, and because the matricide was unbearable for his mind, he preserved her body and took on her personality in order to ease the burden. Moreover, Norman projects his own jealousies onto his mother personality, making her pathologically jealous of any woman that sparked Norman's interest, and thus the mother half of Norman committed the murders. The closing scenes of the film show 'mother' in the police cell and we hear thoughts in her voice.

Subsequent films about multiple personality tend to take one of two different paths. On the one hand, films such as *Sybil* (1976) and *Frankie and Alice* (2010) offer sympathetic depictions of characters who manifest multiple personality as a response to suffering and abuse in early life and whose personalities help them to cope in the adult world. Their behaviour may be puzzling and difficult to integrate at times but criminality is not implied. However, the diagnosis of multiple personality (more corrected termed dissociative identity disorder) is controversial and debated. While some psychiatrists doubt the veracity of the condition, others are concerned that the potential suggestibility of patients leads to false diagnoses based on what therapists assume and are looking for. The case that the film *Sybil* (1976) and the earlier book (*Sybil*, Schreiber: 1973) are based on is one example of this controversy, as both were cast into doubt because of subsequent statements by the patient (Shirley Ardell) and the psychiatrist (Cornelia B. Wilbur) (Rose, 2017).

In other examples, thrillers and police procedural television shows depict the problems that multiple personality raises for questions of criminal culpability. This kind of approach has been criticized by clinicians studying dissociative identity disorder as harmful misrepresentations of the condition which rarely gives rise to criminal acts (Rose, 2017), but despite the inaccuracies, films like *Primal Fear* (1996) and episodes of *Homicide Life on the Street* (1993–9) (ep. 2003) continue to explore anxieties around whether an 'alternate' personality can be tried for committing murder or whether a criminal can act out a multiple personality scenario in order to escape prison. Such anxieties, I suggest, are part of particular understandings of personhood in Western European contexts where the idea that 'one person, one body', an idea that has been shaped by legal, social, political and religious developments, has attained the status of natural and given. It is precisely these kinds of assumptions about what is natural and given that anthropologists interrogate and, as I explore in more depth in Chapter 5, there are many global examples of different models of personhood, many of which include the possibility of benign possession of a human by ancestors, deities and spirits.

Twin Peaks maintains an interesting level of uncertainty about the true status of the relationship between BOB and Leland Palmer. On the one hand, there are clear resemblances between the scene where BOB confesses to the murders in a prison cell and the testimony of the Norman's mother alternate personality in *Psycho*. Sheriff Truman asserts the belief that BOB cannot really exist, and that Leland must be crazy. On the other hand, once BOB has taken over Leland in the police cell and is howling wildly, Ben says 'that's not Leland'. There is also a scene reminiscent of *The Exorcist* (1973) where BOB taunts Cooper about secrets from his past, much as the demon in *The Exorcist* taunts the priest with secret personal information. A possession also is implied when a dying Leland returns to his body and explains that he saw BOB in his dreams and that he invited BOB inside him, whereupon BOB made Leland do terrible things that he could not remember (2009: 'Artbitrary Law'). As I explore in the section about Laura below, it can be argued that the series uses the trope of possession to side-step the thorny issues of incest, rape and murder, but an alternative interpretation is that, because BOB can be regarded as a manifestation of a collective shadow, the series does explore ways in which societies share collective responsibilities for the crimes in their midst.

This idea is supported by the ways in which Jung links the personal shadow with the *collective unconscious*. Applied to the series, BOB's identity goes beyond Leland's personal shadow and encompasses the shadow side of the town of *Twin Peaks* itself. This idea, that the shadow as detected in the personal unconscious can be indicative of wider societal or national problems, is explored by Jung, who suggests that, just as psychological mechanisms work towards balance by throwing up from the collective unconscious that which is lacking in the consciousness mind, similar processes can take place within collectives such as nation states. Moreover, a process that initially aims towards compensation of a deficiency in consciousness can become dangerous and distorted if the contents that have arisen do not become properly recognized, balanced and integrated within the whole, and he uses examples of dictatorships in the 1930s and 1940s Europe to explore how impulses for order can become distorted and perverted by societies that aimed to recover from the chaos after the First World War but instead became subject to dictatorships that appeared to offer order but in fact brought chaos and destruction (Jung, 1995 [1946]: 174–7).

The idea that BOB is a symbol of Twin Peak's collective shadow is aided by the fact that he is seen, often in dreams or visions, by a range of characters, including Sarah Palmer (Laura's mother) and Agent Cooper. Moreover, although the rape and murder of Laura is the most extreme example, this shadow side of the small town is also explored through a range of other characters and situations, many of them related to violence against women. These incidents are potentially linked to spiritual dualities in the programme. For example, when Harry Truman explains to Agent Cooper about the town's secret society, he says,

> Twin Peaks is different, a long ways from the world. That's the way we like it. But there's a back end to that that's kind of different too. Maybe that's the price we pay for all the good things. There's a sort of evil out there, something very very strange in these old woods. A darkness, a presence, call it what you want. It takes many forms but it's been out there for as long as anyone can remember. And we have always been here to fight it. (1004)

A collective shadow side is also suggested through the Black and White Lodges, both apparently portals to other realms that can be accessed through dreams and in specific spots in the woods. Hawk suggests that the White Lodge is a place where spirits that rule man and nature reside and that the Black Lodge is 'the shadow self of the White Lodge. Legend says every spirit must pass through here on its way to perfection. There you will meet your own shadow self' (2011, 'Masked Ball').

The way that this shadow manifests itself in *Twin Peaks* suggests that patriarchy and male violence against women is a recurring and persistent feature of the shadow side of small-town America, and in order to explore that in more depth, I will focus more closely on the character of Laura Palmer, whose murder is the chief driving force of the first half of the series. In doing so, I also draw attention to Jung's analysis of the relationship between the shadow archetype and the archetypes of anima and animus. Linking these archetypes through a discussion of the mechanism of projection, Jung explains that while the shadow is the same sex as the subject, the anima and animus are contra-sexual figures

> whose autonomy and unconsciousness explain the stubbornness of their projections. Though the shadow is a motif as well known to mythology as anima and animus, it represents first and foremost the personal unconscious, and its content can therefore be made conscious without too much difficulty ... the anima and animus are much further away from consciousness and in normal circumstances are seldom if ever realized. (Jung, 1981 [1951]: 10)

This link between the *anima* figure and the mechanism of projection is particularly apt for the character of Laura Palmer, who we only know in the series through other people's accounts of her and who seems to be a repository for a range of projections, positive and negative, rather than a fully fleshed out person in her own right. This linking of female characters with extreme good and evil has a long history in cinema and has been examined in interesting ways by feminist theorists exploring the femme fatale of classical Hollywood's film noir genre and beyond and I therefore utilize some of their work to reconsider the character of Laura Palmer as anima and femme fatale in *Twin Peaks*.

Laura as anima and femme fatale

Scholarly discussions around Laura Palmer often revolve around the question of Lynch's handling of her incestuous rape and murder. I have suggested that by exploring BOB as a shadow figure, one can see how this works on collective as well as personal levels, and the series therefore uses the demonic trope to point to problems in American communities that are rarely discussed at the level of collective responsibility. However, some scholars have argued that by displacing Laura's murder onto a demonic possession, Lynch withdraws from a confrontation with the real issues and thereby participates in the patriarchal structures that perpetuate them. George (1995), for example, situates the way in which *Twin Peaks* revolves around the rape and murder of a young woman in a broader context of crimes against women in American society, arguing that film and television have both reflected and helped to shape a cultural environment in which audiences have a 'love affair with the interfaces of sex and death' and a 'hunger for seeing women dead or maimed or mutilated or suicidal or raped or helpless, especially if they are sexually active' (George, 1995: 110). Further to this, she suggests that the irony, parody and other engaging techniques that the programme uses may obscure fundamental problems with its premise and explores the wider contexts of other female characters in the show to demonstrate ways in which each of them is maimed, deeply flawed, crazy or a victim (George, 1995: 115). She is therefore deeply suspicious of the displacement of Laura's rape and murder away from her father and onto the possessing agent of BOB, arguing that, 'far from holding responsible for their actions the men who abuse and kill under BOB's influence, *Twin Peaks* lets them off the hook by reverting to a simplistic displacement to the supernatural' (George, 1995: 117).

Nonetheless, Laura Palmer is a central character in *Twin Peaks*. Her body is found wrapped in plastic in the pilot episode and the investigation of her murder drives the plot of the initial episodes. Moreover, she has numerous connections to other characters in the show, putting her at the centre of its complex web of social relations. Exhibiting different character traits in different situations, Laura appears to have had a mercurial nature, 'filled with secrets'. Ratings for the show dropped significantly after Laura's murder was solved, leading to critical speculation as to whether later plot lines were more poorly constructed or whether the solving of the central mystery of the series erased a key hook that drew in and retained viewers. The characterization of Laura therefore presents a paradox, being on the one hand central to a plot that draws attention to issues of patriarchal violence in America, while she is at the same time lacking in substance as a person in her own right. Rather, Laura appears to be a repository for numerous reflections and projections of those around her. Her image, both as a smiling 'perfect' schoolgirl and as a body wrapped in plastic, pervades the series and she is also a mirror or a double to other characters in more subtle ways. She looks exactly like her cousin Maddy who is Leland's subsequent murder victim. She is replaced by her best friend Donna as James's love interest, and she is the subject of investigation by another schoolgirl, Audrey, who follows Laura's trail to a brothel named One-Eyed-Jacks where she is sexually pursued by her father, Ben Horne (who is unaware of her true identity), thereby mirroring Laura's subjugation to incestuous rape. These themes of mirroring, doubling and projection are open to a range of interpretations, but I explore here their relevance both to film noir and Jungian psychology, suggesting that Laura can be seen as both a femme fatale of film noir and as an anima figure.

The anima, according to Jung, is an archetype that originates from a point more deeply submerged in the unconscious than the shadow. Jung conceives of anima and animus as contrasexual figures so that the anima manifests itself for men with images of and qualities associated with women, while the animus is a male archetype that manifests itself in women. The depth of these archetypes is one factor that contributes to their tricky and elusive nature. They are rarely perceived directly, but instead tend to manifest themselves in the dynamics of interpersonal relationships and are therefore even more closely associated with the mechanisms of projection than the shadow. Jung suggests that the anima is made up of a number of different elements. The first factor he describes as a female 'imago of a relatively autonomous nature' which has qualities in common with the imago of parental figures as found in, for example, ancestor cults (Jung, 1977 [1928]: 188). Secondly, Jung suggests that men repress their more feminine traits which as a result accumulate in the unconscious. Moreover, 'the imago of woman (the soul image) becomes a receptacle for these demands, which is why a man, in his love-choice, is strongly tempted to win the woman who best corresponds to his own unconscious femininity – a woman, in short, who can unhesitatingly receive the projection of his soul' (Jung, 1977 [1928]: 189). The third is an inherited collective image of woman that is largely unconscious (Jung, 1977 [1928]: 190). Contrasting the anima with the persona, Jung suggests that the persona largely conforms to outward, social expectations, which are thereby somewhat limiting. These limitations lead to an imbalance within the psyche, triggering a process whereby compensating energy is given to other aspects of the person concerned. Because expectations regarding masculinity are important constituents of the persona for many men, Jung suggests that the compensating 'autonomous complex' takes on characteristics associated with the female, and this is often unconsciously projected onto women in the man's personal life (Jung, 1977 [1928]: 192–7). Jung's theories of anima and animus have been the subject of criticism by feminist writers because of concerns about essentialist tendencies in some of his writings about gender. However, despite Jung's slippages into replicating gender prejudices of his time, his work has been the subject of revision and reclamation by a range of feminist scholars (Rowland, 2002). The exploration of the compensatory nature of anima and animus in relation to a person's orientation to public life do suggest an awareness of the social construction of gender relations, and, importantly for this chapter, Jung's mechanism of projection suggests ways in which female characters in fiction can be constructed through the responses of those around them, a point that is key to research into the femme fatale in film and television.

Doane, for example, explores the film *La Signora di Tutti* (1934), suggesting that, 'the narrative of La Signora di Tutti circulates around an absence which seems to reassert the inaccessibility of its central figure' (Doane, 1991: 121). On one level this absence refers to the film within the film (also called *Signora di Tutti*) that is never seen, while on another, the title refers to 'an unnamed woman as the generalized possession of "everybody" ... furthermore, this process of abstracting the woman and transforming her into a signifier of generalized desire is supplemented by the production of a discourse of mechanical reproduction and its techniques of abstraction' (Doane, 1991: 121–2). Woman is also compared to the cinematic apparatus in this film,

> insofar as she constitutes a lure for the male subject – more dangerous even than the cinema since she frequently leads him to his doom. Yet, without knowledge of her effect, she has no access to subjectivity. The narrative of the *Signora di Tutti* is grounded in Gaby's lack of agency. She is the pure object of the desires of men, subject of nothing. As her father points out early in the film, 'The girl is dangerous and she doesn't realize it'. She unwittingly or unknowingly causes death or disaster ... all of Gaby's sexual relations are contaminated by death, but her fatal attraction is not really that of the femme fatale of film noir ... while the femme fatale of film noir is consciously manipulative or conniving, Gaby is apparently devoid of intention or motivation. (Doane, 1991: 122–5)

What Doane does not emphasize, however, is that Gaby is not simply guileless but also a repository for unfounded blame, such as when she is vilified as a school child for being seduced by one of her teachers. Similarly, Neale suggests that 'the force of association between *noir* and *femmes fatales* is such that *"femme fatale"* is often used as a term to label the eponymous protagonists of such canonic *noirs* as *Laura* (Preminger, 1946) and *Gilda* (Vidor, 1946), even though they are not *femme fatales* at all' (Neale, 2010: 188). Even the examples that Neale chooses to better exemplify the stereotype (*Double Indemnity* 1944 and *Human Desire* 1954) also have elements that complicate or even undermine it (Neale, 2010: 188). Neale goes so far as to suggest that *Human Desire* and many of Fritz Lang's other films, 'are full of male bullies, male sex killers and nominally clean-cut male protagonists whose traits are persistently darkened' (Neale, 2010: 197).

Taking this line of enquiry a step further, Grossman (2013: 21) explores 'the striking extent to which "femmes fatales" – seductresses whose desires and malevolence are seemingly unmotivated – don't in fact exist in the noir movies in which so-called bad women appear'. She argues for an alternative close reading of the films, suggesting that 'there are *many* female characters in original-cycle noir who are shown to be limited by, even trapped in, social worlds presented as psychotically gendered' and that therefore their actions are often related to quests for independence and autonomy. Grossman (2013: 2) acknowledges the importance of psychoanalytic and feminist approaches to film noir, for example Copjec (1993) and Kaplan (1998 [1978]), but nonetheless argues for more attention to social context within the films, because 'a large majority of the so-called bad women in noir are not demonized in the films in which they appear and are very often shown to be victims: first, of the social rules that dictate gender roles and, second, of reading practices that overidentify with and overinvest in the idea of the "femme fatale"'.

A particularly relevant example is Otto Preminger's *Laura* (1944). Halskov (2015: 146–7) in his explorations of Lynch's allusions to film noir in *Twin Peaks* suggests that the naming of Laura Palmer may well be a reference to the film *Laura*. In this film, the detective, McPherson, spends much of the early part of the film in Laura's apartment, investigating her murder. Piecing together her life and relationships with other people through their accounts of her, McPherson is drawn into her story with increasing emotion, something illustrated in the film through his 'infatuation' with her portrait. His fantasies are, however, disrupted, when Laura, alive and well, enters her home. Apparently, the body that was mistakenly identified as Laura belonged to another woman, and in McPherson's eyes Laura goes from being murder victim to suspected murderer almost immediately. Grossman (2013: 30) examines the 'obsessive ideation' of Laura by the film's male characters, suggesting that 'McPherson identifies Laura herself with the painting of her – her actual appearance disorients him into casting her as a "femme fatale" and assuming that she is guilty no matter what she says, a point which the character of Laura herself makes in the film'.

In *Twin Peaks*, Laura Palmer, being dead, has no such recourse to protest or challenge the projections of those around her. Instead, the iconic image of her photograph, the last image of every episode, is contrasted with descriptions of her drug-taking and promiscuity. The 'good' Laura is given multiple roles, helping with the Meals on Wheels programme, teaching Josie English and assisting with activities for Audrey Horne's brother Johnny, who has learning difficulties. These multiple roles help to embed her within the network of relationships in the town but also point to a character that is ideational and impossible, in that there are not enough hours in a day to include these activities with a full school life, two boyfriends *and* criminal activity. Instead, Laura's character appears to carry the weight of other people's projections, both good and bad, and is left without subjectivity and depth. Moreover, despite the fact that many characters acknowledge that she was troubled, she is also blamed in ways that allow others to evade responsibility. In one example Bobby tells Dr Jacoby that Laura made him sell drugs and Dr Jacoby theorizes that her bad secrets compelled her to find people's weaknesses and use them to corrupt others because she herself felt corrupted (1006: 'Cooper's Dreams'), an explanation that aims to explore the effects of childhood abuse, but which also exaggerates the role of Laura as the femme fatale.

The link between the absent presence of the central character Laura in the 1944 film and in the series *Twin Peaks* is also explored by Richardson (2004: 78–9) who links their uncertain identities with the mysteries that surround them and the way both are seen from the viewpoint of a range of other characters. In both *Laura* and *Twin Peaks*, the painting and photograph of their respective Lauras 'become the canvas onto which characteristics of the dead protagonist's personality, reconstructed (or imagined?) by the detectives in the course of their investigations, are projected' (Richardson, 2004: 80). Hanson (2007: 84–96) also explores the significance of the portrait in 1940s Hollywood films, suggesting how the absence or presence of paintings or photographs of key characters is used in these films. For example, drawing from Modleski (2016 [1988]: 52), she notes how women's absent presence is particularly powerful because it elides ways in which women are often brought under the male gaze in cinema – a shot of a woman is often immediately followed by that of a man looking at her.

Although Jung's theories of projection in relation to the anima and animus were intended to help people to question the ways in which they relate to others, depictions of projection may not ask enough difficult questions about the mechanism and the lack of depth and subjectivity of female characters in folklore and fiction. In *Twin Peaks*, Laura remains a fantasy figure and a victim in need of rescue that morphs very quickly into a potentially dangerous or sexually manipulative 'bad girl'. Similarly, although there has been some interesting work done by Jungian scholars on film that explores the archetypes, they include strategies that may compound rather than resolve these gender problems.

For example, Beebe's (2001: 209–12) analysis of the anima in film is careful to suggest that not all female characters in a film narrative should be read as animas and he outlines important clues for picking anima figures out. He explores a Jungian reading of films that mirrors in many ways Jungian readings of dreams, folklore and fairy tale, suggesting that

> a way to understand a film psychologically is to take its various characters as signifying complexes, parts of a single personality whose internal object relations are undergoing change. These object relations are represented by the interactions of the characters, who usually include a figure representing the *anima*. Because the relations of the *anima* to other complexes is of particular interest to a therapist. (Beebe, 2001: 212)

Moreover, this method is useful because the material is drawn from the same culture as that of many therapists and their patients and because film-making and watching involve processes of active imagination that have taken on a status like that of a religious activity, providing 'a new ritual context for the immersion into visionary archetypal experience' (Beebe, 2001: 2012). However, I suggest that while this method is intriguing and potentially useful, the method of envisioning all the characters in a story as elements of a singular protagonist reduces the potential for examining other elements of their relational dynamics in sociological and historical context. Taken to extremes, this approach, which tends towards assuming that the central protagonist is male, can reinforce the tendency to miss depth, ambiguity and motivation of female characters in film that Grossman points to.

The evil that men do

Twin Peaks has a reputation for transforming the benchmark for quality television. The way the show plays with genre is of particular note, as it pays homage to the detective drama on the one hand and melodrama on the other. Williams (2005: 46–9), who calls the programme a 'serial-thriller soap', notes the ways that it interweaves styles associated with narrative closure, on the one hand, and the multi-threaded and continuous stories on the other, noting how this combination is used to generate and depict emotion, including tears. This use of soap opera also opens the show to interpretation through the lens of the anthropology of religion. The anthropological eye can feast on multiple interconnected characters and storylines, watching them grapple with important ethical questions with the aid of various spirit beings. As is the case for many of the societies that anthropologists study, dreams and visions are important to the town's inhabitants, and their significance reaches beyond an enhanced understanding of individual psychologies. Agent Cooper and Laura Palmer share a dream that they experience on different dates, a dream that Dale calls 'our dream'. Much of the detective work of the series is based around Dale decoding and remembering this dream with the help of visionary beings including the Giant and the Man from Another Place. Nonetheless, the use of the possession trope as a solution to Laura Palmer's murder is problematic. While possession is an important religious phenomenon in a number of modern societies, it is usually a positive phenomenon that takes place in a guided, ritualized context that offers the medium opportunities to guide the circumstances under which they are possessed. As I discuss in more detail in Chapter 5, mediums are not victims of the deity, they are talented in a form of 'instrumental agency' (Keller, 2002) in which they allow themselves to be played by the gods, ancestors and deities, who thereby form part of the local communities that hold rituals for them. In the case of *Twin Peaks*, the loss of agency that Leland experiences is more total and its loss is more akin to the model offered by the film *The Exorcist*. Child (2008) explores *The Exorcist* (1973) and some features of possession associated with Christian Europe in the Middle Ages, suggesting that even though the latter context is less positive about possession than in other societies studied by anthropologists, there is, nonetheless, often a degree of agency for people reported to have been possessed by demons, in the sense that the possession is regarded as a seduction for which the possessed person is at least partially culpable. *The Exorcist*, on the other hand, creates its horror by depicting an almost entire separation between the young girl, Regan, and the demon that possesses her, suggesting that this manifestation of evil can inhabit the body of any one of us, at any time. This separation is also a feature of BOB on *Twin Peaks*, with only the barest suggestion of resistance from Laura, and no serious exploration of the possibility that Leland, although possessed, may still be culpable for his crimes. The identity of BOB is left unresolved and the episode ends with the possibility that BOB is simply the evil that men do. It is significant that while on one level 'men', is a simple substitute for people, it is men who stand together in the woods trying to make sense of BOB. No women are present. Moreover, although there is this telling reference to men, none of the inhabitants of *Twin Peaks* try to make sense of the murders of three young women and the brutal attack of a fourth with any reference to the constructions of patriarchy. Instead, patriarchy is reproduced in the series in a range of ways. Kuzniar (1995) draws from Silverman (1988) to suggest ways in which the series silences its female characters while giving men the power both to speak and to decipher signs (Kuzniar, 1995: 124). In one example, she notes the ways in which the character of Audrey is punished for her penchant for investigation and her use of her own gaze to obtain information (Kuzniar, 1995: 122). Caught in a failed attempt at undercover work at One-Eyed Jacks, Audrey is bound and drugged, made immobilized and helpless, and she must wait for an overdue rescue attempt by Cooper and some of the Bookhouse Boys. Even more striking is the finale of season two, in which Cooper's love interest Annie is crowned a symbolic queen by winning the Miss Twin Peaks contest before being abducted by the villain Windom Earle and spirited away into the Black Lodge (2022). Mounting another rescue mission, Cooper must 'go alone' through the portal to the Black Lodge, meeting his dark shadow side and becoming possessed by it. This pattern conforms remarkably well to structures in fairy tales and films that are used to illustrate Jung's theories of the processes of descent into the unconscious. However, this is a use of Jung that conforms to patterns of female immobility and male action that are criticized by film theorists such as Mulvey. While *Twin Peaks* hints at an animist sensibility and begins to use the medium of television to multiply character and plot lines to a more social emphasis, at its core, the psychology of a male protagonist remains a central theme. In the next chapter, however, I will examine a series that breaks with these conventions in a range of ways, *Buffy the Vampire Slayer* (1997–2003), arguing that it is possible to use Jungian theories to interrogate patriarchy and to explore story lines in which a range of female and male characters are given more depth and opportunities to explore their own shadows and the societal inequalities that help to shape them.

Bibliography

Bassil-Morozow, H., and Hockley, L. (2017) *Jungian Film Studies: The Essential Guide*. London: Routledge.

Beebe, J. (2001) 'The anima in film', in C. Hauke and I. Alister (eds), *Jung and Film: Post Jungian Takes on the Moving Image*. London: Routledge, pp. 208–25.

Booy, M. (2010) '*Twin Peaks*', in Abbott, S. (ed.) *The Cult TV Book*. New York: Soft Skull Press.

Bulkeley, K. (2003) 'Dreaming and the cinema of David Lynch', *Dreaming*, vol. 13, no. 1 (March), pp. 49–60.

Bourguignon, E. (1989) 'Multiple personality, possession trance, and the psychic unity of mankind', *Ethos*, vol. 17, no. 3 (September), pp. 371–84.

Bowie, F. (2000) *The Anthropology of Religion*. Oxford: Blackwell.

Child, L. (2008) 'Possession in contemporary cinema: Religious and psychological themes', *DISKUS: The Journal of the British Association for the Study of Religion*, vol. 9.

Charet, F. X. (1993) *Spiritualism and the Foundations of C.G. Jung's Psychology*. Albany: State University of New York Press.

Copjec, J. (ed.) (1993) *Shades of Noir: A Reader*. London: Verso.

Creeber, G. (2004) *Serial Television: Big Drama on the Small Screen*. London: British Film Institute and Palgrave MacMillan.

Creed, B. (2007) 'The untamed eye and the dark side of surrealism: Hitchcock, Lynch and Cronenberg', in G. Harper and R. Stone (eds), *The Unsilvered Screen: Surrealism on Film*. London: Wallflower Press, pp. 115–33.

Deacy, C. (2001) *Screen Christologies: Redemption and the Medium of Film*. Cardiff: University of Wales Press.

Devlin, W. J., and Biderman, S. (eds) (2011) *The Philosophy of David Lynch.*
    Kentucky: University Press of Kentucky.
Doane, M. A. (1991) *Femmes Fatales: Feminism, Film Theory, Psychoanalysis.*
    London: Routledge.
Freud, S. (2001 [1921]) 'Psycho-analysis and telepathy', in J. Strachey (trans.), *The
    Standard Edition of the Complete Works of Sigmund Freud*, vol. 18 (1920–2)
    London: Vintage, pp. 173–93.
Freud, S. (2001 [1922]) 'Dreams and telepathy', in J. Strachey (trans.), *The Standard
    Edition of the Complete Works of Sigmund Freud*, vol. 18 (1920–2) London: Vintage,
    pp. 195–220.
Freud (2001 [1923]) 'A seventeenth century demonological neurosis', in J. Strachey
    (trans.), *The Standard Edition of the Complete Works of Sigmund Freud*, vol. 19
    (1923–5). London: Vintage, pp. 69–105.
Gabbard, G. O., and Gabbard, K. (1999) *Psychiatry and the Cinema* (2nd edn).
    Washington, DC: American Psychiatric Press.
George, D. H. (1995) 'Lynching women: A feminist reading of *Twin Peaks*', in D.
    Lavery (ed.), *Full of Secrets: Critical Approaches to Twin Peaks*. Detroit: Wayne State
    University Press, pp. 109–19.
Goudal, J. (2000 [1925]) 'Surrealism and cinema', in P. Hammond (ed.) *The Shadow and
    Its Shadow: Surrealist Writings on Cinema*. San Francisco, CA: City Lights, pp. 84–94.
Grossman, J. (2013 [2009]) *Re-thinking the Femme Fatale in Film Noir: Ready for Her
    Close-up*. Basingstoke: Palgrave Macmillan.
Halskov, A. (2015) *TV Peaks: Twin Peaks and Modern Television Drama*. Odense
    M: University of Southern Denmark.
Hague, A. (1995) 'Infinite games: The derationalization of detection in *Twin Peaks*', in
    D. Lavery (ed.), *Full of Secrets: Critical Approaches to Twin Peaks*. Detroit: Wayne
    State University Press, pp. 130–43.
Hanson, H. (2007) *Hollywood Heroines: Women in Film Noir and the Female Gothic
    Film*. London: I.B. Tauris.
Harvey, G. (2005) *Animism: Respecting the Living World*. London: Hurst.
Hauke, C., and Alister, I. (eds) (2001) *Jung & Film: Post-Jungian Takes on the Moving
    Image*. London: Routledge.
Hauke, C., and Hockley, L. (eds) (2011) *Jung and Film II: The Return: Further Post-
    Jungian Takes on the Moving Image*. London: Routledge.
Hayes, M., and Boulegue, F. (eds) (2013) *Fan Phenomena: Twin Peaks.*
    Bristol: Intellect Books.
Hewitt, M. A. (2014) *Freud on Religion*. Durham, NC: Acumen.
Hirsch, F. (1981) *Film Noir: The Dark Side of the Screen*. Cambridge, MA: Da
    Capo Press.
Hockley, L. (2001) *Cinematic Projections: The Analytical Psychology of C.G. Jung and
    Film Theory*. Luton: University of Luton Press.

Huskinson, L. (ed.) (2008) *Dreaming the Myth Onwards: New Directions in Jungian Therapy and Thought*. London: Routledge.

Izod, J. (2001) *Myth, Mind and the Screen: Understanding the Heroes of Our Time*. Cambridge: Cambridge University Press.

Jeffers McDonald, T. (2019) 'Blueprints from Bluebeard: Charting the gothic in contemporary film', in T. Jeffers McDonald and F. A. Kamm (eds), *Gothic Heroines on Screen: Representation, Interpretation, and Feminist Enquiry*. London: Routledge, pp. 41–54.

Jowett, L., and Abbott, S. (2013) *TV Horror: Investigating the Dark Side of the Small Screen*. London: I.B. Tauris.

Jung, C. G. (1977 [1928]) 'Anima and Animus', in R. F. C. Hull (trans.), *Two Essays on Analytical Psychology*, The Collected Works of C. G. Jung, volume 7. Princeton, NJ: Princeton University Press, pp. 188–211.

Jung, C. G. (2001 [1945]) 'The Phenomenology of the Spirit in Fairytales', in R. F. C. Hull (trans.), *Jung: Four Archetypes: Mother, Rebirth, Spirit, Trickster*. London: Routledge, pp. 101–56.

Jung, C. G. (1995 [1946]) 'The fight with the shadow', in M. Stein (ed.), *Jung on Evil*. London: Routledge, pp. 174–80. (Extract from *Civilization in Transition* (1970) (trans. R. F. C. Hull)) in The Collected Works of C. G. Jung, volume 10. Princeton, NJ: Princeton University Press.

Jung, C. G. (1993 [1946]) 'The psychology of the transference', in R. F. C. Hull (trans.), *The Practice of Psychotherapy*, The Collected Works of C. G. Jung, volume 16. London: Routledge, pp. 163–323.

Jung, C. G. (1981 [1951]) 'The Shadow' and 'The Syzgy: Anima and Animus', in R. F. C. Hull (trans.), *Aion*, The Collected Works of C. G. Jung, volume 9, part 2. London: Routledge, pp. 8–10 and 11–22.

Jung, C. G. (2008 [1955]) *Synchronicity: An Acausal Connecting Principle*. London: Routledge.

Jung, C. G. (1995 [various: 1953–77]) *Jung on Evil* (edited with an introduction by Murray Stein). London: Routledge.

Kaplan, E. A. (ed.) (2012 [1978]) *Women in Film Noir* (revised and expanded edition). London: British Film Institute & Palgrave Macmillan.

Keller, M. (2002) *The Hammer and the Flute: Women, Power, and Spirit Possession*. Baltimore, MD: Johns Hopkins University Press.

Kuzniar, A. (1995) 'Double talk in *Twin Peaks*', in D. Lavery (ed.), *Full of Secrets: Critical Approaches to Twin Peaks*. Detroit: Wayne State University Press, pp. 120–9.

Lavery, D. (1995) 'Introduction: The semiotics of cobbler: *Twin Peaks*' interpretive community', in D. Lavery (ed.), *Full of Secrets: Critical Approaches to Twin Peaks*. Detroit: Wayne State University Press, pp. 1–21.

Lindop, S. (2015) *Postfeminism and the Fatale Figure in Neo-Noir Cinema*. New York: Palgrave Macmillan.

Lynch, J. (2012) *The Secret Diary of Laura Palmer*. London: Simon & Schuster.

Matthees, J. (2005) '"She's filled with secrets": Hidden worlds, embedded narratives and character doubling in *Twin Peaks*', in G. Allrath and M. Gymnich (eds), *Narrative Strategies in Television Series*. Basingstoke: Palgrave Macmillan, pp. 99–113.

Modleski, T. (2016 [1988]) *The Women Who Knew Too Much: Hitchcock and Feminist Theory* (3rd edn). New York: Routledge.

Neale, S. (2010) '"I can't tell anymore whether you're lying": *Double Indemnity, Human Desire* and the Narratology of femme fatales', in H. Hanson and C. O'Rawe (eds), *The Femme Fatale: Images, Histories, Contexts*. New York: Palgrave Macmillan, pp. 187–98.

Nickerson, C. (1993) 'Serial detection and serial killers in *Twin Peaks*', *Literature Film Quarterly*, vol. 21, no. 4, pp. 271–6.

Nieland, J. (2012) *David Lynch*. Urbana: University of Illinois Press.

Nochimson, M. P. (1997) *The Passion of David Lynch: Wild at Heart in Hollywood*. Austin: University of Texas Press.

Nochimson, M. P. (2016) 'Substance abuse: Special Agent Dale Cooper. "What's the matter?"', in J. A. Weinstock and C. Spooner (eds), *Return to Twin Peaks: New Approaches to Materiality, Theory, and Genre on Television*. Basingstoke: Palgrave Macmillan, pp. 47–69.

Richardson, J. (2004) '*Laura* and *Twin Peaks*: Postmodern parody and the musical reconstruction of the absent femme fatale', in E. Sheen and A. Davison (eds), *The Cinema of David Lynch: American Dreams, Nightmare Visions*. London: Wallflower Press, pp. 77–92.

Riches, S. (2011) 'Intuition and investigation into another place: The epistemological role of dreaming in *Twin Peaks* and beyond', in W. J. Devlin and S. Biderman (eds), *The Philosophy of David Lynch*. Lexington, Kentucky: University Press of Kentucky, pp. 25–43.

Rose, S. (2017) 'From *Split* to *Psycho*: Why cinema fails dissociative identity disorder', *The Guardian*, Thursday, 12 January.

Rowland, S. (2002) *Jung: A Feminist Revision*. Cambridge: Polity Press.

Schreiber, F. R. (1973) *Sybil*. New York: Grand Central Publishing.

Sheen, E., and Davison, A. (eds) (2004) *The Cinema of David Lynch: American Dreams, Nightmare Visions*. London: Wallflower Press.

Silverman, K. (1988) *The Acoustic Mirror: The Female Voice in Psychoanalysis and Cinema*. Bloomington: Indiana University Press.

Stables, K. (2012 [1978]) 'The postman always rings twice: Constructing the *Femme Fatale* in 90s cinema', in E. A. Kaplan (ed.), *Women in Film Noir* (revised and expanded edition). London: British Film Institute & Palgrave Macmillan.

Stephen, M. (1995) *A'aisa's Gifts: A Study of Magic and the Self*. Berkeley: University of California Press.

Stephenson, C. E. (2009). *Possession: Jung's Comparative Anatomy of the Psyche*. London: Routledge.

Stoller, P., and Olkes, C. (1989) *In Sorcery's Shadow*. Chicago: University of Chicago Press.

Tacey, D. (1997) *Remaking Men: Jung, Spirituality and Social Change*. London: Routledge.

Thompson, K. (2003) *Storytelling in Film and Television*. Cambridge, MA: Harvard University Press.

Tuzin, D. (1975) 'The breath of a ghost: Dreams and fear of the dead', *Ethos*, vol. 3, no. 4, pp. 555–78.

Von Franz, M. (1995 [1974]) *Shadow and Evil in Fairy Tales*. Boston, MA: Shambala.

Waddell, T. (2006) *Mistakes: Archetype, Myth and Identity in Screen Fiction*. London: Routledge.

Weinstock, J. A. (2016) 'Wonderous and strange: The matter of *Twin* Peaks', in J. A. Weinstock and C. Spooner (eds), *Return to Twin Peaks: New Approaches to Materiality, Theory, and Genre on Television*. Basingstoke: Palgrave Macmillan.

Williams, L. R. (2005) '*Twin Peaks*: David Lynch and the thriller soap', in M. Hammond and L. Mazdon (eds), *The Contemporary Television Series*. Edinburgh: Edinburgh University Press, pp. 37–56.

Wilson, E. G. (2007) *The Strange World of David Lynch: Transcendental Irony from Eraserhead to Mulholland Drive*. New York: Continuum.

Zweig, C., and Abrams, J. (eds) (1991) *Meeting the Shadow: The Hidden Power of the Dark Side of Human Nature*. New York: Penguin.

Filmography

Basic Instinct (1992) Directed by Paul Verhoeven: Tri Star Pictures.

Body of Evidence (1993) Directed by Uli Edel: MGM.

Buffy the Vampire Slayer (1997–2003) Created by Joss Whedon: Mutant Enemy Productions and 20th Century Fox Television. Seasons 1–5, Warner Bros., Seasons 6 & 7, United Paramount Network: 10 March.

David Lynch: The Art Life (2017) Directed by Jon Nguyen, Olivia Neergaad-Holm and Rick Barnes: Duckdiver Films.

Double Indemnity (1944) Directed by Billy Wilder: Paramount Pictures

Frankie and Alice (2010) Directed by Geoffrey Sax: Lions Gates Entertainment.

Gilda (1946) Directed by Charles Vidor: Columbia Pictures.

Homicide: Life on the Street (1993–9) Created by Paul Attansio: NBC: 31 January.

Human Desire (1954) Directed by Fritz Lang: Columbia Pictures.

Laura (1944) Directed by Otto Preminger: 20th Century Fox.

Primal Fear (1996) Directed by Gregory Hoblit: Paramount Pictures.

Psycho (1960) Directed by Alfred Hitchcock: Paramount Pictures.

Rebecca (1940) Directed by Alfred Hitchcock: United Artists.

Spellbound (1945) Directed by Alfred Hitchcock: United Artists.

Sybil (1976) Directed by Daniel Petrie: NBC: 14 November.

The Exorcist (1973) Directed by William Friedkin: Warner Bros.

Twin Peaks (1990 and 1991) Created by Mark Frost and David Lynch, Seasons 1 and
     2: CBS Television: ABC: 8 April.

Twin Peaks (2017) Created by David Lynch and Mark Frost, Season 3: Showtime: 3
     September.

4

A Fairy Tale Heroine: *Buffy the Vampire Slayer*

In the previous chapter I explored *Twin Peaks*, a television series that combines cinematic tropes and genres with a serial format framed by soap opera in order to offer audiences a range of emotional and aesthetic experiences. Its focus on a small town and the extended attention to multiple characters and storylines make it ideal for the casting of an 'ethnographic eye' over television, and *Twin Peaks* also explores a number of phenomena of potential interest to anthropologists of religion, including communicative dreaming, secret societies, spirit possession, and relationships between human communities and their environments. However, I also suggested that the gender dynamics in *Twin Peaks* have raised concerns in feminist scholarship and although the field of action is widened, male protagonists are nonetheless more developed as characters and undertake the majority of the action. In this chapter, therefore, I explore a second television serial drama in which the central protagonist is female and where the characters around her are also strongly developed in sophisticated ways. Lasting for seven seasons, *Buffy the Vampire Slayer* (1997–2003) uses a range of plot devices to give its characters and storylines considerable emotional depth as they respond to events and refer to previous challenges, mistakes and traumas in their reflections, exchanges and strategies in each succeeding episode. Although Joss Whedon is credited with creating the series, the writing and directing team is much broader, a factor which contributes to its nuance and depth (see, e.g. the full episode list and writers in Edwards, Rambo and South, 2009: 211–15). Wilcox and Lavery (2002: xxii, xxiii) use *Buffy the Vampire Slayer* as an example in their analysis of what makes Quality TV, pointing to a large ensemble cast and a 'memory' in which characters and relationships develop and refer back to significant incidents. Moreover, the series lends itself well to analysis from perspectives of anthropologists of religion. They include memories and backstories related to magical powers, ritual and sacred duty. Moreover, the audience, like an anthropologist, can see interactions between different characters that other characters are not privy to. Here, the 'sadistic gaze' is disrupted in favour of a multiplicity of viewpoints.

The idea of the sadistic gaze in cinema is rooted in Mulvey's (1999 [1975], 1999 [1981]) feminist analyses of Hollywood film. In this work Mulvey examines film images and how cinema work shapes ways of seeing and thereby participates in the construction of gender difference. She both utilizes and critiques psychoanalytic theory to do this, explaining that she uses it as a 'political weapon' to reveal the way that 'the unconscious of patriarchal society has structured film form' (Mulvey, 1999 [1975]: 58). In particular, she employs Freud's work on sexuality and Lacan's on the mirror stage of ego development to reveal the pleasures of looking that are utilized and channelled by film. These pleasures include those of looking at others (particularly when one is, oneself, unseen), and identification with images (such as those of characters in movies) (Mulvey, 1999 [1975]: 60–2). She goes on to suggest the ways in which film manages these pleasures with a gendered imbalance, so that men are associated with activity and women with passivity. 'In their traditional exhibitionist role women are looked at and displayed' for the audience and for the pleasure of the main male characters in the film (with whom the audience identifies). Moreover, while these male characters take active roles in the narrative, women are associated with stillness, and their narrative role is much more aligned with the emotions they evoke in the male characters than developed for her individual storyline (Mulvey, 1999 [1975]: 62, 63–4). Men are in control of the action in these stories, and the narrative arc often tames women who at the start of the film are on glamorous display, into a love relation with the hero that brings her into his possession. Moreover, particularly in film noir, men's anxieties about women and their bodies (such as castration anxiety) are worked through with storylines in which women are investigated and punished or forgiven as guilty objects (Mulvey, 1999 [1975]: 65). Thus the gaze of the viewer is implicitly understood to be aligned with the individual male gaze, one that reflects sadistic drives as the protagonist moves the action forward. Similarly, De Lauretis (1984: 103–57) argues, using Freudian Oedipal theory, that while male protagonists in narratives take action and move through space, the roles of female characters are often limited to victims to be rescued, monsters to be defeated or femme fatales to be avoided.

Mulvey's work has been both utilized and critiqued by feminist film theorists, but importantly in this context, it also begs questions about how different modes of telling visual stories, such as multi-authored serial television programs, might impact visual media ways of seeing and gender. For example, Modleski (1979: 14) suggests ways in which soap operas do not conform to conventional gaze theory's pattern. Instead, the action and viewpoint are in continual motion so that 'a viewer might at one moment be asked to identify with a woman finally reunited with her lover, only to have that identification broken in a moment of intensity and attention focused on the sufferings of the woman's rival'. Modleski goes on to suggest that 'the subject/spectator of soaps ... is constituted as a sort of ideal mother' and that 'the connection between melodrama and mothers is an old one' (Modleski, 1979: 14).

Buffy the Vampire Slayer has been referred to as a gothic melodrama by scholars such as Williamson (2005: 78–9) who point to emotional realism in the series and its use of sympathetic vampires with souls. Arguably, one of the reasons that melodrama (the generic grandmother of soap opera) can be regarded as challenging and disruptive to patriarchal power is the ways in which it both celebrates emotion and tends itself to overflow and disrupt traditional generic boundaries. *Buffy the Vampire Slayer* refers to this with some irony, notably by making the 'Big Bad' vampire Spike an avid watcher of soap operas and making this a point of communication that breaks an awkward silence between him and Buffy's mother, Joyce (5012: 'Checkpoint'). Moreover, Giles, a character who holds together somewhat uneasily the roles of librarian, academic, martial arts mentor and sorcerer is embarrassed to admit that he has watched *Passions* with Spike, asking Buffy 'never to speak of it' (5002: 'Real Me'). In the spin off show *Angel*, the action hero Charles Gunn complains that in recent months he feels as if he has got caught up in some 'turgid supernatural soap opera' (4016: 'Players'), which of course, he has! *Buffy the Vampire Slayer* therefore self-referentially utilizes the medium of serial drama to hold focus on multiple characters and their relationships simultaneously (something which I suggest gives this art form something in common with ethnographic writing) and blurs generic boundaries.

Melodrama is also thought to be boundary-breaking because the genre is excessive in its provocation of strong emotional and physical reactions, in particular, tears. Linda Williams has explored this aspect of melodrama and soap operas in the context of a wider enquiry into films that 'promise to be sensational, to give our bodies an actual physical jolt' and are thereby 'on the edge of being respectable' (Williams, 1991: 2). Examining horror films, pornography and melodrama, she suggests that scholars who dismiss these forms as gratuitous, may be wedded to definitions of classical narrative cinema that exclude more emotionally spectacular repetitive formats. Citing as an example Bordwell, Staiger, and Thompson's (1985) study of classical Hollywood style, she suggests that films that are 'characterised as efficient action-centred, goal-orientated linear narratives driven by the desire of a single protagonist, involving one or two lines of action, and leading to definitive closure' tend to be defined as dominant and normative by most film scholars, although, quoting Altman (1989: 345–6) melodrama may actually 'alert us to the existence of a competing logic, a second voice' (Williams, 1991: 3). Williams therefore proposes a more nuanced analysis of excess in horror, pornography, and melodramatic 'weepies' and places at the centre of this the ways bodies on screen can elicit bodily and emotional responses in audiences, including pathos and tears (Williams, 1991: 4). Further to this, she argues for a link between these emotional excesses, and fantasies that have particular time - bound structures. The 'shock' in horror films being linked to a sense of 'too early', and the tears of melodrama and their accompanying sense of loss often being precipitated by a realization or action being 'too late' (Williams, 1991: 9).

Moreover, there are at least two other genres that are held in tension within the *Buffy the Vampire Slayer*; the gothic and film noir, and the conflict between these genres revolves around the fact that the central female character, Buffy, is a young girl with characteristics associated with a male action hero or film noir protagonist, but she also experiences emotional and personal dilemmas more often associated with the gothic heroine. Hanson suggests ways in which gothic cinema and film noir can be thought of as mirror images of one another, particularly as film noir is famous for the treachery of the femme fatale while the gothic women's film often has a heroine who is suspicious of her husband or lover. She strikes a note of caution, however, as analyses through patriarchal lenses have tended to favour film noir as the defining genre while seeing the gothic as derivative and less important. Hanson, on the other hand, asserts the popularity and commercial success of numerous gothic films, arguing for their importance in their own right (Hanson, 2007: 41–7). Hanson (2007: 35) also observes that the gothic as a genre has a number of dynamics that lend themselves to social critique, particularly of gender relations, and notes a complex relationship to the past as one of these dynamics. *Buffy the Vampire Slayer* reflects this trend, interweaving storylines of character development with complex relationships with the past. Age can also be used in an anthropological analysis of the series, so that, for example, one can observe interactions between the vampires (who call themselves the old ones), Buffy and her friends (the students) and the grown-up teachers and parents, as if they are distinct but interpenetrating social groups. However, the focus on complex personal histories also enables a more sophisticated application of Jung's theories of projection. Rather than merely highlighting how women can be the target of projections, the developments of the characters enable us to analyse the impact of those projections from the point of view of the woman concerned, as well as unpack in more detail how mechanisms of projection are shaped by patriarchy and played out in the dynamics of this micro social world.

The heroine and the gothic fairy tale

The central characters, dilemmas and cosmology of the series are set out very clearly in the first two seasons (the focus of this chapter). The picture is constantly refined and made more complex, and the nature of all the persons within it is revealed slowly so that viewers are taken on a maturation journey together with its central character, Buffy Summers, a young girl, who in common with many superheroes, has a dual identity. On the one hand, Buffy is a sixteen-year-old, who has moved with her mother to the Californian small town of Sunnydale, on the other, she has a secret identity that she initially tries to leave behind, she is a Vampire Slayer, a Chosen One, with special strengths and skills. Only women can take this role and there is meant to be only one Slayer alive at any one time. As a Slayer dies (she is often killed by vampires at a young age) a new Slayer is awakened to her powers and takes up the role. Frankel (2012) uses Campbell's (1973) famous mapping of the hero's journey in multiple stories (what Campbell terms the *monomyth*), suggesting ways in which Buffy's progression through each season can be seen to exemplify stages in the journey. She argues, for example, that Buffy's initial refusal of the call to her role has much in common with the Hero's Call to Adventure and his initial reluctance to leave his current life behind (Frankel, 2012: 7). In this model, which borrows ideas from both Freud and Jung, hero stories are metaphors for inner forms of initiation, expressing psychological processes of descent, 'facing the dark side of the self and gaining deep wisdom and self-knowledge from the struggle' (Frankel, 2012: 5). Frankel (2012: 8) also argues that the journeys of female heroes have particular features and that Buffy's progress through the seven seasons becomes more distinctly one of a feminine Chosen One in the later seasons, especially after season three. This proposition certainly has some useful ideas that I explore further. *Buffy the Vampire Slayer* does, for example, emphasize the central protagonist's circle of friends and it has themes and plot lines reminiscent of the *Bluebeard* fairy tale. However, Frankel's emphasis is on the inward journey of the protagonist and she analyses other characters in the series as primarily aspects of her-self. Bringing into play a more anthropological perspective, this chapter explores in more depth the ways in which individual characters are fleshed out. At times these characters are likened to aspects of Buffy's inner conflicts, but they also present a complex and functioning social world, including story arcs in which Buffy is not central. Moreover, paying attention to the social as well as psychological aspects of the series enables an exploration of psychological mechanisms like projection and their impact on Buffy, who is the object of her vampire boyfriend Angel's projections when he loses his soul again and becomes Angelus. There is therefore a *Bluebeard* thread to the story that both highlights and subverts patriarchy, and draws from a wealth of literary and cinematic examples, some of which contribute to a form of 'gothic feminism' (Jeffers McDonald and Kamm, 2019).

Bluebeard is a fairy tale with a storyline that differs considerably from many others such as the Disney versions of *Snow White* (1937) and *Cinderella* (1950). Snow White and Cinderella stories focus on young women and the trials and tribulations they must face before marriage, particularly those inflicted by rival women such as stepsisters, stepmothers and witches. The Prince, on the other hand, is portrayed in an almost completely positive light and once the heroine is married, the story ends with the assumption that her happiness is secured. *Bluebeard*, on the other hand, begins with the marriage of the heroine to the nobleman Bluebeard and emphasizes enigmas and fears related to the early years of marriage in which the wife finds herself trying to understand a virtual stranger and negotiate an unknown space in the form of his home. According to the folktale, Bluebeard leaves his wife often and without much explanation for his trips, giving her the keys to their mansion but forbidding her from entering one specific chamber. On one trip her curiosity is overwhelming, and she opens the forbidden door, finding the bodies of Bluebeard's previous wives behind it. Her efforts to cover up her transgression are not successful and when Bluebeard discovers that she has disobeyed him he tries to kill her as well but is thwarted by her brothers who arrive to rescue her in the nick of time (Tatar, 2004: 12).

Several popular films from the 1940s that can be characterized as gothic women's films echo elements of the Bluebeard story. For example, a section where Hanson (2007: 67) discusses these films is entitled *Prince Charming Becomes Bluebeard*. Two prominent examples are *Rebecca* (1940) and *Secret beyond the Door* (1947). In both films young women are seduced by older men in a whirlwind courtship in a foreign land, but the real action begins once their honeymoon is over and they begin married life in earnest as they try to understand their husbands more fully, negotiate the mysteries of their new homes and uncover secrets related to former wives. In *Rebecca*, the heroine (following the original Du Maurier (2015 [1938]) novel she is never named) must cope with the challenges of marrying Maxim De Winter; a man of a higher social class (she is employed as a lady's companion at the start of the film) and is intimidated by his mansion, Manderlay, and her impressions of Maxim's deceased former wife, Rebecca, who continues to imbue the house with her presence in the form of numerous possessions and the memories of all who knew her. It is only revealed towards the end of the film that Maxim hated Rebecca and accidentally killed her after a particularly violent argument. *Secret beyond the Door* draws out even more sharply aspects of the *Bluebeard* tale, in that the husband, Mark Lamphere, is an architect who collects rooms in which violent murders of women have occurred, a fact that his new wife Celia discovers during their first party together when her husband conducts a grim tour of six of these seven rooms. The seventh room is impenetrable until, echoing the transgressions of Bluebeard's wife, the heroine makes a copy of the key to the room and finds to her horror that it is an exact copy of her own room. In this film psychoanalysis plays a key role. The wife had previously dated a psychoanalyst and is therefore familiar with relevant theories, as is a friend of hers who offers psychoanalytic interpretations of the murders related on the murder-room tour. She takes it upon herself to decode her husband's behaviour rather than leave him and we discover that his frequent, sudden absences, bouts of emotional coldness, alternate temper tantrums and murderous fantasies are rooted in a childhood incident when he is locked out of his mother's room (by his sister but he does not know this and blames the mother). In both films the heroine shows a degree of autonomy and intelligence as the investigator of her husband, but there is considerable ambivalence in his remarkably flimsy redemption. Similarly, while there are themes of the rites of passage that women in the period undergo in their transition from young woman to wife, there is also considerable attention paid to male psychology and the ways in which she applies her detection skills to his history and difficulties rather than simply removing herself from a situation that is potentially dangerous for her.

Buffy's relationship with the character Angel has many elements of this gothic suspicion. A vampire with a soul, Angel enters her friendship circle, helps to fight other vampires and gradually ignites Buffy's romantic interest. It is the relationship with Angel that highlights tensions in the series between Buffy as a gothic heroine (Angel is an older man with a past) and Buffy as a hero in a film noir (Angel can also be regarded as the male equivalent of a femme fatale, an Achilles heel that not only distracts the heroine from her sacred duties but also creates deep rooted tensions in her moral universe entailing difficult decisions). In order to create this dramatic tension, *Buffy the Vampire Slayer* uses the trope of demonic possession as vampirism and then gradually complicates its initial cosmological foundations through the revelation of Angel's backstory.

The vampire with a soul

The nature of vampires in *Buffy the Vampire Slayer* is explained by Giles, a school librarian who is also a Watcher, someone who trains and prepares a Slayer. A key feature of this preparation is his ability to draw from a wealth of arcane knowledge and apply scholarship skills to find apposite texts, many of which are ancient, that offer descriptions, history and behavioural analyses of a range of monsters, especially vampires. After Buffy's friends, Xander and Willow, accidentally become involved in Buffy's secret life and witness vampires, it is Giles who explains that,

> the world is older than any of you know. Contrary to popular mythology it did not begin as a paradise. For untold aeons, demons walked the earth. They made it their home, their hell. But in time they lost their purchase on this reality, the way had been made for mortal animals, for man. All that remains of the Old Ones are vestiges, certain magics, certain creatures … the last demon to leave this reality fed off a human and mixed their blood. He was a human form possessed, infected by the demon's soul. He bit another and another. So they walk the earth, feeding, waiting for the animals to die and the old ones to return. (1002: 'The Harvest')

Later in the same episode Giles further emphasizes the point to Xander, whose friend Jesse has been turned into a vampire. As the group prepare for a confrontation with the vampires, Giles warns Xander that 'Jesse is dead. You have to remember that when you see him you are not looking at your friend. You are looking at the thing that killed him' (1002).

The character of Angel confuses this simple dichotomy between human and vampire, however, firstly through his alliance and romantic relationship with Buffy, and secondly because his vampiric status is complicated by a curse that has restored his soul to him. When Buffy first discovers he is a vampire she does not know about the curse. Rather, Angel slips into his vampiric visage after he and Buffy kiss for the first time. Again turning to Giles, a confused Buffy asks, 'Can a vampire ever be a good person? Could it ever happen?' to which Giles replies, 'A vampire isn't a person at all. It may have the movements, the memories, even the personality of the person it took over but it is still a demon at the core. There is no halfway' (1007: 'Angel'). However, this polar point of view is challenged when Buffy learns that his true identity is complicated by the fact that he was cursed with the return of his soul, as a punishment for having murdered a Romani girl, condemning him to remorse for his past deeds without changing his hungers and other vampiric characteristics. Although he gave up feeding on humans at that point he still needs blood which he obtains from butchers (1007). Buffy and Angel's relationship progresses gradually and is only consummated on her seventeenth birthday. At this point in the story the full nature of the curse is revealed. The restoration of Angel's soul is not final, because the curse should not permit him to enjoy his fate, and one moment of perfect happiness will automatically remove the soul. Buffy is therefore confronted throughout the second half of season two with the vampiric Angel without his soul who reverts to the name Angelus and is an evil killer who becomes obsessed with destroying Buffy emotionally as well as trying to murder her. It is this engagement with the vampire Angelus without a soul that sets in motion some difficult dilemmas for Buffy and her friends and gives audiences opportunities to grapple with the complexities of vampire personhood, demonic possession, the nature of soul and moral responsibility in the Buffyverse, a narrative social world that borrows from religious and folklore traditions in addition to a literary and filmic lineage of vampire stories but cannot be mapped onto one religious tradition or philosophy.

While scholars such as Clements (2011: 57–80) explore themes of sin, sacrifice and redemption in the series from a theological perspective, Abbot (2003) uses Jean-Paul Sartre and a discussion of film noir to assert a largely existentialist perspective on these questions. She argues that when the character Angel stars in a subsequent series named after him (*Angel*, 1999–2004), his identity is explored more fully and suggests that his character is not solely defined by his good soul, but it is rather an exploration of tensions between humanism and vampirism (Abbott, 2003: 1). As such it aligns itself with the philosophical position that 'humanity must define itself through choice and action, rather than assume the possession of an essentialist quality' (Abbott, 2003: 2).

Exploring specifically questions around vampire mythology and the soul in the series, McLaren (2005) argues that it holds in tension two distinct conceptions of the soul, particularly with regard to Angel. On the one hand, following Abbot's analysis, he suggests that the soul in the series acts largely as a metaphor for human agency, but on the other, McLaren argues that this is held in 'an irreconcilable contradiction' with other concepts of the soul in

Buffy the Vampire Slayer that derive from vampiric folklore and forms of early Christianity influenced by the works of the ancient Greek philosopher Plato. More developed than Aristotle's idea of the soul as a force animating the body, Plato attributes to the soul powers to command the body and a role as the seat of all knowledge. Moreover, 'Plato is the first to set forth a doctrine that allows for personal immortality in a separable soul with memories intact', an idea that was built upon by writers such as St Augustine and diffused throughout much of Western philosophy and culture, as a 'concept of the soul as an immortal spirit animating the body as the seat of human will, intelligence, and conscience' (McLaren, 2005: 1–2).

This tension offers an intriguing degree of uncertainty about the relationship between the vampire with a soul, Angel, and his demonically possessed counterpart, Angelus, that leads to questions around Angel's character and ethics, such as why does he take responsibility for Angelus's murderous acts, even though he is not the same person? This leads to a much richer ethical discussion than is possible for *Twin Peaks*, because in the latter Leland and BOB are depicted as almost completely distinct and Leland is hardly rendered culpable, a fact which contributes to feminist critiques of the show for eliding Leland's role in the rape and murder of his daughter. *Buffy the Vampire Slayer* can therefore also be credited with a more accurate evocation of the shadow in the Jungian sense. This is because while in Jung's opinion, archetypes can manifest in ways that appear to be autonomous and 'possess' people, this possession does not absolve the persons affected from responsibilities to engage in the therapeutic work necessary to integrate fragments into a newly balanced whole person. Moreover, while *Twin Peaks* does explore the mechanism of projection onto women as it occurs in patriarchal society, we rarely see Laura Palmer transcend her role as an anima archetype. Buffy, on the other hand, is a fully fledged female hero, and we witness her perplexing and distressing situation when confronted with Angelus and the ethical conundrum in which she is placed. Not only does this demonic character know her intimately enough to wound emotionally but it is also unclear if Angel can be retrieved, and her duty to kill vampires must be balanced against her desire to try to save Angel, a desire that extends beyond her personal involvement with him, because it relates to an injunction against harming human beings that becomes extended to beings with souls and, as the series progresses, even to demonic persons who are not harmful. This conflict is also played out against the development of her own personality, as her contact with some vampire villains involves more complex and upsetting incidents than simply staking them all into dust.

Thrall and trauma in *Buffy the Vampire Slayer*

One example is the climax of season one in which her battle with another vampire, The Master, teaches her a great deal about vampires and about her own potential vulnerability. The Master appears to incarnate the great age of 'the old ones' appearing ravaged by age and much like the vampire in *Nosferatu* (1922). The Master is trying to open a portal between the reality inhabited by ancient demonic creatures and the human mortal world. This portal is located underneath the town of Sunnydale and is referred to by Giles (informed by his textual research) as the Hellmouth. Giles explains that The Master tried to open this portal during an earthquake in the 1920s but, unsuccessful, he became stuck between two worlds (like a cork in a bottle) and resorts to various rituals (guided by prophesies) to try to free himself (1002). One of the prophesies suggests that Buffy will die in the attempt to fight The Master, and she initially tries to abandon her role to avoid this, bringing to a head the phase of the 'refusal of the call' according to Frankel's (2012: 26–41) myth framework. However, events propel her forward and as she dresses in white for a more mundane initiatory ritual; her school prom, she is suddenly called back to duty by a vampire attack on her home territory, the school, which impacts her friend Willow who is visibly shaken by finding the bodies. Comforting Willow, Buffy resolves to go into battle and meet her fate. This encounter is important, in that it shapes both her subsequent emotional responses and development in season two and suggests an important power of vampires which is not depicted so explicitly again until she meets Dracula at the start of season five (5001: 'Buffy versus Dracula'), namely the ability to hypnotize their victims. Using his thrall to draw her to him, The Master reveals that her blood is actually the key to his escape, and biting and killing her, he throws her in a pond, remarking 'love the dress' (1012: 'Prophesy Girl'). I return to the motif of thrall in earlier vampire films in Chapter 6, but in this episode the theme of the vampire as a foe that has hypnotic powers is interwoven with ideas about the dark side of the American cultural infatuation with prom romance, implying an allusion to date rape. It is interesting in this context that Angel is drafted in to help by his rival for Buffy's affections, Xander, who represents a model of true friendship in this sequence because earlier Buffy had turned down Xander's invitation to the prom and thereby rejected his romantic overtures. Nevertheless, Xander overcomes his hurt feelings, resolving to find and rescue Buffy and he is essential because Buffy, technically dead from drowning, needs someone with breath to bring her back to life with CPR. The scene therefore both evokes and puts an original spin on more than one mythological or fairy-tale motif. Like Snow White, Buffy is brought back to life by the kiss of true love, but that love transcends romantic ideals and embodies the power of friendship. In addition, Buffy can be seen as an initiate empowered by her brush with death, as she marches to meet The Master again, informs him he has fruit punch mouth, tells him to 'save the hypnosis crap for the tourists' and dispatches him into a pile of bones (1012).

Nonetheless, as season two opens (2001: 'When She Was Bad') and Buffy returns to Sunnydale after having spent the summer with her father in LA, it quickly becomes clear that the experience has deeply unsettled her. Her behaviour is erratic, she snaps at Cordelia after she mentions The Master and has a dream in which Giles tries to kill her, pulling his face off like a mask to reveal The Master underneath. Worried that she might be possessed, Xander and Willow consult Giles who assures them that it is more likely that Buffy has 'what you Americans call issues' (2001) relating to her near-death experience, leading her to project an unnatural overconfidence to compensate for her feelings of vulnerability. As the episode progresses it is revealed that the remaining vampires from the group originally led by The Master have dug up his bones with the aim of resurrecting him. Her efforts to combat this attempt can be read as a metaphor for the battle going on in Buffy's unconscious. It is no coincidence that the vampires' lair is depicted as being underground in season one, and the religious language that many of these vampires use suggests a mirror image or dark doubling of religious imagery in the show's conscious world. More prosaically, both Xander and Giles refer to Buffy working out her issues, a phenomenon that manifests as a worrying tendency to go it alone and miss wider implications of information relevant to the situation. When the group's research reveals that in order to raise The Master the vampires will need someone close to him, Buffy immediately assumes this must refer to her and the intimacy of mutual murder. She also mistrusts Angel. This may reflect a general fear of intimacy, but she also distrusts his vampire nature. This fight comes to a head when Buffy leaves her friends in the library to rescue Cordelia at the Bronze because of a note thrown into the library (2001: 'When She Was Bad'). Despite protests from Giles and Willow, who points out that the unwritten part of the note says 'p.s. This is a trap!', Buffy insists that it is her fight and accuses Angel of stalking her when he appears and states bluntly that she does not trust him because he is a vampire. Nonetheless, Angel follows her into the Bronze and is suspicious when, instead of Cordelia and the vampire gang, they find a lone vampire, saying, 'there's the bait, but where's the hook?' (2001). Her friends in the library come closer to solving the mystery when Giles realizes that the translation 'closest' specifically means those physically closest to the Master when he died, meaning Giles and Willow. At that moment, the vampires appear just as Giles says, 'It is a trap. It just isn't for her' (2001).

While this particular episode concludes with Buffy's rescue of her friends and a return to her ease with them, the situation with Angel is more complicated. Her trust in him is seemingly restored and subsequent episodes see their budding relationship develop, but there are numerous incidents that sow the seeds of doubt about Angel and that also foreground the dangers of relationships with men that echo the concerns of female gothic cinema.

Bluebeard and the family romance

In order to further explore the social and psychological dynamics of the series the connection between Angel and Giles can be examined. Rein (2014) suggests that *Buffy the Vampire* engages extensively with ideas about the past and memory and this engagement takes multiple intersecting forms, including references to mnemonic objects such as books and weapons, but it also includes persons who are carriers and decoders of memory such as Giles and Angel (Rein, 2014: 132). Giles is a key character who holds arcane knowledge and translates ancient languages from books and artefacts and he imparts research skills to Buffy and her friends who regularly use books in his library to find information about the demons they combat. These skills also become bound up with Giles's emotional role within the group, as a representative of a certain sort of authority. Although this certainly has a paternal strand, the dynamic can also be described in terms of a transmitter of lineage. This lineage has its roots in the convention, rules and training afforded by the Council of Watchers, giving Giles a role that he refers to as a sacred duty. He also earns respect through his interactions with the group and he is often the subject of gentle teasing such as when Buffy says, 'I'm so stuffy give me a scone' (2004: 'Inca Mummy Girl'). He also has a personal history that enriches the character and his relationships.

The fact that vampires have such long lives mean that their memories afford them knowledge that other characters can only acquire from books, a fact that Angel uses to contribute to the research of Buffy and her group. Moreover, Angel also has a kind of lineage, a chain of transmission involving the exchange of blood, in which as he was turned into a vampire by Darla, who in turn was sired by The Master. Angel is also a sire. As part of his evil past as Angelus, he turned a young woman called Drusilla into a vampire, and she, in turn, transformed a young man called William (who as a vampire calls himself Spike), and Spike and Drusilla come to Sunnydale in season two. Once Angel has reverted to Angelus again, he returns to them, and the three vampires can be seen in terms of a small social world. Moreover, prior to turning her into a vampire, Angelus inflicted mental tortures onto Drusilla, including killing her family, driving her mad and perverting her gift of having visions which remains with her vampire self but is used for evil purposes (2007). Drusilla therefore plays a role not unlike the first wife that is found in a multitude of gothic romances with an undercurrent of the *Bluebeard* tale running underneath them. It is intriguing that the first time that Buffy sees Drusilla the latter is talking with Angel. They are out of Buffy's earshot, but as Angel is trying to compel Drusilla to leave town with Spike, Drusilla tries to seduce him back into a more vampiric lifestyle by suggesting that this is his true nature. Sounding like a ghostly version of the murdered first wife, she predicts what will happen to Buffy, her successor, telling Angel that 'your heart stinks of her. Poor little thing. She has no idea what's in store' (2007: 'Lie to Me'), a particularly chilling comment given that when he later reverts to the Angelus persona, he not only tries to kill Buffy but also delights in attacking her emotionally and threatening her family and friends in ways reminiscent of his previous behaviour towards Drusilla. Moreover, Drusilla's comment can be read more generically, suggesting that women in the early stages of a romantic relationship (particularly if they are young or inexperienced) are unaware of its emotional dangers.

In addition to the *Bluebeard* thread, the series plays with fairy tales more broadly. As Zipes (2006 [1983]) has so effectively argued, each telling of these stories has a specific social and historical context. For example, European oral folktales were transformed into literary products by people such as Charles Perrault (2010 [1697]) in seventeenth-century France and turned into a 'type of literary discourse about mores, values, and manners so that children and adults would become civilized according to the social code of that time' (Zipes, 2006 [1983]: 3). *Sleeping Beauty* and *Cinderella*, for example, have beautiful but passive, obedient heroines who wait for the prince to rescue them. Some literary retellings of fairy tales deliberately play with these narratives, in some cases to revive the folk tales that seeded them, but often to both highlight and subvert their gender dynamics. A famous example is the work of Angela Carter (2006 [1979]). There are also film adaptations of fairy tales that try to revise their gender implications, but scholars such as Bacchilega and Rieder (2010) and Williams (2010) explain that although films such as *Ever After* (1998) rework classical fairy tales to offer audiences more well-rounded and interesting heroines they often leave the patriarchal structures unchallenged. Snowden (2010: 159) goes further, arguing that this kind of limited re-visioning runs counter to the concerns of second- and third-wave feminism and aligns itself instead with a post-feminist agenda that falsely implies that activism is redundant because there is nothing left to fight for. Nonetheless, the range of adaptations of fairy tales in film potentially disrupts ideological hegemony and offers feminist interpretations and Zipes rightly counters the false impression that fairy tales are universal and ageless and explores their diversity and historical and sociopolitical contexts (Zipes, 2006 [1983]: 1). However, fairy-tale themes and motifs can also strike particularly powerful resonances in storytelling and thereby have the kind of emotional impact associated with myth. From this perspective it is easy to see why Jung (2001 [1945]) and prominent Jungian thinkers such as von Franz (1995 [1974]) use fairy tales to explore archetypal figures.

The episode 'Halloween' (2006) both evokes the mythical dimensions of fairy tales and offers feminist critiques and revisions when Buffy, for example, explores a Cinderella fantasy. She and Willow clandestinely look through the diaries of previous Watchers to try to imagine the kind of women that Angel might have dated in the past and spy a drawing of a woman dated 1775 with an old-fashioned gown and styled hair that lead to Buffy fantasizing aloud about going to a ball like a princess in a 'fantabulous gown' (2006) that provokes a rye comment from Willow about her preference for women's right to vote. Buffy's initial curiosity about Angel's previous taste in women has been sparked by her arriving to a date with him unkempt from slaying vampires and looking more careworn than most girls her age. Her fantasies suggest that she would like, even if only at times, to transcend her duty and leave behind its preoccupation with violence and the 'cinders' of dirt and untidiness associated with battling in graveyards. This Cinderella fantasy appears to have an outlet when, shopping for a Halloween outfit, she finds a beautiful dress in a costume shop and the owner of the shop remarks when she holds the dress up to herself and looks in the mirror, 'meet the inner princess … I think we've found a match' (2006). It transpires that the shop owner is in fact an evil sorcerer called Ethan Rayne who casts a spell during Halloween that will transform everyone into the beings suggested by the costumes that they have rented from him. The significance of this transformation goes beyond the magic of costume, however, and reveals hidden desires and strengths in the Scoobies that the audience (and in many cases the characters themselves) were previously unaware of. It marks a major turning point in the series and can be fruitfully read using a Jungian paradigm to explore archetypal characteristics such as the shadow sides of the group's personalities. Drusilla points to the depth of the transformations when she has a vision foreseeing that outer and inner parts of the gang will be switching. For Xander, who was embarrassed earlier in the episode by Buffy intervening before he could get in a fight for her honour, the inner warrior is unveiled, and his toy gun and army clothes turn him into a soldier. Buffy becomes a helpless noblewoman from 1775 who cowers and clings to men in the hope of protection while Willow has the most complex inner journey in this episode as she wears two outfits. She wears a leather outfit with a short skirt, hoping to impress Xander. However, Willow is not ready to reveal herself and covers this ensemble with a ghost costume that is a sheet with BOO written on it. When the transformation occurs, Willow becomes a ghost, leaving the sheet behind and walking around (and through walls) in her leather costume. She is therefore essentially herself and does not suffer amnesia about her identity as Xander and Buffy do. Moreover, she also gains confidence in her intelligence, problem-solving skills and the ability to direct other members of the group in a crisis. At the end of the adventure, restored to her physical body, Willow throws away the sheet and confidently strolls home, catching the eye of her soon-to-be boyfriend Oz, who exclaims 'who is that girl?' (2006).

Compared with her friends in the 'Halloween' episode therefore, Buffy's inner self or shadow appears to be the least developed and the most dangerous. Her helpless dependence on others nearly gets her bitten by Spike, and Cinderella is not so much integrated into herself as rejected once the spell is broken. This resonates with the statement of intent by the show's creator Joss Whedon, who explains that 'the original kernel of an idea for *Buffy* came with the reversal of an image from traditional horror: a fragile-looking young woman walks into a dark place, is attacked – and then turns and destroys her attacker' (Wilcox and Lavery, 2002: xvii), but the attractions of the Cinderella fantasy are bound up with the fantasy of being relieved from the burdens of her sacred duties. For example, in 'Reptile Boy' (2005) Giles pressures Buffy about her training, telling her off for dawdling with her friends and Angel prevaricates about developing their relationship. Buffy makes the mistake of rebelling by attending a ball, or more prosaically, accompanying Cordelia to a party in a university fraternity house. Unfortunately, the frat boy princes are in fact members of a secret cult who sacrifice young women to a hungry monster who offers the cult members wealth and power in exchange. This episode is one of several in which Buffy encounters dangerous men, suggesting that while Angel is a risk for her, he is a preferable risk, because of their genuine attraction to each other. Nonetheless, the scene in which she tries to invite Angel for coffee, and he expresses uncertainty, has echoes of Bluebeard themes, with Angel reminding her that he is two hundred and forty-one years old and she is sixteen and suggesting that she doesn't know what she wants. Insisting that he is trying to protect her, he argues that if they date one thing could lead to another and things could get out of control, to which Buffy counters that one thing has already led to another and things are meant to get out of control. Angel responds with a sterner but more passionate warning, admonishing her by saying that 'this isn't some fairy-tale. When I kiss you, you don't wake up from a deep sleep and live happily ever after' to which she replies, 'No. When you kiss me I wanna die' and runs away (2005). This scene demonstrates ways in which evoking and subverting fairy-tale themes can resonate on a deep emotional level, specifically linking sexuality and death. It suggests both the more general gaining of emotional and sexual maturity by Buffy through this relationship and the dangers of these processes, compounded by unscrupulous men and patriarchy. I will suggest, however, that certain patriarchal trends can also be seen in her mentor Giles's behaviour. Although these need to be teased out from the narrative more, they are crucial for demonstrating the social dynamics of the season and how projection (in the Jungian sense) goes beyond internal processes and has an impact on social worlds, especially between the generations (or within the context of the show, the adults, students and vampires).

Modleski (2008 [1982]), in her book *Loving with a Vengeance*, explores possible relationships between patriarchy, intergenerational dynamics and gothic novels for women. She suggests that a common plot feature in these novels is the suspicion of the heroine that her husband or lover is trying to kill her, has killed someone else (particularly his first wife) or that he is trying to drive her insane. She dismisses Russ's (1973: 681) assertion that this may reflect a justified paranoia and instead explores the idea that while most men are not lunatics or murderers, there may still be a core of truth to the paranoia of the novels that rests with the unequal relations between men and women (Modleski, 2008 [1982]: 53). Drawing from Meissner's (1978) exploration of *The Paranoid Process*, she suggests that unequal gendered power dynamics between the parents often manifest in a domineering father and submissive mother. Women, therefore, even in relatively 'normal' circumstances, need to work through ambivalence towards male figures that includes anger at their aggression but relief that a man stands between the woman and her potential over identification with the mother figure. In addition to childhood needs to separate from the maternal figure that are exacerbated in women because they are the same gender, women may have anger towards maternal figures for their apparent submission, which can be worked through to transform into greater understanding of the mother's position and difficulties. Working through may be seen in gothic novels when male husband or lover figures turn out to be trustworthy after all and mother-substitute figures such as first wives or other female relatives of the hero are better understood by the heroine (Modleski, 2008 [1982]: 58–76).

Although Modleski (2008 [1982]) is careful to explain that her use of analyses of paranoia in relation to gothic texts is not intended to identify gothic readers as neurotic or unstable, there is potentially a problem with broadly aligning the thought processes of female protagonists in novels or drama with mental illness in this way. Women as witnesses are still less likely to be regarded as credible in multiple modern contexts, particularly if they are also socially disadvantaged or marginalized. Dramatizations of such cases include *Three Girls* (2017) and *Unbelievable* (2019). Modleski also explores instances when audiences and critics do not properly acknowledge rape scenes in the Hitchcock films *Blackmail* (1929) and *Marnie* (1964) (Modleski, 2016 [1988]: 127–8). The idea that the gothic formula almost inevitably vindicates the suspected husband or lover is also questionable. On the contrary, as Hanson (2007: 42–3) argues in the context of discussions of the gothic film cycles of the 1940s and 1950s 'it is actually very rarely the case that the gothic heroine's perceptions are proved to be imagined or incorrect at the close of the gothic film' and the plot of a number of these films explores husbands deceiving their wives and tricking them into doubting her own perceptions in order to try to cover committed or intended crimes, a pattern perhaps best exemplified by the film *Gaslight* (1944).

Nonetheless, Modleski does identify narrative patterns that are found in a number of gothic texts that are also reflected upon within the series. One example is the idea of the female protagonist telling herself that 'true love means absolute faith in the loved one' (Modleski, 2008 [1982]: 68). In the case of *Buffy the Vampire Slayer*, the conflict between this true love and faith and a healthy suspicion of abusive behaviour is played out using the device of contrasting Angel (who is a vampire but possesses a soul) with Angelus, who Buffy describes at one point as 'the demon who's wearing his face' (2019: 'Only Have Eyes for You'). While in some places this contrast seems absolute, in others the core of truth beneath the gothic suspicions of lovers being potentially violent is alluded to in two instances when Buffy tries to talk about what happened, firstly to her mother (2017: 'Passion') and later in the series to a school guidance counsellor (3004: 'Beauty and the Beasts'), neither of whom are aware of the existence of vampires at the time of the conversation. In both cases, Buffy's stumbling attempts to explain the conflict between love and self-protection that she is going through and the emotional pain arising from the situation are interrupted by her hearers with the phrase 'he changed', suggesting that dangers also exist in relationships not affected by supernatural circumstances and alluding to the core of truth that Modleski suggests lies buried within the 'paranoid' gothic text. Most importantly, Modleski (2008 [1982]: 73) places that core of truth within the systematic oppression of women in society connecting the social with the psychological and the personal with the political in ways that suggest how it is transmitted across generations and it is this process that I want to examine in *Buffy the Vampire Slayer* through a focus on the pivotal role that Giles plays in the relational dynamics of the series.

The role Giles plays is to some extent paternal. Buffy's parents are divorced, and her father is mostly absent, having remained in Los Angeles while Buffy and her mother have moved to Sunnydale. In contrast, she trains with Giles most days and at times Giles and Joyce appear to act as co-parents for her. On the other hand, his role is clearly one step removed and guided by extra-familial authorities (such as the Council of Watchers based in England) and his engagement with the more hidden forces in the Buffyverse are suggestive of a lineage that resembles lines of transmission in religious sects. The true extent of Giles's magical history and the complexities of his personal history are only hinted at until the episode 'The Dark Age' (2008), which begins with references to the students' comfortable misapprehension that Giles was always the familiar figure of order and authority, that he must have worn tweed diapers as a child and loved school. They are gently enthusiastic about his budding romance with a fellow teacher, Miss Jenny Calendar, who teaches computer science and identifies as a techno-pagan, having an interest in magic in common with Giles but contrasting him with her modern outlook that extends to taking the lead in their courtship, and suggesting that they 'stay in' on a coming Saturday (presumably to consummate their relationship).

However, Giles's engagement with the past extends beyond his knowledge of arcane languages and lore, he has a personal history that catches up with him in Sunnydale in the form of a demon that he and some friends had conjured in a reckless game when they were young. The demon re-emerges and starts to kill Giles's old friends one by one and when Giles realizes what is happening, his behaviour becomes erratic. He is plagued by strange dreams, drinks far in excess of his normal habits and, staring into a mirror, comments 'so you're back' (2008). These scenes suggest that we are learning about not only Giles's past but also his shadow-side in the Jungian sense of the word, a point reinforced when the Scoobies are trying to figure out what is wrong and Xander remarks, somewhat astutely, that 'Yeah. Yep. I knew this would happen. Nobody can be wound as straight and narrow as Giles without a dark side erupting' (2008). What is key here is the idea that archetypes such as the shadow and the anima emerge into dreams or consciousness as compensating factors that participate in processes that keep the psyche in balance. A man whose outer life is defined by authority, respect and convention is precisely the example most likely to be overcome (or possessed) by a spontaneous projection of the anima, because his more irrational instincts have been repressed to the extent that the psyche has become imbalanced. References to psychological phenomena continue in the episode with the idea that the demon (called Eyghon) is a Sleepwalker Demon who can only exist in this reality by possessing a dead or unconscious host, and the demon that inhabited Giles's old friend Philip jumps into Jenny after she is accidentally knocked unconscious. Giles, still insisting that the problem is private, takes a shaken Jenny home and there is a scene where the demon possessing Jenny tried to seduce Giles, and Jenny's face is transformed into a demonic visage. This scene depicts the mechanism of anima projection very well, as not only is a demon created by Giles able to possess a woman significant to him, but his unconscious fears about her sexual confidence are also manifested. Moreover, after the demon escapes a confrontation with Buffy, Giles tells her about his past and he admits that he is terrified because he does not know how to kill the demon without killing Jenny along with it, a classic Jungian problem of integrating shadow or anima archetypes into the psyche and being able to distinguish them from projections onto other persons. Willow alights upon the idea of using Angel to attack the demon possessing Jenny, tricking the demon into jumping from her into Angel, who is dead, but not dead, and whose inner demon battles Eyghon and triumphs, leaving the group to adjust to a new understanding of Giles.

On the surface, this episode offers a relatively positive development. Buffy explains that she was surprised to learn that far from being just a grown up, Giles is a person who makes mistakes sometimes, thus she indicates the episode as part of her maturation process. Giles's dark side also reveals a capacity for violence that can be interpreted as adding strength to his character and additionally provides considerable humour, most memorably in the season-three episode, 'Bad Candy' (3006), in which Ethan Rayne also reappears, this time as the distributer of cursed candy bars that leads adults to regress to their teenage selves. A deeper examination of events in the 'Dark Age' (2008) episode, however, suggests a much darker side to Giles that is more in keeping with the kind of Jungian analysis that Xander references (albeit in an offhand and humorous way). In addition, Giles's attitudes to gender and sexuality as they play out in his relationship with Jenny can be seen as not just projections of the individual psyche, but as personal expressions of wider societal imbalances imbued in patriarchy. Moreover, when the demon is transferred to Angel, it can be suggested that Giles's patriarchal projections are also transferred to Angel, depicting how patriarchy gets transmitted across generations. In the series, this event is not referred to again, and is not therefore specifically depicted as a factor in the events leading up to Angel's fall and the restoration of the demon Angelus, but I suggest a reading of the season in that way, where the patriarchal aspects of Giles's projections onto women, and Jenny in particular, are transmitted to Angel in this scene, and that they therefore play a role in Angelus's murder of Jenny and in his cruelty to Buffy. In other words, the Angelus storyline can be seen to explore Angel's projections onto Buffy, and taken in the context of Giles's dark side, can also be seen as patriarchy transmitted across generations. Moreover, Jenny's murder is also entwined with Jenny's own backstory and ways in which her past is connected with Angel's.

In episodes 2013 ('Surprise') and 2014 ('Innocence') it is revealed that Jenny, too, has a hidden identity, as she is a descendant of the Romani family whose daughter was murdered by Angelus and who therefore cursed him with a soul. The endowment of this soul is regarded by Jenny's family not as an opportunity for him to atone, but as a vengeance that must be a continual torment for him. One minute of happiness would therefore reverse the curse, remove the soul, and bring back Angelus. After a difficult battle with Spike and Drusilla. Buffy and Angel run from the scene and in the heat of the moment, make love, thus giving Angel a moment of true happiness and leading to the removal of his soul and the re-emergence of the evil vampire Angelus (2013: 'Surprise').

In subsequent episodes the series explores the idea that vampires are not necessarily simply a demonic being inhabiting a human body. Rather, they appear to be human/demonic hybrids with many characteristics and emotions remaining from the human that was turned. Angelus is cruel to Spike, and even more so to Buffy. Rather than simply killing her, as Spike suggests would be expedient, Angelus has what Spike calls a 'real yen to hurt this girl', a remark that Angelus responds to with the statement that 'She made me feel like a human being. That's not the kind of thing you just forgive' (2014: 'Innocence') and he proceeds to stalk her, torment her and threaten her mother and her friends. The apparently thin line between Angel and Angelus evokes themes of his shadow side, while his obsessive spite towards Buffy suggests that she is the object of his projections. The explicit link between Angel losing his soul and the preceding 'true happiness' associated with him having sex with Buffy therefore provides very important clues as to the nature of his conflict which can be elaborated both in terms of re-considering the tropes of femme fatale and homme fatal and through a deeper analysis of splitting, projection and the desire for wholeness in Jungian theory.

Examining the femme fatale in a range of artistic images, Allen (1983: 2–3) observes that these images often appear to portray

> an orgasmic vision; if you will, an erotic swoon … precisely that moment of abandonment in the sex act – a loss of self-awareness following the conscious seduction of the male. The *petite morte* of the orgasm … moreover … expresses the idea that a woman's erotic power can destroy her as well as her male victims … however … even though she might die, she will not be obliterated. She will rise to claim another victim, perhaps as one of the living dead, a vampire.

Key here is the idea that projection (of the image of the femme fatale onto a woman) is tied in with eroticism and specifically the ways in which orgasm can lead to a temporary abandonment of individual identity – a loss of self within the couple. While both men and women may find sexual intimacy threatening to individual identity, the framing of masculine identities and power compound these issues for men and legitimize cruelty as a coping strategy. Doane (1991: 2) refers to Allen's argument to emphasize the ways in which punishment of the femme fatale in texts 'involves a desperate reassertion of control on the part of the threatened male subject. Hence, it would be a mistake to see her as some kind of heroine of modernity. She is not the subject of feminism but a symptom of male fears about feminism.'

Moreover, these narratives often position female characters who are targeted for this kind of abuse as psychoanalytic detectives who offer investigations, care and understanding. This kind of positioning is dangerously deceptive, in that it appears to confer power on female characters while actually rendering them responsible for the projections placed upon them, and it often fails to challenge the root causes and true power dynamics of the situation. Baxter remarks upon her observations when teaching students about Bluebeard, as their comments are often sympathetic to him (Baxter, 2019: 13). Examples from classic Hollywood cinema appear to take this tendency even further, making the woman responsible for unravelling her husband's psychological state and healing him. Modleski (2016 [1988]: 41–53) explores in some detail the ways in which Hitchcock's film version of *Rebecca* glosses over Maxim's murder of his first wife in an almost eerie manner, focusing on the heroine's sense of triumph over her rival when she is told she is loved and seemingly blind to the dangers of her position once she has unveiled her husband's secrets. *Secret beyond the Door* appears to deflect the husband's bizarre compulsion to contemplate women's murders and his re-creation of multiple crime scenes in his multi-roomed home, attributing his problems to the behaviours of his mother and sister, and, by resolving this psychological mystery, the heroine is able to put on one side his menacing behaviour, emotional disconnection, irritation and coldness.

Hanson (2007: 68) refers to Warner (1993: 29) to suggest that marriage in fairy tales is characterized as a rite of passage for young women. It is interesting in this context that in *Buffy the Vampire Slayer* the consummation of Buffy's relationship with Angel (her first sexual experience) coincides with her seventeenth birthday. Similarly, in a number of 1940s gothic films, the period following the consummation of a relationship or marriage is deeply ambiguous. Both *Rebecca* and *Secret beyond the Door* contain subtle and slightly edgy or ironic references to traditional fairy tales. In *Secret beyond the Door*, Mark in his first conversation with Celia refers to her as a Sleeping Beauty figure, a comment that is embedded in scenes that associate the whirlwind romance with the pleasures and dangers of sexual awakening. An interview between Hitchcock and Truffaut about the film *Rebecca* raises the idea that the film has motifs reminiscent of Cinderella (Truffaut, 1983: 132; see also Hanson, 2007: 70). However, these films eschew the 'Happily Ever After' of many fairy-tale stories and they focus instead on the new wives contending with suspicions about the murderous thoughts, intentions or passed deeds of a new husband, often accompanied by dismissive attitudes, unexplained absences or angry outbursts. In other words, Prince Charming becomes Bluebeard. The storyline of *Buffy the Vampire Slayer*, however, is distinguished by the way in which vampire personhood is constructed as a form of demonic possession and the idea that in certain vampires demonic possession can be overridden or suppressed by the return of the soul of the original human being. While in the gothic women's films of the 1940s the dilemma of women trying to judge their husband's or lover's motives and intentions is usually framed in terms of discovering facts about them or delving deeper into their psychological make-up, in *Buffy the Vampire Slayer* the problem is re-framed using the trope of possession. On the one hand, Buffy has the comfort of believing that the evil Angelus is nothing more than a demon wearing her lover's face, leaving Angel and his love for Buffy intact, but on the other hand, little clues appear throughout the second season that suggest ways in which that division is not so sharp. Moreover, several of Buffy's friends are wary of Angel even before he reverts to his Angelus persona. An interesting example is Kendra, a vampire slayer who was activated when Buffy briefly died at the hands of The Master, and who comes to Sunnydale to help for a short while (2009 and 2010: 'What's My Line?' Parts 1 and 2). Although Kendra impresses Buffy with her dedication and dutiful studies of vampire-related books, she is less experienced in more ordinary emotions and friendships. In many ways, her character can be read as another aspect of Buffy's inner world, but in complete contrast to the Cinderella archetype or fantasy, Kendra represents a feminine knight. Understood in this way, it is particularly telling that Kendra the Vampire Slayer is not comfortable with the ambiguity of Angel's status or his relationship with Buffy, saying that he is a vampire and he should die. Kendra's character also highlights the show's racial imbalances. As one of the very few non-white characters (she is depicted as a young African Jamaican woman) her sudden death later in season two limits the fleshing out of her character and role, aligning her with the 'tragic mulatta' in Edwards's (2002: 87) reading. Nonetheless, Kendra not only offers an alternative inner voice to Buffy that questions Angel's identity, but her representation of the female knight also offers women valuable alternatives to Cinderella motifs.

Interestingly, in the final episodes of season two, Angelus's attacks combine emotional betrayal with a strategy that displays and revels in his knowledge of Buffy's past mistakes. He uses them to create a trap, that, for the second time in the season, is not for her. Tricking Buffy into a fight with him that leaves Giles and her friends vulnerable in the library, Angelus mocks: 'This wasn't about you. This was never about you' (2021: 'Becoming'). In addition to showing how he uses knowledge of her weaknesses, however, this line also suggests a more hidden but nonetheless significant link between Angelus and Giles.

From an ethnographic perspective, both Giles and Angel cross between the realms of the 'old ones', students and grown-ups the most and both have access to arcane knowledge. Furthermore, the transmission of the demon that Giles created, Eyghon, to Angel can be read in terms of the transmission of patriarchy and its imbalances that trigger projections onto women. However, as Buffy races back to the library to try to save her friends, and the voice-over ominously talks about the big life-altering moments, it is neither Giles, nor Angel that are truly centre stage. While Angel has been distracting Buffy, Drusilla has invaded the library with a group of followers in order to kidnap Giles and before carrying him off, Drusilla combats Kendra, who has been charged with protecting the group in Buffy's absence. Drusilla enacts one of the relatively rare acts of vampiric hypnotism in the show. Telling Kendra to look into her eyes, she sways like a snake in sync with a snake charmer and slashes Kendra's throat with her fingernail. When Buffy rushes in, minutes later, she sees her dead warrior friend and kneels in a combination of tribute and sorrow in the last moments of the penultimate episode of the season.

In the final scene of the episode Buffy is bent over her dead friend, and stages powerfully the 'too late' that Williams refers to in relation to the tears of melodrama (Williams, 1991: 9). While there are other significant scenes in the final episodes, including where Buffy must kill Angel even though his soul has been restored to him, this death of the inner feminine knight is deeply significant. Even though the characters never refer to it again, Buffy's character evolves further in season three and a new Slayer arises, Faith, whose problematic character suggests a personification of the traumas connected with Kendra's death.

While both *Twin Peaks* and *Buffy the Vampire Slayer* use the trope of demonic possession to explore splitting, projection and the nature of evil, *Buffy the Vampire Slayer* offers much more emotional depth and a more nuanced critique of patriarchy. The central figure is female and the character developments of her and her social network trace ways in which mechanisms of projection impact the person who receives them. Angel's backstory and the ways in which his loss and return of soul are explored offer audiences an opportunity to see points of continuity as well as difference between Angel and Angelus that highlight problematic questions about the nature of evil and situate them within a social context that includes patriarchy, a context informed by a history of gothic melodrama films that position newlywed women as facing dilemmas akin to those of Bluebeard's wife, and thus raising painful questions about fairy tales such as *Cinderella* and *Snow White* in which rescue by and marriage to a prince are framed as happy endings in themselves. However, in line with many popular films and television programs, in *Buffy the Vampire Slayer*, the device of possession assumes that this is a demonic phenomenon, and this is largely shaped from ideas drawn from a Christian historical background, even though the series itself does not depict Christianity except with cross and holy water symbols. This is in contrast to many anthropological examples of societies in which possession is regarded in comparatively positive or neutral terms and the possessing entities can be deities, spirits or ancestors. Therefore, the next chapter will examine some of those examples of positive possession and offer comparisons of their dynamics with encounters of spirits in film and television.

Bibliography

Abbott, S. (2001) 'A little less ritual and a little more fun: The modern vampire in Buffy the Vampire Slayer', *Slayage: The Online International Journal of Buffy Studies*, vol. 1, no. 3, June.

Abbott, S. (2003) 'Walking the fine line between Angel and Angelus', *Slayage: The Online International Journal of Buffy Studies*, vol. 3, no. 1, August 2003.

Abbott, S. (2007) *Celluloid Vampires: Life after Death in the Modern World*. Austin: University of Texas Press.

Allen, V. M. (1983) *The Femme Fatale: Erotic Icon*. Troy, NY: Whitston Publishing.

Altman, R. (1989) 'Dicken, Griffith, and film theory', *South Atlantic Quarterly*, vol. 88, pp. 321–59.

Baccilega, C., and Rieder, J. (2010) 'Mixing it up: Gender complexity and gender ideology in early twenty-first century fairy-tale films', in P. Greenhill and S. E. Matrix (eds), *Fairy Tale Films: Visions of Ambiguity*. Logan: Utah State University Press, pp. 23–41.

Barber, P. (1990) *Vampires, Burial and Death: Folklore and Reality*. Yale: Yale University Press.

Bassil-Morozow, H., and Hockley, L. (2017) *Jungian Film Studies: The Essential Guide*. London: Routledge.

Baxter, G. M. (2019) 'Bluebeard's women fight back: The gothic heroine in contemporary film and Heidi Lee Douglas' *Little Lamb*', in T. Jeffers McDonald and F. A. Kamm (eds), *Gothic Heroines on Screen: Representation, Interpretation, and Feminist Enquiry*. London: Routledge, pp. 13–26.

Beebe, J. (2001) 'The anima in film', in C. Hauke and I. Alister (eds), *Jung and Film: Post-Jungian Takes on the Moving Image*. London: Routledge, pp. 208–25.

Bordwell, D., Staiger, J., and Thompson, K. (1985) *The Classical Hollywood Cinema: Film Style and Mode of Production to 1960*. Abingdon: Routledge.

Campbell, J. (1973) *The Hero with a Thousand Faces*. Princeton, NJ: Princeton University Press.

Carter, A. (2006 [1979]) *The Bloody Chamber and Other Stories*. London: Vintage.

Charet, F. X. (1993) *Spiritualism and the Foundations of C. G. Jung's Psychology*. Albany: State University of New York Press.

Clements, S. (2011) *The Vampire Defanged: How the Embodiment of Evil Became a Romantic Hero*. Grand Rapids, MI: Brazos Press.

De Lauretis, T. (1984) *Alice Doesn't: Feminism, Semiotics, and Cinema*. Bloomington: Indiana University Press.

Doane, M. A. (1991) *Femmes Fatales: Feminism, Film Theory, Psychoanalysis*. London: Routledge.

Du Maurier (2015 [1938]) *Rebecca*. London: Virago.

Edwards, L. (2002) 'Slaying in black and white: Kendra as tragic mulatta in *Buffy*', in R. V. Wilcox and D. Lavery (eds), *Fighting the Forces: What's at Stake in Buffy the Vampire Slayer*. Lanham: Rowman & Littlefield, pp. 85–97.

Edwards, L. Y., Rambo, E. L. and South, J. B. (eds) (2009) *Buffy Goes Dark: Essays on the Final Two Seasons of Buffy the Vampire Slayer on Television*. Jefferson, NC: McFarland.

Frankel, V. E. (2012) *Buffy and the Heroine's Journey: Vampire Slayer as Feminine Chosen One*. Jefferson, NC: McFarland.

Groom, N. (2018) *The Vampire: A New History* New Haven, CT: Yale University Press.

Hallab, M. Y. (2009) *Vampire God: The Allure of the Undead in Western Culture*. Albany: State University of New York Press.

Hanson, H. (2007) *Hollywood Heroines: Women in Film Noir and the Female Gothic Film*. London: I.B. Tauris.

Hanson, H., and O'Rawe, C. (eds) (2010) *The Femme Fatale: Images, Histories, Contexts*. Basingstoke: Palgrave Macmillan.

Hirsch, F. (1981) *Film Noir: The Dark Side of the Screen*. Cambridge, MA: Da Capo Press.

Hubner, L. (2018) *Fairy Tale and Gothic Horror: Uncanny Transformations in Film*. London: Palgrave Macmillan.

Huskinson, L. (ed.) (2008) *Dreaming the Myth Onwards: New Directions in Jungian Therapy and Thought*. London: Routledge.

Jeffers McDonald, T., and Kamm, F. A. (eds) (2019) *Gothic Heroines on Screen: Representation, Interpretation, and Feminist Enquiry*. London: Routledge.

Jowett, L. (2005) *Sex and the Slayer: A Gender Studies Primer for the Buffy Fan*. Middletown, CT: Wesleyan University Press.

Jung, C. G. (1995 [various: 1953–77]) *Jung on Evil* (edited with an introduction by Murray Stein). London: Routlege.

Jung, C. G. (2001 [1945]) 'The phenomenology of the spirit in fairytales', in R .F. C. Hull (trans.), *Jung: Four Archetypes: Mother, Rebirth, Spirit, Trickster*. London: Routledge, pp. 101–56.

Jung, C. G. (1977 [1928]) 'Anima and Animus', in R .F. C. Hull (trans.), *Two Essays on Analytical Psychology*. The Collected Works of C. G. Jung, volume 7. Princeton, NJ: Princeton University Press, pp. 188–211.

Kaveney, R. (ed.) (2001) *Reading the Vampire Slayer: An Unofficial Critical Companion to Buffy and Angel*. London: Tauris Parke Paperbacks.

Keller, M. (2002) *The Hammer and the Flute: Women, Power and Spirit Possession*. Baltimore, MD: John Hopkins University Press.

Krentz, J. A. (ed.) (1992) *Dangerous Men and Adventurous Women: Romance Writers on the Appeal of Romance*. Philadelphia: University of Pennsylvania Press.

Levine, E., and Parks, L. (eds) (2007) *Undead TV: Essays on Buffy the Vampire Slayer*. Durham, NC: Duke University Press.

Lutz, D. (2006) *The Dangerous Lover: Gothic Villains, Byronism, and the Nineteenth-Century Seduction Narrative*. Columbus: Ohio State University Press.

Masse, M. A. (1992) *In the Name of Love: Women, Masochism and the Gothic*. Ithaca, NY: Cornell University Press.

Meissner, W. W. (1978) *The Paranoid Process*. New York: Jason Aronson.

Modleski, T. (1979) 'The search for tomorrow in today's soap operas: notes on a feminine narrative form', *Film Quarterly*, vol. 33, no. 1 (Autumn), pp. 12–21.

McLaren, S. (2005) 'The evolution of Joss Whedon's vampire mythology and the ontology of the soul', *Slayage: The Online Journal of Buffy Studies*, vol. 5, no. 2, September.

Modleski, T. (2008 [1982]) *Loving with a Vengeance: Mass-Produced Fantasies for Women*. New York: Routledge.

Modleski, T. (2016 [1988]) *The Women Who Knew Too Much: Hitchcock and Feminist Theory* (3rd edn). New York: Routledge.

Mulvey, L. (1999 [1975]) 'Visual pleasure and narrative cinema', in S. Thornham (ed.), *Feminist Film Theory: A Reader*. Edinburgh: Edinburgh University Press, pp. 58–69. (Originally published in *Screen*, vol. 16, no. 3, pp. 6–18).

Mulvey, L. (1999 [1981] 'Afterthoughts on "Visual pleasure and narrative cinema" inspired by King Vidor's *Dual in the Sun* (1946)', in S. Thornham (ed.), *Feminist Film Theory: A Reader*. Edinburgh: Edinburgh University Press, pp. 122–30. (Originally published in *Framework*, 15–16–17, pp. 12–15).

Perrault, C. (2010 [1697]) *The Complete Fairy Tales* (trans. with an introduction by Christopher Betts). Oxford: Oxford University Press.

Plato (2002) *The Collected Dialogues of Plato Including the Letters* (ed. E. Hamilton and H. Cairns). Princeton, NJ: Princeton University Press.

Rein, K. (2014) 'Archives of horror: Carriers of memory in *Buffy the Vampire Slayer*', in S. Bacon and K. Bronk (eds), *Undead Memory: Vampires and Human Memory in Popular Culture*. Oxford: Peter Lang, pp. 131–55.

Rowland, S. (2002) *Jung: A Feminist Revision*. Cambridge: Polity Press.

Russ, J. (1973) 'Someone is trying to kill me and I think it's my husband: The modern gothic', *Journal of Popular Culture*, vol. 6, no. 4, pp. 666–91.

Sartre, J. P. (2001 [1945]) 'Existentialism and humanism' October 1945 lecture reprinted in S. Prince (ed.), Jean-Paul Sartre *Basic Writings*. London: Routledge, pp. 27–38.

Short, S. (2015) *Fairy Tale and Film: Old Tales with a New Spin*. Basingstoke: Palgrave Macmillan.

Snowden, K. (2010) 'Fairy tale film in the classroom: Feminist cultural pedagogy, Angela Carter, and Neil Jordan's *The Company of Wolves*', in P. Greenhill and S. E. Matrix (eds), *Fairy Tale Films: Visions of Ambiguity*. Utah: Utah State University Press, pp. 157–77.

Spicer, A. (2002) *Film Noir*. Essex: Pearson Education.

Stephenson, C. E. (2009). *Possession: Jung's Comparative Anatomy of the Psyche*. London: Routledge.

Tacey, D. (1997) *Remaking Men: Jung, Spirituality and Social Change*. London: Routledge.

Tatar, M. (2004) *Secrets Beyond the Door: The Story of Bluebeard and His Wives*. Princeton and Oxford: Princeton University Press.

Truffaut, F. (1967) *Hitchcock*. New York: Simon & Schuster.

Von Franz, M. (1995 [1974]) *Shadow and Evil in Fairy Tales*. Boston, MA: Shambala.

Warner, M. (1993) 'The uses of enchantment', in D. Petrie (ed.), *Cinema and the Realms of Enchantment: Lectures, Seminars and Essays by Marina Warner and Others*. London: BFI.

Wilcox, R. V., and Lavery, D. (2002) 'Introduction', in R. V. Wilcox and D. Lavery (eds), *Fighting the Forces: What's at Stake in Buffy the Vampire Slayer*. Maryland: Rowman & Littlefield, pp. xvii–xxix.

Williams, L. (1991) 'Film bodies: Gender, genre and excess', *Film Quarterly*, vol. 44 (Summer), pp. 2–13.

Williams, C. (2010) 'The shoe still fits: *Ever after* and the pursuit of a feminist Cinderella', in P. Greenhill and S. E. Matrix (eds), *Fairy Tale Films: Visions of Ambiguity*. Utah: Utah State University Press, pp. 99–115.

Williamson, M. (2005) *The Lure of the Vampire: Gender, Fiction and Fandom from Bram Stoker to Buffy*. London: Wallflower Press.

Zipes, J. (2006 [1983]) *Fairy Tales and the Art of Subversion: The Classical Genre for Children and the Process of Civilization*. (2nd edn). New York: Routledge.

Zipes, J. (2011) *The Enchanted Screen: The Unknown History of Fairy-tale Films*. New York: Routledge.

Zweig, C., and Abrams, J. (eds) (1991) *Meeting the Shadow: The Hidden Power of the Dark Side of Human Nature*. New York: Penguin.

Filmography

Angel (1999–2004) Created by Joss Whedon and David Greenwalt: Mutant Enemy Productions and 20th Century Fox Television. Seasons 1–5, Warner Bros: October 5.

Blackmail (1929) Directed by Alfred Hitchcock: British International.

Buffy the Vampire Slayer (1997–2003) Created by Joss Whedon: Mutant Enemy Productions and 20th Century Fox Television. Seasons 1–5, Warner Bros., Seasons 6 and 7, United Paramount Network: 10 March.

Cinderella (1950) Directed by Hamilton Luske, Wilfred Jackson, and Clyde Geronimi: Walt Disney Productions, R.K.O. Pictures.

Ever After (1998) Directed by Andy Tennant: 20th Century Fox.

Gaslight (1944) Directed by George Cukor: Metro-Goldwyn Mayor.

Hitchcock/Truffaut Interviews (1962) Selection on the film *Rebecca* included in the Blu Ray edition of *Rebecca* (2017 [1940]) *Carlotta Films*.

Marnie (1964) Directed by Alfred Hitchcock: Universal Pictures.

Nosferatu (1922) Directed by Friedrich Wilhelm Murnau: Film Arts Guild.

Rebecca (1940) Directed by Alfred Hitchcock: United Artists.

Secret beyond the Door (1947) Directed by Fritz Lang: Universal Pictures.

Snow White (1937) Directed by David Hand: Walt Disney Productions, RKO Pictures.

Three Girls (2017) Directed by Philippa Lowthorpe: BBC One: 16 May.

The Two Mrs Carrolls (1947) Directed by P. Godfrey: Warner Bros.

Unbelievable (2019) Created by Susannah Grant, Ayelet Waldman and Michael Chabon: Netflix: 13 September.

5

Ghosts and Spirits: *Ghost, Poltergeist* and *Afterlife*

The previous two chapters have explored television series that use the trope of demonic possession to raise complex questions about the nature of personhood and evil. While *Buffy the Vampire Slayer* has a more sophisticated and ambivalent exploration of demonic possession than *Twin Peaks*, it nonetheless depicts possession as a negative displacement of the soul that leads to criminal behaviour and both programs draw inspiration from demons in horror films as well as movies that explore the darker sides of human nature from more psychological perspectives. While possession is almost always a negative and frightening phenomenon in film and television, anthropologists in numerous fieldwork contexts have found something very different. Mediums can use possession to help the bereaved talk with their loved ones who have died, or they can open themselves to temporary inhabitation by spirits or gods of their religious traditions. These gods and spirits can perform many positive functions, including expressing individual, community and cultural moods and situations and offering advice and healing to attendees of possession rituals. In this chapter, therefore, I explore in more depth a range of possession traditions examined by anthropologists and offer for comparison some of the most common examples of positive encounters with spirits in film and television, including the ghostly romance.

One of the challenges of this kind of comparison is the wide range of perspectives that scholars have on key aspects of possession. While many find instances of positive possession, there are differences of opinion about the extent to which spirits and gods are active possessing agents, with many scholars emphasizing instead the social and psychological benefits of possession ceremonies. For example, as ritual dramas they may allow people to express tensions related to gender identity and erotic fulfilment (Boddy, 1994: 415–22), raise issues rarely openly discussed (Lambek, 1981: 78) or highlight and engage with issues and personalities related to colonialism (Henley, 2006: 735; Stoller, 1994: 636). While these analyses do not necessarily entail the dismissal of the idea that the spirits are also 'real', they do suggest that their characters and activities are shaped in part by the concerns of the medium and their community. The famous study of ecstatic religion by Lewis (2003 [1971]) is even more emphatically sociological in orientation. Although he asserts that this does not mean the explaining away of belief in spirits (Lewis, 2003: 24), his agnostic position tends to lean more in the direction of the social circumstances of possessed persons. He notes, for example, that many possession rituals are dominated by women, who can gain respect through the spirits that speak through them and thereby improve their situation in patriarchal societies and that 'the empowerment conferred by possession on those disadvantaged by gender and other social disabilities provides an adequate explanation of mystical experience' which is 'more logically compelling and inherently plausible than taking religious experience at face value' (Lewis, 2003: xv). Moreover, in the preface to the third edition of his book he critiques scholars who place too much emphasis on what the spirits say and argues for more questions addressed to the testimony of mediums and their situation. It is telling in this discussion that he suggests that 'what the possessing spirits actually say' is nonetheless useful, because they 'in effect speak for their human vehicles' (Lewis, 2003: xii).

While Lewis's approach represents one end of the spectrum, other anthropological studies offer alternative approaches. Schmidt (2017) for example, pays careful attention to sociological factors such as race and class in her analysis of spirits and trance in Brazil, but she also explores in considerable detail the ways in which possession is experienced. She explains how practitioners and different groups vary in their understandings about the degree of agency of possessing deities and spirits, and deities' relationships with mediums and others in a ritual setting. Santo (2015) emphasizes ways in which communications with the dead and other spirits may give mediums and other practitioners of Cuban Espiritismo expanded and porous selfhood. Blanes and Santo (2014) have collected articles that reject theories of spirits that relegate them to the role of symbols of something else, arguing instead that spirits have agency and examining their social interactions in some detail.

Keller's (2002) work analyses possession trance in the context of broader issues in religious studies, anthropology and the study of gender. She highlights flaws in many sociological and psychological approaches to possession trance, arguing that they tend to underestimate the significance of the 'radical receptivity' of possessed women's bodies and the power of possessing agents (typically ancestors, deities and spirits) (Keller, 2002: 2–3). Possession disrupts many of the assumptions about subjectivity and agency that inform dominant paradigms of scholarship in twentieth-century Europe and America, and as a result, she argues, this scholarship tends to observe the bodies of possessed women with a kind of horrified fascination, while at the same time feigning indifference to the things that make possession interesting, including its complex engagement with penetrable personhood (Keller, 2002: 7). Keller therefore proposes a concept of 'instrumental agency' in order to advance theoretical understandings of possession trance that reflect more accurately indigenous perspectives. In other words, although deities, ancestors and spirits may have agency and choose to enter mediums during a ritual, the mediums are neither helpless nor completely passive. On the contrary, allowing oneself to be played like an instrument by a deity is a skill (Keller, 2002: 9, 10). While Keller does not use the term 'animism' in her approach, there are important ways in which debates about possession trance intersect with contemporary animist approaches to religion. For example, contemporary animist studies tend to emphasize the ways in which practitioners act in the world, negotiating with spirits and other persons, rather than concerning themselves with the more nebulous and often dismissive question of the 'beliefs' of indigenous peoples. Moreover, as Keller highlights, mediums challenge paradigms of personhood that underlie in subtle ways the perspectives that traditional scholars bring to the table when studying possession, and one of the key threads in contemporary animist scholarship is to suggest how the study of indigenous religions can provoke a radical critical re-evaluation of common Western understandings of personhood and challenge scholars to expand those understandings.

Given the range of approaches taken by scholars who study possession trance and spirits, it is perhaps unsurprising that popular films and television also depict different attitudes to the ghosts and spirits in their narratives. The ghostly romance or melodrama is particularly difficult to place, because, unlike the fantasy horror film, it is harder to separate the themes from emotional circumstances and questions in everyday life outside the film. For example, although part of the premise of *Buffy the Vampire Slayer* is that vampires are real, this premise takes place within an established fictional literary and filmic genre that is separate from commonly accepted notions in modern Western cultures. The divide between the fictional world of ghosts and spirits and the everyday worlds of the audiences who enjoy these stories is less clear-cut. For example, Striner (2016), who explores a number of films featuring love stories that continue into the afterlife or that take place with ghosts, including *Truly, Madly, Deeply* (1990),

The Ghost and Mrs Muir (1947) and *Always* (1989), suggests that many of them can be analysed using mythical themes such as those of classical Antiquity, and that, moreover, such films offer a form of underground religion that does not always conform to conventional scientific, philosophical or theological norms. Deacy (2012: 14) is able not only to offer some detailed comparisons between the afterlife as depicted in film and debates about it in Christian theology, but he is also able to assert that 'rather than dismiss afterlife-themed films as a throwback to a pre-scientific way of thinking, such movies can shed new light on the way in which religious, theological and philosophical themes are being conducted in a "secular" setting'. Moreover, Spiritualist churches and gatherings where mediums can communicate with the spirits of deceased loved ones are not uncommon in twentieth and twenty-first-century contexts and have been studied by anthropologists in settings such as Edinburgh (Wilson, 2013) and Bristol (Hunter, 2014).

Spiritualism's survival can be linked, not only to its attractions as a religious practice but also to the ways in which its growth in the nineteenth and twentieth centuries took place alongside of technological innovations of modernity (Natale, 2016). For example, the increasing use of and discourse around electricity as an invisible force also fed into ways in which spirits and communications with them were conceived (Weinstein, 2004). The 'uncanny' aspects of photography made the practice ghostly in itself and the technology was soon used to try to capture spirits on film (Gunning, 2015). Schüttpelz (2015: 63–5) asserts a clear relationship between Spiritualism and modernism, citing early comparisons between Spiritualists' telepathic practices and the telegraph and 'the steady search for empirical evidence of imponderable and telecommunicative forces and fluids'. These relationships between trance, spirits and visual media have continued to expand and develop into the twenty-first century and in some cases have become an important part of the ways in which indigenous practitioners communicate about their religions (Behrend, Dreschke and Zillinger, 2015).

Nonetheless, despite these developments, many Hollywood films about ghosts and spirits take the audience somewhat hesitantly down the path of engagement with these beings, depicting characters who initially display scepticism about them, before gradually accepting their existence and interacting with them. In addition, the focus of scholarly interest in these films is social and emotional tensions as depicted through the development of characters and the communication between them, which is why the films are often deemed generically a form of melodrama (Kovacs, 1999; Walker, 2017).

Ghost

One famous example is the film *Ghost* (1990), a romance that suggests that emotional forces and attachments, together with unresolved conflicts, may hold a person in between the worlds of the living and the dead. The film follows Sam Wheat, who at the start is moving into a new home with Molly, his girlfriend, and they are helped by their friend Carl. Sam works in finance with Carl and appears to have a comfortable and happy lifestyle but is anxious that he may lose his happiness in the future. He hesitates to discuss marriage with Molly and does not use the word love with her, but instead responds whenever she says that she loves him with the word 'Ditto'. His fortunes suddenly change when he is shot in the street by a mugger, and he does not realise at first that this shooting has killed him. We see Sam running after the escaping mugger and then turning back to see a distraught Molly holding his body and calling for help. As the story progresses, we learn that ghosts are the dead who have not allowed themselves to be taken away to their next destination. For the virtuous, it is lights that descend and invite the spirit, while when the villains in the film die, they are taken by sinister shadows.

Although the light and dark heralds appear to be related to Christian beliefs, there are other ideas in the film that resonate with a wider range of cultures, such as the idea that ghosts do not realize they are ghosts, and that they are held in a betwixt and between state that is neither alive nor dead. A study of early anthropology theorized by Hertz (1960 [1909]) looks at examples such as the Dayak of Borneo to draw links between burial ceremonies, beliefs about ghosts and mourning the dead (both for individuals and as a collective enterprise). Modern Western societies tend to view death as happening at one time, although the ambivalence of this attitude is depicted, for example, in television shows such as *ER* (1994–2009), where the instant of death is not always obvious but is shaped by a procedure where a doctor working on a patient declares a time of death at the point where they feel no more can be done for them. However, many other societies regard death as a process that can take weeks or even months to complete. Hertz explores this is in relation to the double-burial, a broad term that identifies where societies have two rituals following the death of one of their members. The first is a relatively brief ceremony, that is followed by a period in which the body is laid out in a special way while it goes through the natural process of decay. A second ceremony takes place once the bones are dry and is a much more lavish and expensive ritual (Hertz, 1960 [1909]: 29–31). It is during this period between the two ceremonies that those close to the deceased have the most stringent prohibitions placed upon them, and this is linked to the idea that the soul is also going through a transitional period, no longer living but not yet a member of the community of ancestors (Hertz, 1960 [1909]: 34–5). During this time the soul is often regarded as restless and potentially malicious, particularly if the living friends and relatives do not attend to mourning customs correctly, and it is only once the second burial is complete that the soul is thought to have joined the collective community of ancestors. Once the soul has transitioned to a place within the society of the dead, they are thought to have much more stable and positive relationships with the living (Hertz, 1960 [1909]: 36–7).

Although double burial is not a common feature of death rites in the modern Western context, ghost films often contain narrative themes that suggest that ghosts are restless beings that have not transitioned into a further stage of existence after death. The ghosts that kidnap the little girl, Carol-Anne in the film *Poltergeist* (1982) are characterized in that way by the medium, Tangina, who further explains that this final stage in the death process can be completed when the ghosts walk into a light, and that the light is therefore dangerous to Carol-Anne as she is not really dead. When Carol-Anne's mother, Diane Freeling, rescues her daughter from the alternate dimension in their house that the ghosts inhabit, images of birth are evoked as the mother has a cord wrapped around her waist and both her and her daughter emerge covered in what looks like birth fluids. Creed (1993: 55) in her exploration of the feminine in horror draws attention to ways that haunted houses resemble wombs, giving *Poltergeist* as an example. Moreover, links between birth and death ceremonies are of considerable interest to anthropologists, with one of the most well-known examples being Turner's theorizing of the tripartite nature of many rites of passage, including those surrounding death, birth and initiation (Turner, 1995 [1969]).

For Sam Wheat in *Ghost*, his betwixt and between or liminal ghostly state is perpetuated because of love for his wife and his fears for her safety. Sam learns that, rather than being accidentally shot by a mugger, he was murdered by someone who was hired by his friend Carl (who is laundering money at the bank where he and Sam work) to retrieve a computer code. Carl's continuing search for the code places Molly in danger and Sam, searching for a way to warn her, stumbles across a con artist posing as a psychic – Oda Mae Brown – only to find that she overhears his sarcastic comments about her overacting. The suspension of disbelief in this film is thereby combined with its comic elements through a charlatan spirit medium, who discovers that she actually can communicate with the dead and be possessed by them. There are therefore features in this film that resonate with ethnographic accounts, including the fact that the medium is able to negotiate to a certain extent with the spirit and Oda Mae allows her body to be borrowed for certain purposes, such as allowing Sam to touch Molly.

What this suggests about contemporary Western attitudes to possession is debatable. It could be argued that such films are employing possession in a metaphorical sense that allows a temporary belief in ghosts to enable the audience to explore the dimensions of human love using imagery which still holds power over the imagination, but which is not necessarily part of explanatory processes in the everyday contemporary West. This temporary belief, moreover, engages with more sceptical viewpoints in *Ghost*. Molly is convinced only gradually of Oda Mae's sincerity, initially by her references to things only Sam and Molly would know about, and finally by Sam's ability to move objects (in this case, a penny). Between these events, both the police and Carl express other views, including the idea that grief makes people vulnerable and spirit mediums take advantage of this.

The suspension of disbelief

This proposition, that ghosts in film are simply a manifestation of redundant ideas, could be analysed using the notion of the uncanny in the sense suggested by Freud. For Freud, the uncanny is frightening because it is a sense of something both familiar and unfamiliar at the same time, something that 'ought to have remained secret and hidden but has come to light' (Freud, 2001 [1919]: 220–4, 225). He goes on to describe two interrelated kinds of repressed material that might come to light in this connection, the first being related to the unconscious processes of the individual mind, in particular those related to emotions and experiences of childhood (Freud, 2001 [1919]: 236) and the second being more related to Freud's proposition that Western society as a whole has undergone certain evolutionary processes that have led, under ordinary circumstances, to a greater scepticism about the existence of spirits than is in evidence in societies that Freud describes as 'primitive'. However, more concrete encounters with death may have a strong emotional impact and awaken feelings of dread or hope in relation to the possibility of the return of the dead as spirits or ghosts (Freud, 2001 [1919]: 241–3). He explores accounts of uncanny experiences, such as when someone dies soon after another person has wished them dead, or when one meets a person unexpectedly just after thinking about them, and argues that,

these last examples of the uncanny are to be referred to the principle which
I have called 'omnipotence of thoughts', taking the name from an expression
used by one of my patients. And now we find ourselves on old familiar ground.
Our analysis of the uncanny has led us back to the old, animistic conception
of the universe. This was characterised by the idea that the world was peopled
with the spirits of human beings; by the subject's narcissistic overvaluation of
his own mental processes; by the belief in the omnipotence of thoughts and the
technique of magic based on that belief; by the attribution to various outside
persons and things of carefully graded magical powers, or '*mana*'; as well as by
all the other creations with the help of man, in the unrestricted narcissism of
that stage of development, strove to fend off the manifest prohibitions of reality.
It seems as if each one of us has been through a phase of individual development
corresponding to this animistic stage in primitive men, that none of us has
passed through it without preserving certain traces of it which are still capable of
manifesting themselves, and that everything which now strikes us as 'uncanny'
fulfils the condition of touching those residues of animistic mental activity
within us and bringing them to expression. (Freud, 2001 [1919]: 240–1)

Freud's work on the uncanny has been used extensively by theorists of both
literature and film and television (Balanzategui, 2018; Bényei, 2016; Hubner,
2018; Royle, 2003). His explorations of the double, themes of repetition, trauma
and the juxtaposition of the familiar offer valuable insights for film theorists
(Walker, 2017: 31–4). However, his assertions about religious attitudes he
calls 'animistic', and especially his dismissal of engagements with spirits are
more problematic. If Freud's analysis is correct, then it would follow that those
images of possession in fantasy films are effective largely because they engage
with ideas and emotions that are rarely acknowledged in contemporary society,
but which, nonetheless, retain a degree of power. Carroll's treatment of horror
films is useful here, as he explores theories that suggest that the pleasures of
emotional excitation that such performances generate are made possible by a
kind of suspension of disbelief that retains certain limits, allowing the viewer
to make leaps of imaginative exploration within the context of the film, without
necessarily applying the same principles to everyday life (Carroll, 1990: 60–88).
While this kind of approach has some attractions, particularly as there
appears to be more examples of possession in cinema than in other contexts
of contemporary Western life, it may also be self-limiting if fascination with
possession phenomena is regarded as nothing more than the psychological
equivalent of an appendix, a functionally redundant anomaly connected to our
evolutionary past. For example, Walker (2017: 27), drawing from a Freudian

perspective, suggests that, 'a belief in ghosts was once commonplace but is now dismissed by science'. This view glosses over the possibility that those who watch ghost films may have a range of attitudes to the phenomenon, and that these attitudes may be fluid and contextual. Moreover, the science that Walker refers to is unclear, and may be rooted in Freud's own attempts to distinguish his emerging science of psychology from other movements spearheaded by his contemporaries, such as the Society for Psychical Research (Hewitt, 2020: 24–6).

Moreover, the specific characterization of the relationship between ghost and medium in *Ghost* has come under scrutiny in comparison with earlier ghost films. Kovacs (1999: 147), for example, has suggested that 'the ghost of the 1990s is a pale shadow of his predecessors' and that the comparative helplessness of Sam, who relies on the medium Oda Mae to act in the world and speak on his behalf, is a comment on, as well as a product of the problems of modernity in the period, and that he is an example of an 'almost cataclysmic decline of the fearsome Gothic apparition' (Kovacs, 1999: 150–8, 159). Fowkes (1998) takes this view further, suggesting that Sam's invisibility and difficulties with moving objects are part of a scenario driven by masochistic fantasies.

Such a view, however, elides the complexity of relationships between mediums and spirits as found in ethnographic studies. Placido (2001), for example, in her study of the Venezuelan cult of Maria Lionza, explores ways in which a number of modern media, including anthropological writings, documentaries and contemporary cinema, are utilized by mediums and their circle of believers. On one level, this use helps to shape the characters of 'spirit persons' in the context of a particular medium and the circumstances surrounding him/her. This is possible because

> unlike the Catholic saints and the Santeria Orishas with whom they are often compared, spirits have very undefined identities. Everything about the spirits – even the Three Powers, Maria Lionza, el Negro Felipe, and el Indio Guaicaipuro – is very vague … the spirits are general characters, and it is up to mediums and believers to transform them into social persons with a particular identity. (Placido, 2001: 214)

While anthropological books and films might inform this process, it is far from a one-way flow of information. On the contrary,

> when the spirits descend … they not only affirm or reject the knowledge and information mediums have acquired through books and videos, but they also often give new stories and unknown versions of the events and thus provide people with new knowledge about them. Many of these new tales and stories

then appear in the books that researchers produce on the basis on information acquired through contact with spirits. (Placido, 2001: 216)

This sense that the spirit's identity is somehow negotiated with, rather than simply imposed upon, the medium can also extend to the way in which the medium is entered because the spirit may be 'brought down' or *led into* the medium if they have sufficient skill (Placido, 2001: 217). Placido also explains how examples from popular culture, such as the film *Ghost*, are also sources from which mediums and believers draw to explore spirit phenomena. Placido explains this in connection with her argument that anthropologists tend to emphasize the *form* of spirit possession as an activity, rather than focusing on what is actually said during possessions. The speech content is, however, of paramount importance to believers,

> Spirits love talking. In fact they are desperate to speak because, mediums and believers insist, spirits need to speak in order to 'exist'. The idea that spirits could be wandering around without being able to express themselves is a cause of great worry and distress for many of those who believe in them. Virginia, a believer, offered a clear explanation of this, as she burst into tears while we were watching the film *Ghost*. The tape of this film had been rented for me to watch so that I would understand better what spirit-human relations are like. *Ghost* was considered very accurate at describing those relations. It is about a young man, killed by someone he knows, who desperately tries, once he has become a spirit, to find a medium, to communicate with his fiancée, who is in danger of being killed by the same man. *Ghost* was a cult movie (in more than one sense) among some mediums and believers I met: they had learned bits of it by heart and they were very keen that I should understand how terribly difficult it is for the spirits to be heard, seen, and felt; that is, to exist. (Placido, 2001: 213–14)

Fiction films are therefore one of a number of examples of the ways in which the creative relationship between mediums and spirits is dynamic and subject to contemporary cultural influences. Far from fading from view, spirits may play important roles in a community's response to economic and political changes generated by encounters with modernity, and may be part of a dynamic engagement with the past (Lambek, 1998; Lan, 1985). Lambek, for example, uses Aristotle's concept of *poiesis* to explore spirit possession in Madagascar, because this concept suggests that history-making can be both objective and creative simultaneously (Lambek, 1998: 110–13). Thus, 'if becoming possessed is a kind of mimetic surrender to history, when the spirits rise they are understood as rational historical agents' (Lambek, 1998: 113). Lambek questions sharp distinctions between the mythical and the real, partly because such distinctions miss the diversity of cultural forms, but also because 'the commonsense "real" world itself is culturally constituted and to a degree contingent and variable' (Lambek, 1998: 114).

Spirits and prejudice: *I Walked with a Zombie* and *White Zombie*

While scepticism about ghosts and spirits in Hollywood films and academic writings about them may be informed by a focus on the psychological vulnerability of the bereaved and the idea that science has superseded engagements with spirits in the modern West, there are also prejudices about spirit religions that are rooted in more global colonial attitudes. Arguably, Freud's dismissal of 'animistic' religion is itself a product of the influence of colonial attitudes on scholarship concerning indigenous religions in the early twentieth century. However, there is also evidence of very specific prejudices directed at indigenous African religions and those of the African diaspora that have influenced Hollywood cinema. These themes are important because they offer another strand to the way possession is treated in film. Moreover, ethnographies of African religions (including diaspora) are some of the key resources for academics studying the phenomenon of possession in fieldwork.

Important examples are the traditional religious practices of the Yoruba, Fon and Ewe peoples, located in the regions of Africa later designated as Southern Nigeria, Benin and South-West Nigeria, and Ghana and Togo, respectively (Hurbon, 1995: 14–15). Ceremonies included elements such as drumming, dance and ritual sacrifice, intended as offerings for deities collectively known as Vodun and these acts can also be interpreted as an invitation for the deities to participate, through their possession of celebrants. Although Christianity and Islam have become important religious traditions on the African continent, traditional indigenous religions remain, including those worshipping the Vodun (e.g. Ben Amos, 1994; Montgomery, 2017). Moreover, as the slave trade shipped African people to various parts of South America and the Caribbean, their traditions were also exported from around the 1500s onwards. This process brought with it change, as traditions that had been very localized were subject to mutual influences brought about by the co-participation of members originating in different African locations. There were also fusions with

Christianity that helped to disguise their origins. There are multiple examples of these traditions, that include Vodou (also spelt Voodoo and Vodu) in Haiti where the deities are called Iwa or Loa, Obeayisne in Jamaica, Candomblé in Brazil and Santería in Cuba, where the deities are called Orixas or Orishas. Many religious traditions in these regions have a multiplicity of influences, so that, for example Santo Daime in Brazil includes indigenous Amazonian components as well as Afro-Brazilian traditions and Catholic Christianity (Dawson, 2011: 144). Moreover, Santo Daime and other Brazilian religions, including Umbanda, were also inspired by Western Spiritualist movements such as those of the Frenchman Rivail (1804–1869) who from around 1855 onwards took the name of one of the spirits, Kardec, as an alias for his writings on Spiritualism, and Kardecism became the name by which his ideas were known in Brazil (Brown, 1994; Dawson, 2011: 147; Schmidt, 2016: 32–7). Subsequent voluntary migrations have meant that these religious traditions can be found globally, with, for example, substantial communities in America (Murphy and Sanford, 2001; Schmidt, 2008).

One important ethnography of a New York Vodou community in Brooklyn uses stories told by the community as family histories to explore the tradition's complex links with Africa and Haiti, and the ways in which historical and social circumstances have helped to shape practices (Brown, 2001 [1991]). The book offers detailed explorations of several of the Vodou deities, including Ogou (Brown, 2001 [1991]: 94–139), a warrior deity sometimes twinned with the Roman Catholic Saint James; Danbala (Brown, 2001 [1991]: 272–309), a serpentine deity associated with Saint Patrick; and Gede (Brown, 2001 [1991]: 330–81), the deity of death and sexuality. The reputation of Haitian Vodou has been impacted by a slave rebellion that began in 1791 and resulted in a declaration of an independent state of Haiti in 1804 that challenged French rule and more fundamentally European colonialism and the slave trade more generally (Hurbon, 1995: 41–50; Schmidt, 2008: 56). Much of the negative publicity around Vodou can therefore be said to have originated in the fears generated by the slave rebellion and its associations with religion. Examples include negative commentaries from that time but continued in ways that influenced depictions in Hollywood films (Brown, 2001 [1991]: 111).

Krzywinska (2000: 157–200) explores the complex associations highlighted in cinematic references to Vodou, including films such as *White Zombie* (1932), *I Walked with a Zombie* (1943) and *The Serpent and the Rainbow* (1988). She explores the motifs in these films that perpetuate confusing links in the colonial imagination between Haiti, Vodou and a range of signifiers of 'otherness' (whether romanticized or vilified), noting, for example, the ways in which these films offer enticing or repellent representations of alterity that contrast the 'rationality' of colonial white culture. Interestingly, such representations are themselves highly emotive fantasies. Examples include the use of African drumming in these films and the sensationalized depiction of people participating in Vodou ceremonies, often with a focus on women in trance (Krzywinska, 2000: 172). Moreover, Vodou in these films is represented in very similar ways to films sensationalizing witchcraft and demonic possession. While some of these films offer a passing acquaintance with Vodou, their tone and structure are more related to cinematic and literary gothic forms than an engagement with African religions. The motif of the zombie is particularly confusing in this regard. Although mythologies and practices related to zombies can be found in Haiti, they are not integral elements of the Vodou religion, and are more properly understood in the context of fears of slavery (McAlister, 2012). In American films, the associations between zombies and economics, power and control remain (Botting, 2013), but they are divorced from any real engagement with Haiti, and instead they become signifiers of gothic monstrosity that at times may highlight racial injustice, but more often exemplify colonial fantasies about race. An American occupation of Haiti (1915–34) also contributed to the shaping of these associations (Krzywinska, 2000: 161) as did ongoing racism within America itself, a country that had also benefitted economically from African slave labour. Although Abbott's study of zombie films focuses on later examples, she explains how ambivalent emotions about slavery fuse with gothic motifs in early examples. She suggests that the casting of Bela Lugosi as the villain in *White Zombie*, Bokur, is used to maximum effect and resembles his characterization of Dracula in the 1931 film *Dracula*. Bokur is a white mill owner who uses Haitians whom he has enslaved as zombies to work in his mill and he suggests that others should also use similar slaves on their plantations (Abbott, 2016: 63). Importantly for the purposes of this chapter, there is often little effort to distinguish between Vodou possession and zombification in film depictions. The subtle lending of agency to the spirits in Vodou ritual is not explored and both possession and zombies become fused in fears and fantasies about loss of rationality and control.

Brown's analysis of Vodou suggests that issues of power, control and submission to deities are much more complex. This is in part because Vodou is a highly flexible system which adapts to people's needs in times of difficulty and social change, both in the broad sense (such as when women gain a more prominent place in the growing urbanization of Haiti and the urban contexts of the Diaspora) (Brown, 1991: 221, 255) and in the ways that rituals are often tailored to meet specific individual needs for empowerment in difficult situations, such as when Cecile, a woman unhappy about her husband's infidelity, is instructed to hold a ritual plant and say (not beg for) what she wants (Brown, 1991: 343). A relationship with the spirits, therefore, although characterized on one level as 'service', does not turn practitioners into victims. 'Those who serve the spirits do not fall on their knees and implore a god to solve their problems for them. A Vodou spirit is not a *deus ex machina* but a catalyst who mobilizes the will and energy of human beings' (Brown, 1991: 254). Moreover, while possessions in Vodou rituals can be spontaneous, there are numerous activities that are aimed at inviting specific deities to specific rituals, including putting out the deity's favourite foods and drinks and the liturgies chosen for that day (Brown, 2001 [1991]: 55).

With regard to questions of agency during the possession itself, Keller points to the problems involved in studying a phenomenon where the possessed person may not remember all or some of what took place during the possession. On the one hand, this mysterious aspect of spirit possessions can help indigenous practitioners to define authenticity in ways that resist outside influences (van de Port, 2005) (see also Johnson (2002) on circulations of secrecy in Candomblé). On the other hand, this 'blotting' of consciousness 'is viewed suspiciously as a traumatic and negative event, especially from a psychologically informed perspective. Consciousness itself is viewed as the source of an individual's agency, so that possessions represent a troubling event' (Keller, 2002: 4). As Keller cogently argues, while possessions themselves are certainly fascinating and worthy of study, some of the 'problems' thrown up by these rituals may have more to do with limitations and cultural bias inherent in the perspectives of scholarly analyses than with the phenomena itself. Schmidt (2017: 96) uses Taves (1999) to explain ways in which understandings of agency may differ between cultures and that the emphasis on control stressed in Western contexts may not apply in other societies such as African traditional religions or practices derived from them, 'she insists therefore that seemingly involuntary acts that include uncontrolled bodily movements, spontaneous vocalizations, unusual sensory experiences and alterations of consciousness and/or memory should not be regarded as symptoms of mental weakness or an expression of false religion, but should be understood in terms of skill development' (Schmidt, 2017: 96–7). Moreover, Schmidt also uses her own detailed ethnography of spirits and trance in a Brazilian context to explain that there are considerable differences between different religious traditions (e.g. Candomblé, Umbanda and Spiritism) and even between informants in the same tradition, with regard to the degree of consciousness mediums experience during possession. For example, Spiritist mediums tend to remain fully or semiconscious because their practices emphasize offering clients advice dispensed by the spirits for whom the mediums are interpreters as well as go-betweens (Schmidt, 2016: 119). By contrast, most Candomblé practitioners she spoke to and observed appeared to be largely in an unconscious state during possessions, and rarely spoke, unlike the Venezuelan mediums studied by Placido (2001) that I discussed earlier. In Brazilian Candomblé, the deities that possess mediums express themselves through body language, movement and dance, and a separate process of oracle readings is used to convey messages in words (Schmidt, 2016: 109). Moreover, informants disputed the term 'possession', explaining that the process of initiation for mediums gradually shapes and cultivates relationships with deities that are already present in their bodies but which remain dormant without training (Schmidt, 2016: 111).

This idea, that the medium and the deities that possess them, cultivate one another's personhood during processes of initiation and practice, is interesting from a contemporary animist point of view and is also suggested by Sered (1994: 189) who refers to Jacobs and Kaslow (1991: 132) to argue against the idea that the medium's own identity is erased by the spirit's during possession, rather she is often working with a further social self in subtle ways. Sered's theorizing walks a fine line, as she does not subscribe to the idea that possession is largely a mechanism to redress social or psychological problems, but notes with amusement (drawing from Leacock and Leacock, 1972) how Brazilian Batuque women mediums 'often engage in "male" behaviour such as smoking cigarettes or cigars, drinking alcoholic beverages, and shouting vulgarities. (The entranced medium is unaware of all this so cannot possibly be enjoying herself!)' (Sered, 1994: 183). The subtlety of the distinction can be totally missed in Western films and television that depict possession as simply a licence for criminal behaviour.

Continuity between the medium and the possessing agent?

Buffy the Vampire Slayer offers an interesting example in this regard. As explored in the previous chapter, the show constructs the vampire myth in a way that categorizes it as a kind of possession phenomena. It combines filmic traditions of demonic possession and cinema that explores psychological explanations of serial violence in its tropes, but at the same time complicates the debate with the plot device of Angel's restored soul. Similarly, in season four, technology is installed into Spike's head that causes him pain when he hurts humans and that also curbs his demonic behaviour. Although there is no evidence to suggest that the writing team engaged with the anthropology of spirit possession, the results of their reflections on the vampire and personhood offer some interesting results when cast in the light of ethnographic insights. For example, in *The Wish* (3009) Cordelia, hurt by her discovery of her boyfriend Xander's affair with Willow, wishes that Buffy had never come to Sunnydale. Her wish is granted by a vengeance demon called Anyanka and she is transported into an alternate reality in which Buffy has not come to Sunnydale, many of her friends are dead, and Xander and Willow have been turned into sadistic vampires (and much to Cordelia's chagrin are *still* together)! This alternative reality is only dissolved when Anyanka's 'power centre', an amulet, is broken by Giles. In a subsequent episode (3016), Anyanka attempts to retrieve the amulet and regain her powers by tricking Willow into performing a spell with her that links them with the alternate reality. Instead, Vampire Willow enters the normal Buffy-verse and Willow meets her 'self', transformed by vampiric possession. Willow, a normally rather excessively conventional student, engages with a version of herself that is not only sadistic but also exhibits an interest in lesbian sexuality. Once the vampire is captured, she discusses her discomfort with her friends, and Buffy tries to reassure her by suggesting that the vampire's personality has nothing to do 'with the person that was', whereupon Angel (a character whose insight is complicated by the fact that he is a vampire who has had his soul returned to him) remarks 'well actually …'. Later, in the fourth season, Willow does embark upon an important lesbian relationship with a fellow student, Tara, and when her partner is murdered, she realizes a capacity for extreme sadism when taking her revenge, using a phrase her vampire self was fond of as a prelude to violence – 'bored now' (6020).

Sexuality is also an example used by ethnographic writers exploring the question of whether there are characteristics in common between a possessed person and the possessing agent. In studies informed by psychological models of possession it may be suggested that possession allows someone to act out desires and emotions, including homosexual desire, which might otherwise be repressed either by society's disapproval or their own personal conflicts. Brown takes a more pragmatic approach to the same question. She explores a number of forms of Ezili, a female deity of Haitian Vodou, and argues that the social circumstances and personal preferences of the spirit medium may have an impact on which spirits are more likely to frequently manifest within that person. She suggests that

Alourdes and her spirits create one another, a relationship recognized within her Vodou family, where someone is as likely to speak about 'Alourdes's Danto' as about Ezili Danto in general. Alourdes is a heterosexual woman, in mid life, who grew up in Port-au-Prince and has lived in the United States for twenty-five years. Her situation as a woman relating to the three Ezili is naturally different from that of a man relating to mother and lover figures. Her heterosexuality suppresses the acknowledged lesbian dimension of Ezili Danto, a part of the *lwa's* character that could be very important for other women. (Brown, 2001 [1991]: 222)

Possession as a Metaphor for Emotions: *Practical Magic*

In addition to exploring personhood, film and television can also use possession themes to consider emotional states and relationships. One example is *Practical Magic* (1998). The film focuses on two sisters, Sally and Gillian, who possess magical powers but are ambivalent about using them. This bringing together of the themes of sisterhood and magic is also found within the television series *Charmed* (1998–2006) (see also Beeler, 2007) and may be a reflection of the way in which magical practices have become associated with feminism in the contemporary West. Both women have problems with their personal relationships, Sally enjoys a happy marriage that is suddenly cut short by her husband's accidental death, while Gillian's more rebellious nature leads her to indulge in a passionate relationship with a man called Jimmy that has dark side that spins out of control and becomes violent. She calls on Sally for help, and when she administers an overdose of belladonna in an attempt to render Jimmy unconscious, he is killed. In fear of the consequences of murder, the women attempt to bring him back from the dead, but unable to control the 'dark and unnatural' manifestation, kill him a second time and bury him in the garden. This is, however, not the end of the matter and his spirit continues to trouble the sisters, eventually possessing Gillian – and – to borrow a phrase from the film – 'squatting inside her like a toad'. This possession is clearly a metaphor for his control over Gillian's emotions and state of mind, something implied by the way in which the supernatural situation is described in Western terms by other women called upon to help with the exorcism. They use phrases such as, 'apparently her sister just got out of a very bad relationship and now the guy just will not leave her alone' and her admittance to magical abilities is described as 'coming out'.

While one reading of the possession metaphor focuses on the psychological hold that Jimmy exercises on Gillian, a second reading can suggest that the experiences of both sisters actually explore Sally's psychological condition following her husband's death. Her initial shock and disbelief are expressed in a request to her aunts to resurrect her husband, but they refuse on the grounds that while the returning entity might superficially appear to be him, the reality would be something 'dark and unnatural'. Sally accepts this explanation and continues her grieving with a period of time in bed, where Gillian finds her and encourages her to continue with her life and care for her children. Later in the film, Sally shows some hesitation in her budding romance with a policeman, but the darker aspects of her emotional state can best be regarded in the light of the parallel story of Gillian's relationship with Jimmy. Firstly, when Sally kills Jimmy, and secondly when they use the resurrection spell that was Sally's first impulse when her husband died. This is partly justified by the fact that Jimmy always was 'dark and unnatural', but his resurrected self is unmanageable and Sally is compelled to kill him a second time, whereupon he haunts the girls and possesses Gillian. Jimmy's disappearance brings the policeman into Sally's life and the haunting therefore takes place at the same time as her struggle with the challenges of forming a new relationship. Moreover, it can also be suggested that stories that portray the dead's hold over the living explore a kind of transference stimulated by the ways in which survivors may become locked into a series of problematic emotions concerning their dead. Attig, for example, refers to the way in which grief often causes a person to hesitate, withdrawing from their normal social world, and experiencing the emotional pain associated with a longing for the return of the deceased (Attig, 1996: 34). However, he clearly distinguishes between the most immediate emotion of grief and the long-term process of grieving which he suggests is an active learning to live in a world in which the deceased is absent.

> When mourners go on as if a temporary retreat from reality is a sustainable posture in the world, they do something far different from temporarily indulging a wish that the world were other than it is. Grief leads some mourners to long for the return of the deceased in a way that if it persists, becomes irrational and dangerous. When they enter what I call extreme grief emotion, their disposition to expect, and their quite rational wish for, the presence of the deceased becomes a fervent, pervasive, preoccupying, and irrational desire. As they wholeheartedly and persistently desire the impossible and dwell in intense longing for what is irretrievably lost and recognized by them to be so, they experience something far different from ordinary grief ... a suppression of the belief and a consequent refusal to face and come to terms with death's reality. (Attig, 1996: 35)

From this perspective, Jimmy's possession of Gillian may also be a metaphor for Sally's battle with the attractions of extreme grief, and the way that the sisters reaffirm bonds with each other and their wider social world is therefore given additional significance. An episode of *Buffy the Vampire Slayer* explores grief in a similar way (5017). When Buffy's mother dies, Dawn (Buffy's sister) performs a resurrection spell that she finds in one of Giles's books. She ignores warnings from Tara that such spells should never be cast because there are some aspects of the natural order of the universe that can never really be changed, and also from a practitioner of dark magic that Joyce may not come back exactly as she was. When a conversation with Buffy reconciles Dawn with her sister, Dawn breaks the spell by tearing through a photograph of her mother just before the being she has conjured knocks on the door. Such storylines may in part reflect ideas held within contemporary pagan witchcraft circles, including the idea that magic is a legitimate force in certain circumstances, but potentially dangerous in others. However, there is also a sense that grieving persons are psychologically vulnerable, and this idea contributes to suspicions of mediumship activity in film and television.

Mediums and the dead: *Afterlife*

The early 2000s were popular years for fictional television shows about mediums, including *Ghost Whisperer* (2005-10) and *Medium* (2005-11). These shows do depict characters that are unsure of the medium's abilities, but *Medium* in particular suggests that the medium is believed, as her insights enable her to work closely with the police to solve crimes. It is loosely based on the life and writings of Allison DuBois (2005), the name given to the show's central character. Scepticism about the potential abilities of mediums is explored in much more depth in the British series *Afterlife* (2005-6). Set in Bristol, the programme revolves around two principal characters: Alison, a reluctant spirit medium, and Robert, a university psychologist who makes her the subject of his research publication. Early in the first episode, Robert explains ways in which fake mediums can elicit information from clients through 'cold reading', a kind of detailed, but wholly material form of observation, and takes them 'into the belly of the beast' (a psychic evening in Clifton). Alison, however, defies expectations on several counts. She continues with her detailed description of a spirit standing behind one of the students, although the student gives her no encouragement, and Alison does not really want to accept money for her services. Most importantly, she asserts that she has no control over which spirits she sees, 'I'm not in charge you see. They are' (1001). This notion continues to be an important theme in the discourse between her and Robert, not least because Alison has spent time in hospital with mental health problems. She explains that medication does not work, saying 'I don't have any choice. You don't choose the spirits, they choose you'. Moreover, in ways reminiscent of Keller's argument, she asserts the agency of the spirits in a way that suggests that it is not only the living that need resolution but also the dead, and that sometimes there can be conflict between the two. This is dramatically illustrated in the case of Robert's student, the sole survivor of a family suicide pact. Although initially Alison believes that the spirit of this girl's mother wants to see her daughter move on, the reality is that this spirit is only satisfied when the daughter also commits suicide (1001). This idea, that spirits may envy the living and may try to take them with them into death, is also recorded in ethnographic studies, and is a particular concern when people dream about a dead person. Stephen, for example, describes Mekeo ideas about a dream-self, which, when it leaves the body,

> is exposed to many potential dangers. It encounters the dream-selves of other living people, of the dead, and of spirit beings such as the water spirits, all of which may try to influence, control, or destroy it. If a person's dream-self accepts food offered by dead relatives, or their embraces, or agrees to leave with them on some journey, the bodily self will wither and perish; if it refuses, no harm will be done. (Stephen, 1995: 125)

The agency of the dead is an important part of the tension between Alison and Robert, because while Robert wants to examine Alison (and her 'delusions') from a critical distance, she insists on a more personal engagement, based on her ability to see and communicate with Robert's dead son. Robert resents the possibility that she is manipulating him, a concern that is shared by his ex-wife (Jude) and his friend (Barbara) who both feel that involvement with a medium will hinder, rather than help, his grieving process, and he argues with Alison about which one of them is in denial (1002). The problems between them come to a head when it appears that Alison has been deceived by a journalist who stages a haunting in a flat in which no one has died. Alison has seen spirits committing a murder in the flat and will not relinquish her perceptions although they fly in the face of the facts. Robert becomes impatient with her insistence, saying, 'The truth is you don't want to be helped, do you? You don't want the spirits to leave you alone', whereupon Alison replies, 'No. They *won't* leave me alone. Your dead son won't *leave me alone!*' (1005). The conflict is only finally resolved during a séance in the final episode of the series, where Alison is possessed by Josh. Once the boy and his father are reconciled, Josh feels that he can move on but tries to take Alison with him and she falls into a coma.

This kind of emphasis on the agency of the spirits, and the conflicts of this world view with psychological perspectives, is also discussed by Vitebsky in the context of his ethnographic study of the Sora people of eastern India. Here, the medium provides a vehicle through which the dead can engage in lengthy, often painful dialogues with their living relatives, in which

> speakers persuade, cajole, tease, remind, deceive, and plead with one another. Dialogues represent a mutual quest for awareness about the other person's state of mind. At the same time, they are the medium through which each person's being is constantly moulded. Living and dead people cause each other to do things through dialogues at the same time as they themselves are changed by these encounters. Each person is an agent, but at the same time is acted upon and does not simply return to his or her previous state. (Vitebsky, 1993: 5)

Vitebsky contrasts this process with the ideas laid out in Freud's *Mourning and Melancholia* (2001 [1915]), suggesting that there is no room for the agency of the dead in Freud's model, there is simply normal mourning (in which the bereaved person withdraws libido from the beloved person, having accepted their loss) or melancholia (when the bereaved person cannot accept the death and loses interest in staying alive) (Vitebsky, 1993: 239). There are similarities between Sora thinking and Freud's ideas, including

> a comparable intense attachment, based on memory, between the bereaved and the deceased; a comparable gradual, painful withdrawal which eventually leaves the successful mourner 'free'; an ambivalence between compassion and hostility; a risk of shared fate through an identification between the two parties; and, where the entire process fails, a comparable loss of the will or ability to live. (Vitebsky, 1993: 240)

However, for the Sora,

> the deceased does continue to exist. But he does so in a way which modifies the dynamics of his relationship to the living since these dynamics are not the same as when both parties were still alive ... Freud reverses the Sora model and takes the initiative out of the hands of the dead ... it is not the Sora mourner who finds it difficult to "abandon a libidinal position" (Freud, 2001 [1915]: 244) but the deceased. Indeed, the dead may even be more articulate than the bereaved about their sense of loss. (Vitebsky, 1993: 241)

Ghosts and deities as social beings:
Always and *Truly, Madly, Deeply*

Fiction films that depict encounters with ghosts and possession often explore strong emotions and complex relationships in ways that lend themselves to psychological theoretical frameworks. The ghostly romance in particular explores the grieving process and the manifestation of the ghost that holds the attention of the bereaved on the love that they have lost, and this is often juxtaposed simultaneously with attempts to move forward with a new life and form new relationships. In *Always* (1989) the ghost Pete is given a mission to help another man, Ted, succeed as a flyer, but he must also let go of the love he left behind, Dorinda, who is starting a courtship with Ted (Fowkes, 1998: 42–3). In *Truly, Madly, Deeply* (1990) the ghost, Jamie, appears to his widow, Nina, who is initially overjoyed to see him but gradually wants to claim the new flat she has bought as her own and explore a budding relationship with Mark. In addition to Freudian models of the grieving process, these films also explore tensions between conceptions of intense love relationships that can overcome all boundaries, even death, and conceptions of individuality that allow for conflict and separation in personal relationships. Fowkes (1998: 75) draws attention to this in the context of her exploration of masochism in ghostly romance films. She notes how in *Ghost* and *Always* the reprise of a piece of music from a previous romantic scene where the ghost was still alive 'is employed nostalgically because it re-creates the lost scene of union between the two lovers before the untimely death of the male ... and its association with romantic oneness' and suggests (in a way reminiscent of Freudian theory) that this echoes the pre-Oedipal maternal bond (Fowkes, 1998: 75). While I agree that there is a tension between romantic oneness and individuality explored in these films, I suggest that this can also be explored beyond the limits of Freudian theory, and considered in light of broader tensions between individual and collective conceptions of consciousness and personhood. By this I mean that although romantic films focus on the union between two individuals that are known to each other, they can still be thought of as forming a tiny 'collective' between them. Moreover, using Hertz's ideas that I explored earlier in the chapter, it is possible to see how the ghost in many romantic ghost movies is transitioning from a web of relationships on earth to alternative connections in the afterlife, with the film exploring the period of adjustment for them and their loved ones 'betwixt and between' those states.

In *Truly, Madly, Deeply* (1990) this is hinted at by the ghostly Jamie hanging out with his ghostly friends in Nina's flat. Although these characters are ghosts rather than ancestors, they give the impression that when Nina chooses the new life she is building, rather than to keep the ghost, her dead husband has not been abandoned to exist alone, but has an alternative community to fall back on. This film is also interesting because it does not use the character of a medium to mediate Jamie and Nina's encounter and the 'suspension of disbelief' is very subtle. At the start of the film we hear Nina talking to a counsellor about Jamie, who she thinks she can hear as a comforting presence in the most difficult times of her grief. The implication is that this is Nina's imagination reliving typical conversations between herself and her husband, although now he sometimes speaks to her in Spanish (a language he did not know in life). The story shifts however, when one day Nina is playing the piano and she sees Jamie playing the cello, realizing that he is a much more real and substantive ghost, she rushes into his arms in tears. The boundaries are blurred between perceptions of imaginative and substantive apparitions when Nina tentatively tries to talk about her experiences, as other people do not respond with disbelief. A friend from Chile who Nina helps with English-language skills explains to Nina that she used to be a film-maker who explored spirit engagements in her country, asserting that they are everywhere and walk among us. George, a friendly man who is trying to exterminate rats in Nina's apartment explains to her that he regularly speaks to his wife who died years ago, and that both he and Nina know that Death has no dominion. Even Nina's counsellor does not meet Nina's suggestion that her encounters with Jamie are more substantial with scepticism but in response to Nina's assertion that the whole thing is ridiculous, asks why.

Rather than drawing the tension between belief and disbelief, *Truly, Madly, Deeply* contrasts the blissful moments when Nina and Jamie's love first reasserts itself in their initial ghostly encounter with the problems of her trying to live with the ghost. He starts to rearrange the new flat she had bought, interfering with her assertion of a new project and personhood after his death, and instead of being alone together, Jamie constantly inhabits her home with his ghostly friends. In the end, Nina chooses life and lets Jamie go, allowing the film to work as both real ghost depiction and metaphor.

In many of the African and African diaspora traditions that I have explored in this chapter, spirits have an even more collective dimension, as in addition to the spirits of the dead, deities communicate with and possess celebrants. When I suggest that deities are collective, I mean that more people know and relate to them, although, as I have suggested, the personhood of deities can be refined by the needs and circumstances of locality and their relationships with individual mediums. I have also argued elsewhere that Durkheim's theories of *collective consciousness* can be useful for exploring possessing deities (Child, 2007, 2010).

Many ethnographic studies of possession refer to spirits, ancestors or deities who are important to the community at large. Ben-Amos, for example, in her exploration of the Olokun cult among the Edo in Benin City, Nigeria, argues (counter to Lewis's (2003 [1971])) theories about possession) that

> women's religious associations are not necessarily peripheral or low in status. On the contrary, worship of Olokun is at the very centre of Edo cosmology and has a major part in ongoing religious practices ... the status that urban Edo women achieve in this cult is permanent not temporary, and the psychological benefits of participation are not temporary outlets but a real redefinition of self. (Ben-Amos, 1994: 119)

This is because the mediums are in touch with a deity (Olokun), thought to rule a spiritual kingdom under the sea, a representation of power that mirrors and at times acts as a balancing force with regard to temporal power (Ben-Amos, 1994: 120). This engagement with collective forces and ideas is an important part of the continuing vitality and success of spirit mediumship in ethnographic contexts.

Although it is much more rare for deities to be depicted in Western film, there are nonetheless features to be found in common with ethnographic accounts. *Buffy the Vampire Slayer* offers depictions of possession that are complex and where the inhabiting demon appears to have characteristics similar to the human they possess, although the show is not informed by ethnography and this feature is probably a reflection of ideas about human psychology. In *Afterlife*, possession itself is portrayed only rarely, and usually Alison's connection with spirits is in being able to hear and see spirit persons (who look much like living persons). Nonetheless, it is suggested that in addition to her natural gifts, her mediumship has been propelled by the suffering of a near-death experience during a train crash, and this notion, that practitioners are called by the spirits through suffering, is also found in ethnographic accounts (Ben-Amos, 1994: 121).

While depictions of mediums on film often express anxiety about the dangers of fake mediumship (*Séance on a Wet Afternoon*, 1964) and the vulnerability of their clients, studies of contemporary Spiritualism such as that of Wallis (2001: 137) suggest that extreme grief may be discouraged rather than encouraged by Western mediums, and that while the opportunity to converse with dead relatives may be an initial attraction to the movement, there are other factors that sustain the interest of long-term members, including its philosophical ideas and the sense of belonging to the community of attendees (Wallis, 2001: 141–2).

I would therefore like to suggest that these anxieties and tensions in films that depict ghosts and spirits have deeper roots than a simple rejection of the possibility of their existence. Rather, ghosts and spirits are reminders of collective and religious dimensions of personhood and society that have not been relegated to a distant evolutionary past but remain very much a part of modernity, and subject to transformation and adaptation within it. Rather than being superseded by psychological frameworks of explanation, collective emotions remain in tension with them, and this tension is particularly acute in late capitalist modernity because of the ways in which it defines itself and maintains power through particular notions of individuality.

Moreover, these tensions are also evident in depictions of love and romantic relationships in film. In part, tensions between absorption into the collective consciousness of the couple and the assertion of oneself as an individual are a part of the human condition that film depicts in a range of ways, including the grieving processes explored in the ghostly romance. *Buffy the Vampire Slayer* explores them even more starkly, highlighting the dangers of losing oneself in love, a frequent theme of gothic films and novels. However, the attractions and dangers of love as collective consciousness are depicted with even more ambivalence in films that explore shared dreams and fantasy worlds of lovers, and as I go on to explore in the next chapter, I suggest that these fears are in part an expression of broader social tensions around an imagined centrality of individuality in late modernity that is in conflict with the attractions of more social and penetrable models of personhood.

Bibliography

Abbott, S. (2016) *Undead Apocalypse: Vampires and Zombies in the 21st Century.* Edinburgh: Edinburgh University Press.

Attig, T. (1996) *How We Grieve: Relearning the World.* New York: Oxford University Press.

Balanzategui, J. (2018) *The Uncanny Child in Transnational Cinema: Ghosts of Futurity at the Turn of the Twenty-First Century.* Amsterdam: Amsterdam University Press.

Beeler, K. E. (ed.) (2007) *Investigating Charmed: The Magic Power of TV.* London: I.B. Tauris.

Behrend, H., Dreschke, A., and Zillinger, M. (eds) (2015) *Trance Mediums and New Media: Spirit Possession in the Age of Technical Reproduction*. New York: Fordham University Press.

Ben-Amos, P. G. (1994) 'The promise of greatness: Women and power in an Edo spirit possession cult', in T. D. Blakely, W. E. A. van Beek and D. L. Thomson (eds), *Religion in Africa*. London: James Currey. pp. 119–34.

Bényei, T. (2016) '"I'm from Brooklyn": Detection, myth and religion in *Angel Heart*', *Hungarian Journal of English and American Studies*, vol. 22, no. 1, pp. 153–66.

Blanes, R., and Santo, D. E. (eds) (2014) *The Social Life of Spirits*. Chicago: University of Chicago Press.

Boddy, J. (1994) 'Spirit possession revisited: beyond instrumentality', *Annual Review of Anthropology*, 23, pp. 407–34.

Botting, F. (2013) 'Undead-ends: Zombie debt/zombie theory', *Postmodern Culture*, vol. 23, no. 3, n.p.

Brown, D. D. (1994) *Umbanda: Religion and Politics in Urban Brazil*. New York: Columbia University Press.

Brown, K. M. (2001 [1991]) *Mama Lola: A Vodou Priestess in Brooklyn*. Berkeley: University of California Press.

Carroll, N. (1990) *The Philosophy of Horror or Paradoxes of the Heart*. New York: Routledge.

Child, L. (2007) *Tantric Buddhism and Altered States of Consciousness: Durkheim, Emotional Energy and Visions of the Consort*. Aldershot: Ashgate.

Child, L. (2010) 'Spirit possession, seduction, and collective consciousness', in B. Schmidt and L. Huskinson (eds), *Spirit Possession and Trance: New Interdisciplinary Perspectives*. London: Continuum, pp. 53–70.

Creed, B. (1993) *The Monstrous Feminine: Film, Feminism, Psychoanalysis*. London: Routledge.

Dawson, A. (2011) 'Spirit, self and society in the Brazilian new religion of Santo Saime', in A. Dawson (ed.), *Summoning the Spirits: Possession and Invocation in Contemporary Religion*. London: I.B. Tauris, pp. 143–61.

Deacy, C. (2012) *Screening the Afterlife: Theology, Eschatology and Film*. London: Routledge.

De Certeau, M. (1996 [1970]) *The Possession at Loudun* (trans. Michael B. Smith) Chicago: University of Chicago Press.

DuBois, A. (2005) *Don't Kiss Them Goodbye*. New York: Fireside.

Fowkes, K. A. (1998) *Giving Up the Ghost: Spirits, Ghosts, and Angels in Mainstream Comedy Films*. Detroit: Wayne State University Press.

Freud, S. (2001 [1915]) 'Mourning and melancholia', in James Strachey (trans.), *The Standard Edition of the Complete Psychological Works of Sigmund Freud*. vol. 14 (1914–16). London: Vintage, the Hogarth Press and the Institute of Psychoanalysis, pp. 237–60.

Freud, S. (2001 [1919]) 'The Uncanny', James Strachey (trans.), *The Standard Edition of the Complete Psychological Works of Sigmund Freud*, vol. 17 (1917–19). London: Vintage, The Hogarth Press and the Institute of Psychoanalysis, pp. 217–56.

Gunning, T. (2015) 'Phantom images and modern manifestations: Spirit photography, magic theater, trick films, and photography's uncanny', in M. Leeder (ed.), *Cinematic Ghosts: Haunting and Spectrality from Silent Cinema to the Digital Era.* New York: Bloomsbury, pp. 17–38.

Henley, P. (2006) 'Spirit possession, power, and the absent presence of Islam: Reviewing *Les Maîtres Fous*', *Journal of the Royal Anthropological Institute*, 12, pp. 731–61.

Hertz, R. (1960 [1907]) *Death and the Right Hand* (trans. Rodney and Claudia Needham) London: Cohen & West.

Hewitt, M. A. (2014) *Freud on Religion*. Durham, NC: Acuman.

Hewitt, M. A. (2020) *Legacies of the Occult: Psychoanalysis, Religion, and Unconscious Communication*. Sheffield: Equinox.

Hubner, L. (2018) *Fairy Tale and Gothic Horror: Uncanny Transformations in Film.* London: Palgrave Macmillan.

Hunter, J. (2014) 'Mediumship and folk models of mind and matter', in J. Hunter and D. Luke (eds), *Talking with the Spirits: Ethnographies from Between the Worlds.* Brisbane: David Grail, pp. 99–129.

Hunter, J., and Luke, D. (eds) (2014) *Talking with the Spirits: Ethnographies from Between the Worlds*. Brisbane: David Grail.

Hurbon, L. (1995) *Voodoo: Truth and Fantasy*. London: Thames & Hudson.

Jacobs, C. F., and Kaslow, A. J. (1991) *The Spiritual Churches of New Orleans*. Knoxville: University of Tennessee Press.

Keller, M. (2002) *The Hammer and the Flute: Women, Power, and Spirit Possession*. Baltimore, MD: John Hopkins University Press.

Kovacs, L. (1999) *The Haunted Screen: Ghosts in Literature and Film*. Jefferson, NC: McFarland.

Krzywinska, T. (2000) *A Skin for Dancing In: Possession, Witchcraft and Voodoo in Film.* Trowbridge: Flicks Books.

Johnson, P. C. (2002) *Secrets, Gossip, and Gods: The Transformation of Brazilian Candomblé*. Oxford: Oxford University Press.

Johnson, P. C. (2006) 'Secretism and the Apotheosis of Duvalier', *Journal of the American Academy of Religion,* vol. 74, no. 2, pp. 420–45.

Lambek, M. (1981) *Human Spirits: A Cultural Account of Trance in Mayotte.* Cambridge: Cambridge University Press.

Lambek, M. (1998) 'The Sakalava Poiesis of history: Realizing the past through Spirit possession in Madagascar', *American Ethnologist*, vol. 25, no. 2, pp. 106–27.

Lan, D. (1985) *Guns and Rain: Guerrillas and Spirit Mediums in Zimbabwe.* London: Currey.

Leacock, S., and Leacock, R. (1972) *Spirits of the Deep: A Study of an Afro-Brazilian Cult.* New York: Doubleday Natural History Press.

Lewis, I. M. (1966) 'Spirit possession and deprivation cults', *Man*, vol. 1, no. 3, pp. 307–29.

Lewis, I. M. (2003 [1971]) *Ecstatic Religion: An Anthropological Study of Spirit Possession and Shamanism*. London: Routledge.

McAlister, E. (2012) 'Slaves, cannibals, and infected hyper-whites: The race and religion of zombies', *Anthropological Quarterly*, vol. 85, no. 2, pp. 457–86.

Montgomery, E. J. (2017) '"Visual Voodoo": Photo-voice in Togo', *Visual Anthropology*, vol. 30, no. 4, pp. 287–309.

Murphy, J. M., and Sanford, M. (eds) (2001) *Òsun across the Waters: A Yoruba Goddess in Africa and the Americas*. Bloomington: Indiana University Press.

Natale, S. (2016) *Supernatural Entertainments: Victorian Spiritualism and the Rise of Modern Media Culture*. Pennsylvania: Pennsylvania State University Press.

Placido, B. (2001) '"It's all to do with words": an analysis of spirit possession in the Venezuelan cult of Maria Lionza' *The Journal of the Royal Anthropological Institute*, vol. 7, no. 2, pp. 207–24.

Royle, N. (2003) *The Uncanny*. Manchester: Manchester University Press.

Santo, D. E. (2015) *Developing the Dead: Mediumship and Selfhood in the Cuban Espiritismo*. Florida: University of Florida Press.

Schmidt, B. E. (2007) 'Misuse of a religion: Vodou as political power rooted in "magic" and "sorcery"', *Diskus*, vol. 8, pp. 1–19. http://www.basr.ac.uk/diskus/diskus8/schm idt.htm.

Schmidt, B. (2008) *Caribbean Diaspora in the USA: Diversity of Caribbean Religions in New York City*. Aldershot: Ashgate.

Schmidt, B. (2016) *Spirits and Trance in Brazil: An Anthropology of Religious Experience*. London: Bloomsbury.

Schüttpeltz, E. (2015) 'Trance mediums and new media: The heritage of a European term', in H. Behrend, A. Dreschke, and M. Zillinger (eds), *Trance Mediums and New Media: Spirit Possession in the Age of Technical Reproduction*. New York: Fordham University Press, pp. 56–76.

Sered, S. S. (1994) *Priestess, Mother, Sacred Sister: Religions Dominated by Women*. Oxford: Oxford University Press.

Sluhovsky, M. (2007) *Believe Not Every Spirit: Possession, Mysticism, and Discernment in Early Modern Catholicism*. Chicago: University of Chicago Press.

Stephen, M. (1995) *A'aisa's Gifts: A Study of Magic and the Self*. Berkeley: University of California Press.

Striner, R. (2016) *Love in the Afterlife: Underground Religion at the Movies*. Madison: Fairleigh Dickinson University Press.

Stoller, P. (1994) 'Embodying colonial memories', *American Anthropologist*, vol. 96, no. 3, pp. 634–48.

Taves, A. (1999) *Fits, Trances and Visions: Experiencing Religion and Explaining Experience from Wesley to James*. Princeton, NJ: Princeton University Press.

Turner, V. (1995 [1969]) *The Ritual Process: Structure and Anti-Structure*.
New York: Aldine de Gruyter.

van de Port, M. (2005) 'Circling around the *really real*: Spirit possession ceremonies and the search for authenticity in Brazilian Candomblé', *Ethnos*, vol. 33, no. 2, pp. 149–79.

Vitebsky, P. (1993) *Dialogues with the Dead: The Discussion of Mortality among the Sora of Eastern India*. Cambridge: Cambridge University Press.

Walker, M. (2017) *Modern Ghost Melodramas: 'What Lies Beneath'*.
Amsterdam: Amsterdam University Press.

Walliss, J. (2001) 'Continuing bonds: Relationships between the living and the dead within contemporary Spiritualism', *Mortality*, vol. 6, no. 2, pp. 127–45.

Weinstein, S. (2004) 'Technologies of vision: Spiritualism and science in nineteenth-century America', in A. Weinstock (ed.), *Spectral America: Phantoms and the National Imagination*. Madison: University of Wisconsin Press, pp. 124–40.

Wilson, D. G. (2013) *Refining Shamanisms: Spiritualist Mediums and Other Traditional Shamans as Apprenticeship Outcomes*. London: Bloomsbury.

Filmography

Afterlife (2005) Created by Steven Volk: Seasons 1–2, ITV: 24 September.

Always (1989) Directed by Steven Spielberg: Universal Pictures.

Buffy the Vampire Slayer (1997–2003) Created by Joss Whedon: Mutant Enemy Productions and 20th Century Fox Television: Seasons 1–5, Warner Bros., Seasons 6 and 7, United Paramount Network: 10 March.

Charmed (1998–2006) Created by Constance M. Burge: Seasons 1–8, The WB: 7 October.

Dracula (1931) Directed by Tod Browning: Universal Pictures

ER (1994–2009) Created by Michael Crichton: Seasons 1–15, NBC: 19 September.

The Exorcist (1973) Directed by William Friedkin: Warner Bros.

Ghost (1990) Directed by Jerry Zucker: Universal Pictures.

The Ghost and Mrs Muir (1947) Directed by Joseph L Mankiewicz: 20th Century Fox.

The Ghost Whisperer (2005–10) Created by John Gray: Seasons 1–6, CBS 23 September.

I Walked with a Zombie (1943) Directed by Jacques Tourneur: RKO.

Medium (2005–11) Created by Glenn Gordon Caron: Seasons 1–7, NBC: 3 January.

Poltergeist (1982) Directed by Tobe Hooper: MGM.

Practical Magic (1998) Directed by Griffin Dunne: Warner Bros.

Séance on a Wet Afternoon (1964) Directed by Bryan Forbes: Rank Organisation.

The Serpent and the Rainbow (1988) Directed by Wes Craven: Universal Pictures.

Truly, Madly Deeply (1990) Directed by Anthony Minghella: Samuel Goldwyn Company.

White Zombie (1932) Directed by Victor Halperin: United Artists.

6

Dreams Reprise: Mad Love, Mesmerism and Mystical Participation in *Heavenly Creatures* and *Bram Stoker's Dracula*

In this book I have explored a range of filmic representations of dreams, vampires and ghosts and utilized insights from the anthropology of religion to suggest alternative and additional ways in which these motifs can be understood. This chapter revisits a number of these themes, considering how an analysis of collective, in addition to individual consciousness, may enhance our understanding of the depiction of sexual relationships in film. It begins with an examination of *Heavenly Creatures* (1994), a film that explores the 'mad love' between two young women in Christchurch, New Zealand, and their murder of one of the girl's mothers. Based on a real case, the film uses a combination of the diaries of one of the girls and some creative filmic techniques to illustrate a lively mystical collective realm between them, inhabited by characters from their collective writing projects. The film has received a good deal of critical and scholarly attention, much of it focused on the politics of gender, class and place. Writings about the way that lesbian relationships are treated expose the imbalanced depictions in film and television of lesbian couples, with dysfunctional and often murderous storylines dominating our screens while healthy and positive lesbian relationships are often invisible (Wilts, 2009). Hart (1994: ix) suggests that the problem goes even deeper than this, exploring ways in which depictions of aggressive women are 'pathological repetitions of a profoundly paranoid heterosexist/patriarchal culture that persistently and ostentatiously exhibits and produces its necessary other in order to keep it under erasure'. Quoting Diana Fuss, she also notes that 'lesbian and gay theory is infused with the rhetoric of "hauntings", and observes a striking, repetitive fascination 'with the spectre of abjection, a certain preoccupation with the figure of the homosexual as spectre and phantom, as spirit and revenant, as abject and undead' (Fuss, 1991: 3, 6; Hart, 1994: ix). This participates in a peculiar logic inherent in many representations of women. On the one hand, women are tantalizingly portrayed as desiring subjects and capable of taking roles as aggressive protagonists, but only to reveal such traits as a threat so that they may be returned to the subjection of patriarchal control. Although Hart does not develop the relationship of this mechanism to vampirism further, Deb Verhoevan (1993) looks closely at how media representations of convicted murderer Tracey Avril Wigginton in the early 1990s linked constructions of her lesbianism to ideas of vampirism, thereby demonstrating a remarkable persistence of this mythological connection in a supposedly rational secular context (Bevan, 2014). The trope appears again in reporting of the Parker murder case that was the basis of the film *Heavenly Creatures* (1994), where the 'blurring of boundaries between reality and fantasy amusingly challenges contemporaneous religious and medical homophobia' and a newspaper suggests that 'what happens to these imaginative girls is a real-life illustration of vampire bonding' (Boyle, 2002: 42 – quoting the *New Yorker* 21 November 1994, 131).

Similarly, many scholars and fans were disturbed by the way in which the narrative depiction of Willow and Tara's relationship in *Buffy the Vampire Slayer* (1997–2003) was developed in the later seasons. Tara's murder and Willow's addiction to magic and subsequent violence were seen by some critiques as a betrayal of the positive lesbian role models that they had initially established and a descent into stereotypes all too common in Western media (Wilts, 2009: 44–6). While Tara and Willow were depicted as vampire-fighting witches, their location in a television show about vampires evokes an ambiguous history of gender and sexuality in the vampire film, a genre in which 'the monsters' were often coded as gay or bisexual and in which conventional patriarchal sexual identities are both disrupted and reinforced by vampire storylines.

Part of the reason that vampires are so easily identified with gay sexuality is the way in which the vampire's bite is associated with sex and can be performed by either gender (see Creed, 1993: 59–72 and Heller-Nicholas, 2017 for further discussions of lesbian vampires). Weinstock (2012: 31) argues that, 'although vampire sex takes a variety of forms – from the decorously heterosexual to the polymorphously perverse – my argument is that vampires are nonetheless inevitably "queer"; by recklessly transgressing gender expectations and sexual mores they foreground the social constructedness of gender and sexual codes, as well as the hegemonic devices that attempt to naturalize those constructions. And nowhere is the queer sexuality of the vampire more readily apparent than in the prominence of the lesbian vampire character.' Moreover, even when films appear to restore the heroine to the loving arms of patriarchy in the form of a conventional male suitor, they may nonetheless suggest the attractions of other forms of desire. As Weinstock (2012: 34) drawing from Benshoff (1997) suggests, not only is the vampire quintessentially queer because of the way the figure transgresses numerous boundaries, but the delights of those transgressions can also remain with audiences long after the monster has been staked, 'in other words, films like *Dracula's Daughter* must first conjure up monsters of alternative erotic desire before staking them; but if the cinema has taught us anything about vampires, it is that vampires in all their queer glory are impossible to kill completely'. This argument is useful, partly because it potentially expands the definition of queer, but also because of the idea that when films attempt to manage and suppress desires outside of patriarchal norms, these strategies can backfire and simultaneously indicate the attractions of desire beyond the boundaries of convention. As Berenstein (1996: 90) suggests, 'most hypnosis films, by which I mean vampire, mummy, and zombie movies, are inverted fairy tales. Girl gets boy at the conclusion, but her best times, the moments that give her free reign to throw all caution to the wind, are spent with the monster in the narrative middle.'

While this chapter does benefit from scholarship that asks important questions about the way in which lesbian and gay relationships are depicted, I want to extend those questions and examine them from another point of view, arguing that media ambivalence about sexual relationships is also related to uncertainty when depicting any sexual relationships that are intense or share mystical qualities. I suggest that the reason for this is related to a broader series of questions about contemporary societal attitudes to conceptions of personhood that challenge notions of individual self-containment. Films such as *Heavenly Creatures* (1994) and *Bram Stoker's Dracula* (1992) each depict disturbing aspects of sexual life, including dream communication, seduction and mystical participation in alternate dimensions. In other words, sexual relationships can be portrayed as having a kind of *collective consciousness* that is subject to the same kind of attractions and repulsions for film-makers as other kinds of collective phenomena explored in this book.

Mad love and *collective consciousness*

The idea of *collective consciousness* is most closely associated with the sociological theories of Durkheim. He argued that society was more than a collection of the individuals and that

> if collective consciousness is to appear a *sui generis* synthesis of individual consciousnesses must occur. The product of this synthesis is a whole world of feelings, ideas, and images that follow their own laws once they are born. They mutually attract one another, repel one another, fuse together, subdivide, and proliferate. (Durkheim, 1995 [1912]: 426)

The language that Durkheim uses here is highly suggestive of energetic or electrical metaphors and this is intentional, because for Durkheim, society is not just held together by rules and institutions, it has an emotional and energetic quality. Using examples from the ethnographies of Aboriginal Australia available to him at the time, Durkheim analysed their rituals and suggested that these ceremonies excited a bubbling up of collective emotions that he termed *collective effervescence* and which he suggested was the basic component of both religion and society, including those of the modern Europe of his day (Durkheim, 1995 [1912]: 218–21). Because of its energetic nature, this collective consciousness not only blurs boundaries between individuals, but it also has a contagious quality that potentially contaminates everything it comes into contact with, entailing prohibitions for any persons or objects imbued with this quality (in other words anything sacred) (Durkheim, 1995 [1912]: 322–8). Under certain circumstances the contagious and volatile nature of collective effervescence can be dangerous, 'stirred by passions so intense that they can be satisfied only by violent and extreme acts: by acts of superhuman heroism or bloody barbarism' (Durkheim, 1995 [1912]: 213). However, despite needing the prohibitions and constraints of social order to channel and contain them, the energies of collective consciousness (closely associated with the sacred in Durkheim's thought) are also at the core of moral and social personhood (Durkheim, 1995 [1912]: 224).

While Durkheim's work aimed to offer theoretical frameworks for the study of society and religion more broadly, scholars have since used his models to consider collective consciousness between two people. Child (2007) explores the consort relationship in tantric Buddhism and Mellor (2002) considers the implications of Durkheim's theories for the study of sacred love and also *l'amour fou* (in the sense that the surrealists used the term). Arguing against more utilitarian understandings of the marriage 'contract', Mellor explores the potentially sacred, world-transforming character of love (Mellor, 2002: 121). He argues that, 'romantic relationships can be interpreted in Durkheimian terms because they clearly have a strong emotional basis, they naturally give rise to ritual, symbolic and conceptual representations of themselves, and they imbue an experience of social solidarity with a transcendent character in the sense that they connect us with something that surpasses us' (Mellor, 2002: 129–30). Exploring the *l'amour fou* of the surrealists, Mellor suggests that the movement saw itself as trying to redress modernity's hatred of the marvellous with mad love, using it as a path to exaltation. The transcendent character of this phenomenon is key here, in that through mad love, individual selves become merged, as they are dissolved into one being (Mellor, 2002: 133–4).

Film and television depictions suggest highly ambivalent attitudes to mad love. While stories are woven and re-woven around its criminal extremes with relish, and vampires use mesmeric powers and dangerous spells to enthral their victims, examples of visionary or telepathic aspects to normal loving relationships are rare. While the blurring of boundaries between people appears to be a source of fascination in these films, they also link seduction with negative portrayals of hypnosis and mesmerism in ways that suggest that experiencing the mini-collective in the love relation is like falling into a trance, and automatically relinquishes power to a dangerous other. The loss of individualized 'rational' control is a source of fascination and delight, but also abject terror in these films.

An emphasis on individual psychology in theory leads to somewhat different readings of *l'amour fou* in film. Creed's (2005: 88) analysis of *Bram Stoker's Dracula* (1992) suggests that Dracula represents the dark side of the primal uncanny. Describing the relationship between Mina and Dracula in terms of a kind of surrealist *l'amour fou*, she does not frame this with Durkheim's sociological passions but in psychological terms, arguing that 'Coppola's *Dracula* argues against the possibility of the fulfilment of desire. The individual subject (given that the vampire is in all of us) remains a prisoner of his/her unsatisfied desires, yet continues to believe that desire can be fulfilled' (Creed, 2005: 87). Similarly, Krimmer and Raval (2002: 153–4) utilize Lacan's (1975) work to explore the relationship between Buffy and Angel in *Buffy the Vampire Slayer* (1997–2003), suggesting the narrative pleasures of the impossibility of their relationship are rooted in fundamental psychological tensions between 'love … as the merging of two beings into one. But as life is always the life of an individual, this dream of oneness is thwarted by the realisation that … trapped in our bodies, we cannot achieve oneness without dissolving our very selves'. However, as I have contended in this book, the assertion of this specific understanding of self is one that is rooted in European and American cultural and intellectual milieus, and even in these contexts these understandings of bounded individuality are subverted as well as asserted. By exploring Buffy's relationship with Angel and using Jung's conception of 'the shadow' I suggested that *Buffy the Vampire Slayer* explores the gendered power dynamics behind the 'impossible relationship'.

Moreover, the show also suggests that there may be virtues in *amour fou* as a willingness to abandon narrow conceptions of the self. It is the driving force of Spike's transformation from an evil, monstrous villain into a person striving for a soul and duty, and is shown much earlier in the series than his attraction to Buffy is revealed. Spike and Drusilla, a psychic woman driven mad by Angel and then turned into a vampire, are rejected by the Judge as not being evil enough because they stink of love and jealousy, emotions that lead Spike to form his first tentative alliance with Buffy in order to rescue Drusilla from Angelus (2013: 'Surprise').

In *Bram Stoker's Dracula* the relationship between Mina and Dracula is certainly doomed, but it is not impossible. At the beginning of the film we see them as a married couple who are only later separated by tragic circumstances and I suggest that one of the appeals of the film is its depiction of something that Lacan argues against, a connection between people unbroken by time and distance that can be illuminated by anthropological perspectives on themes of memory, rebirth, and telepathic communication.

Heavenly Creatures

The film *Heavenly Creatures* (1994) is based on the murder, in June of 1954, of Honora Mary Parker by her daughter, sixteen-year-old Pauline Yvonne Parker and her close friend, fifteen-year-old Juliet Marion Hulme. The murder was a brutal killing. Honora's body was found on a deserted path in Victoria Park in Christchurch, New Zealand with forty-five wounds to her head, neck, face and hands, and the murder weapon, a half brick, was found shortly afterwards (Boyle, 2002: 37). The case was closely followed by the media and its legendary status and reputation for shocking the nation were based on several factors. Firstly, as Boyle (2002: 35–6) explains, the fact that the perpetrators were young women was disturbing, not least because patriarchal societies suppress or ignore both aggression and desire in young women (deeming both to be essentially masculine traits), and when one of these traits bursts untamed into public consciousness it is inevitably linked to the other. In the Parker case, desire – in the form of women's homosexual desire – was brought to the public's attention in several ways, most prominently through Pauline Parker's diaries that documented their intense friendship and that they had *planned* the murder together (Boyle, 2002: 37) but also in the way that the defence of insanity in the trial was inextricably linked with a homosexuality 'diagnosis'. Both women denied a physical relationship with one another, but Dr Francis Bennett, a psychiatrist who had seen Pauline and diagnosed her with homosexuality prior to the murder, argued in the trial that the girls were '*folie à deux* homosexual paranoiacs of the elated type' (Boyle, 2002: 38 – quoting from *The Times*, 26 August 1954: 5). Although the jury found the women to be both sane and guilty, it was a condition of their release that they never see one another again, a condition that implies that in addition to the girls' individual guilt, the relationship between them was culpable (Boyle, 2002: 38).

The case and the Peter Jackson's film have been examined from a range of critical perspectives. In addition to gender and sexuality, Thornley (2002) draws attention to the complex references to class tensions in the film, highlighting how New Zealand's specific history differentiates its class culture from that of England. Rueschmann (2000: 110) notes how *Heavenly Creatures* highlights the prejudices surrounding homosexuality in 1950s New Zealand, observing Henry Hulme's attempts to keep the girls apart and his recommendation to Honora Parker that she take her daughter to a psychiatrist, Mr Bennett, who 'shares Hulme's conservative prejudices, [and] "diagnoses" Pauline a homosexual. Peter Jackson satirizes the doctor's ignorance and paranoia, and his homophobia masquerading as science precipitates the girl's increasingly violent responses to the hypocritical adult world'. Offering an alternative psychological analysis of the film, Rueschmann (2000: 101) explores the girls' desire to be sisters and their conflicts with their mothers, arguing that pre-oedipal attachments between girls and their mothers can resurface in adolescence and turn violent. She nonetheless emphasizes that while the violence of the Parker case is unusual, intense friendships between young women and ambivalent feelings towards their mothers are not (Rueschmann, 2000: 105). Analysing the broader family dynamics depicted in the film, she explores how, although Honora Parker shows concern and care for her daughter, it is she who becomes the 'bad object' of the girls' delusions, while at the same time Henry and Hilda Hulme are idealised, despite their frequent abandonment of Juliet, to the extent that Pauline had fantasies about becoming part of their family (Rueschmann, 2000: 109). Moreover, this idealization is inflated by the Hulme's English background and upper-class pretensions, which in reality cover some troubling family dynamics. Wilson (2003: 197–201) explores the film in the context of New Zealand's 'cinema of unease', a range of films that explore tensions in late-twentieth-century New Zealand between its Protestant religious conservatism, myths of the country as a pastoral paradise and the complex realities of class, gender and racial conflict.

While the shared fantasies in *Heavenly Creatures* are most often talked about from psychological theoretical perspectives, a detailed analysis of Jackson's (1994) depiction of the 'Fourth World' suggests religious and mythical elements that have points in common with accounts of visionary experiences. This shared world begins in the film through shared play in which an imaginary world, Borovnia, is created by Juliet and Pauline who write extensively about its characters and make clay images of its inhabitants. Moreover, they identify themselves with this world's King Charles and Queen Deborah. In another scene, play that has a ritualistic character is shown with Juliet and Pauline lighting candles and placing pictures of their favourite stars, including the opera singer Mario Lanza, in a structure that they have constructed outdoors. The stars are termed 'saints' and they offer prayers to them. It is in this scene that Juliet first speaks about the 'Fourth World' which she describes as 'like heaven' but better because it does not have the trappings of conventional Christianity.

Boundaries between the girls and between them and their fantasy life dissolve in a later scene where Juliet, distraught at the news that her parents intend to leave her for several weeks, sees a gateway through the clouds and into the Fourth World. Both girls appear to share a hallucination with gorgeous gardens and unicorns that they understand as a mark of their status as two of the few special people given a key to the Fourth World. In other scenes, both together and separately, Pauline and Juliet have visions of Borovnia and its inhabitants who are depicted in the film with giant clay figures. These visions are depicted as becoming increasingly violent, such as when Pauline in her imagination sees one of these figures attack the psychiatrist, but a sense of real danger or suspense about the impending murder is largely absent from the film with the exceptions of the opening sequence (in which the young women are seen screaming and bloody running from the scene of the murder) and in the build-up to Honora's murder at the end of the film. In between, the film largely follows Pauline's viewpoint and uses excerpts from her diaries, and while this conveys a sympathetic portrait of the emotional situation, it can also be read in a more sinister way, as a suggestion that, caught up in their own psycho-social world, Pauline and Juliet were unaware of the danger they posed to themselves or others, and that this world, rather than any moral or psychological flaws in either young woman as an individual, was solely responsible for the crime.

Bram Stoker's Dracula

A number of scholars have expressed exasperation with Coppola's (1992) film *Bram Stoker's Dracula*. Botting's (2008: 1) comments are perhaps the most scathing, as his analysis of what he considers to be the problematic combination of the gothic with the romance genres begins with his expressing of irritation with the film. The issue therefore appears to be largely located in differences between Stoker's book and Coppola's film and in particular the backstory of a romantic link between the vampire Dracula and the primary heroine of the story Mina Harker. There are clear differences between the book and the film, as I explore in more depth below, but it is interesting to note that both Stoker's book and famous previous adaptations of it do explore the idea of a telepathic connection between Dracula and Mina. It is only that Coppola's film creates a backstory that re-evaluates telepathy, moving the phenomena from mere power and manipulation into the realms of shared memories of a past life and mutual recognition. Interestingly, Botting suggests that 'romance, as it frames the gothic, seems to clean up its darker counterpart, sanitising its depravations; it tries to transform, even ennoble, violent gothic energies as a quest for love in the face of death; it recuperates gothic excesses in the name of the heterosexual couple, occluding the homosocial tensions and cultural anxieties of Stoker's novel' (Botting, 2008: 1). In this chapter I aim to suggest an alternative perspective. That while the analysis of homosexual and lesbian desires remains critically important to scholarship of vampire cinema, the dynamics of *l'amour fou*, shared creative visions, perceptions of shared past lives, and telepathy are also key, whether they are portrayed in homosexual or heterosexual relationships. While it is certainly true that fantasies about the dangers of obsession have been more often projected onto homosexual characters in fiction and film, and that this is in part related to strategies of dominance and power related to patriarchy, what I aim to explore here is how telepathy itself is transgressive, particularly in its positive manifestations.

As Freeland (2000: 137) explains, Coppola's film *Bram Stoker's Dracula*, despite its title, diverges in important ways from Stoker's book. By presenting a pre-story that is absent from the novel, Coppola is able to present the monstrous vampire as a 'tragic hero'. The film begins with an episode set in Transylvania in 1462 in which Dracula is presented as a 'Rumanian knight of the Sacred Order of the Dragon – Vlad the Impaler, known as Draculea' (Coppola and Hart, 1992: 12). This knight wins a battle against the Turks and in defence of Christianity, but the opposing army takes revenge through a false message conveyed to his wife, Elisabeta, who believing him dead, flings herself from the castle turret and into the river below. Overcome with despair and rage, Dracula renounces God and turns himself into a monster in a ritual drinking from the sacramental cup. While this story is not in Stoker's novel, it is interesting in its resemblance to mythical motifs about tragic lovers. In Shakespeare's *Romeo and Juliet*, it is Juliet who appears to die, having been given a drug than feigns death as a ruse to escape her family and an unwanted arranged marriage. Romeo, unaware of the ploy, believes Juliet to be dead and commits suicide. Juliet, when she wakes, finds the body and kills herself in turn. In Coppola's film, this motif is combined with the vampire myth, so that instead of committing suicide in turn, Dracula chooses to remain on earth, *undead*, and able to pursue Mina, the reincarnation of his lost wife, in London 400 years later. *Bram Stoker's Dracula* gives the notion of reincarnation a peculiarly modern significance in its link with romantic love, and also in its self-conscious references to cinema itself.

Freeland (2000: 139), for example, notes a number of Coppola's techniques, including keyhole opening and closing lens, the overlays of Dracula's shadow or eye stalking Jonathan or Mina and framed film inserts, arguing that the film maintains 'a patent artificiality' and that the story is 'meant to be seen as a story'. Describing Dracula's movements, she observes that when he is in his wolf form the audience are given his 'predatorial point of view' and as he moves in his guise of a young handsome aristocrat in London, Coppola's use of the pathé camera allows the audience to 'see him as if experiencing an old movie' (Freeland, 2000:140).

Weinstock (2012: 74) goes so far to suggest that 'our thinking about the cinema itself has been influenced by the idea of vampirism'. He uses *Bram Stoker's Dracula* as an illustrative example, focusing initially on a scene that

> opens with an effect that perhaps more explicitly than any other scene in the film self-referentially foregrounds the celluloid nature of the cinematic text the viewer is watching as it is made to appear as if the circular iris of an antique camera is opening onto a sepiationed street scene. In the background is heard the sound of a projector, furthering the impression that the viewer is watching a silent film. The motion of the camera as it descends from above to street level is jerky and the movements of the horse-drawn carriages and Victorian-garbed pedestrians are mechanical and sped up, as if the product of an under-cranked camera. All of this creates the impression of 'vintageness' and indeed the beginning of the sequence was shot with a turn-of-the-century hand-cranked Pathé camera owned by Coppola. This is modern cinema masquerading as antique cinema. (Weinstock, 2012: 74–5)

This sequence sets the scene for the first social encounter between Dracula and Mina. He asks her to show him to the 'wonder of the civilized world': the cinema, and they continue their date with four silent sequences in the background, including scenes evocative of cinematic techniques developed by the Lumière brothers and Méliès. This scene is analysed in some detail by Weinstock (2012: 76–7) who argues that Coppola has juxtaposed the vampire, modernity and the cinema, because of the ways in which the cinema itself is uncanny in its preservation of the dead on film. Quoting Abbot (2007: 43) he writes that 'made up of still images, ghostly shadows of the dead that are reanimated through technological means, film bears striking parallels with vampirism' (Weinstock, 2012: 77).

Examining the same scene, Freeland (2000: 141) argues that

> Mina is compelled not by fascination with the screen images but by the sheer force of her attraction to Vlad/Dracula. Vlad speaks to Mina in Romanian, and she *recognizes* him ... it is no accident that this crucial scene of recognition takes place within a movie theatre. This setting suggests that we in the audience are also not merely passive before the screen but active – like Mina, we, too, engage in acts of memory and recognition in response to Vlad. We recognize him as the famous film character taking on a new shape and persona in this movie ... True, the vampire has physically swept Mina away into the shadows and bent down over her; he must struggle with himself not to violate her, and his eyes glow red. He holds back because he wants Mina to succumb to him voluntarily, from recognition and desire.

The seduction continues with a subsequent date in an absinthe bar, where Vlad uses the drink to induce an altered state of consciousness in Mina, who thereby remembers her past with him more vividly, although it is not until a later scene where Dracula has confessed to his true monstrous identity and Mina demonstrates her desire to join him by sucking blood from his bared breast that their relationship is 'consummated'. Before Mina meets Dracula in his aristocratic garb on the Victorian street, Mina unwittingly comes across the vampire in a bestial form mating with Lucy. He commands her not to see him, only to reverse that command in the Victorian Street scene previously discussed. Moreover, Mina initially attempts to rebuff his advances in this street scene by asking 'Do I know you sir? Are you acquainted with my husband? Shall I call the police?' Once inside the cinema, however, she is literally swept off her feet, saying 'My God – who are you? I know you ...' It is here that Dracula 'holds back' and the theme of the beast is introduced into the narrative once again because a wolf is running loose in the cinema. Commanding the animal, Dracula brings it under his control and invites Mina to stroke it with him, explaining that there is much to be learned from beasts.

The telepathic connection between Mina and Dracula gains prominence towards the end of the film, when Dracula, returning to his homeland to regain his strength, is pursued by Van Helsing, Jonathan Harker (who is married to Mina at this point in the story) and two suitors of Mina's friend Lucy, who had become involved when they tried to save Lucy from vampirism and finally destroyed her body in order to save her soul. Van Helsing recognizes the strong bond between Mina and Dracula and hypnotizes Mina in order to get clues about the vampire's location. While this bond is thought to be in part from the usual mechanism that occurs through blood exchange, the film suggests that the shared memories of past lives in the incident in the absinthe bar is a key point in the connection between Mina and Dracula as it awakens her to an 'inner voice' that speaks to her when she is alone, and that she now identifies as Dracula.

The idea that Mina and Dracula shared a past life is unique to Coppola's film version of the story and gives the film a quality that has features in common with ghostly romance films where love conquers death through communication with the ghost. From an anthropological viewpoint, although reincarnation and rebirth are most well-known from South Asian religious traditions such as Hinduism and Buddhism, there are many more examples, including African traditional religions, Native American and Canadian traditions, and some philosophical traditions from ancient Greece (Obeyesekere, 2002). Obeyesekere argues that within the South Asian traditions impersonal ethics are key to rebirth. Behaviour in previous lifetimes determines each rebirth much more than geographical location or personal ties. However, this is not the case for many other rebirth traditions. For example, the reborn person is often identified as an ancestor, relative or family friend in a number of indigenous contexts, so that rebirth traditions are much more closely tied up with kinship (Mills and Slobodin, 1994; Obeyesekere, 2002: 40). Ideas about rebirth also appear to have a complex relationship with Spiritualism. Wilson (2013: 51) explains that in Britain it is generally accepted that reincarnation should not be taught from the platform, and Spiritualists' National Union tutors told him that reincarnation is not itself a part of Spiritualism. Nonetheless, many of his informants expressed some interest and belief in reincarnation. Similarly, Meintel (2014: 81) found that a good number of her Spiritualist informants in Montreal believed in reincarnation while acknowledging that such beliefs are not necessarily integral to Spiritualism itself. Offering some historical context to ideas about reincarnation that circulated from the mid-nineteenth century in European and Euro-American circles, Bender (2007: 594) identifies the French Spiritist Kardec (1804–1869) as a key figure. Kardec is also identified as a key proponent of the idea of 'soul mates', figures with whom one had strong connections in previous lives such as family members and lovers, an idea that also fed into the notion that love is stronger than death (Bender, 2007: 595–6). I suggest here that key to these developments is the attraction of forming kinship bonds based on affinity rather than birth, and also of affirming and exploring perceptions intuited in altered states of consciousness. Waterhouse (1999) has noted the rise in numbers of people reporting reincarnation beliefs in late-twentieth-century Britain, arguing that this has less to do with specific religious affiliations and is more impacted by a societal context in which people can seek information about and affirmation of personal experiences through a wide range of available reading materials and looser communities of support. This background offers some insight into the potential attractions of Coppola's rebirth backstory to Dracula but leaves complex questions about its distinction from Stoker's novel and from other Dracula films. The more 'genuine' horror gothic that Botting appears to refer to when he expresses concern about its dilution with romance needs further examination, particularly with reference to those who come in contact with the vampire or other monsters. In the absence of past life romance, what is the connection between these monsters and their 'victims'? Is a telepathic or supernatural connection between them simply a case of charismatic or mesmeric mind control?

Hypnotism, mesmerism, thrall and spells in *The Mummy*, *Dracula* and *Dracula's Daughter*

Although the past life backstory is not found in Stoker's book or in other Dracula films, the device is not entirely unfamiliar in gothic cinema. *The Mummy* (1932), directed by Karl Freund, uses similar themes to connect the monster with the heroine. The past life scenes are set in Ancient Egypt where a princess Anck-es-en-Amon is dying and her lover, Imhotep steals a scroll, The Scroll of Thoth, and speaks its incantations in an attempt to raise the princess from the dead. He is caught and punished for doing what is described as an unholy thing by being bound like a mummy (but alive and with his internal organs intact) and buried, along with the scroll and a curse that threatens death and eternal punishment for anyone who opens the casket. Imhotep is revived when a 1921 British museum expedition led by Sir Joseph Whemple, finds the Mummy and the scroll, and a foolish assistant reads transcriptions from the scroll that he had retrieved despite the misgivings of a certain Dr Mueller, who warns that the ancient Egyptian gods still live in their ruined temples and although their spells may be weaker, they have not lost their potency altogether. Upon witnessing the Mummy come alive, the assistant goes mad and it is not until ten years later that a further expedition, led by Sir Joseph's son, Frank Whemple, that the Mummy reappears, in the guise of a man called Ardeth Bey, to lead the expedition to the site of the burial of his beloved princess. At the same time we learn of a young woman, Helen Grosvenor, who is staying with Dr Mueller in Cairo, and who appears to fall into a trance when Ardeth Bey, in an attempt to revive the Princess, starts to chant words from an ancient language near her remains (now housed at Cairo Museum). Helen leaves a party and heads to the museum, also chanting in an ancient language and saying Imhotep's name, and is found by Frank, having fainted at the door of the museum. In a later scene, after Helen has again been moved to go to Ardeth Bey by his chanting and glowing eyes, she remains in a trance while Ardeth shows her, through a pool in his home that can reveal happenings at a physical distance or from the past, the story of their past life selves. The fact that she is hypnotized is implied by the fact that he suggests that she will not remember what she has seen when she awakes. Helen later explains to Frank that although she is aware that Ardeth Bey represents death for her, there is something else inside her that is alive too and fighting for life by drawing her to Bey. She therefore articulates much more clearly than Mina in *Bram Stoker's Dracula* a conflict between her past life and present self, and, moreover, rescues herself from being killed by Bey at the end of the film by calling upon the deity Isis to save her. Bey's plot to kill Helen and resurrect her as the Princess is thus thwarted by Helen's own insistence that despite being aware of her previous love for Imhotep, he is now dead and her present self is alive, but it is the goddess Isis who sets fire to the scroll, finally defeating the Mummy. There is therefore a conflict in the film between ancient Egyptian religion and the sacrilegious behaviour of Imhotep, who, despite his displays of power, is defeated by his own gods. Similarly, Dracula in *Bram Stoker's Dracula*, turns his back on his religion (Christianity) and thereby obtains unholy powers, but his demise, partially facilitated by Mina, is depicted as more of a reconciliation than a defeat, as Dracula asks her to bring him peace (by killing him).

The Mummy is analysed by Berenstein as an example of a hypnosis movie, in which heroines do the creature's bidding and are transformed into doubles of the fiend, while signifying some kind of trance with a vapid stare that 'is a physical sign of her plunge into a nether world of monstrous control' (Berenstein, 1996: 90). Berenstein sometimes uses the words hypnosis and mesmerism interchangeably but her real focus is on the gaze and how it is used in classic horror (Berenstein, 1996: 91). Utilizing Williams (1984) she suggests that Mulvey's (1999 [1975]) analysis of the male sadistic gaze often does not fit well with classic horror cinema because in these films the hero's gaze is ineffectual compared to the mesmerizing stare of the monster or even the actions of the heroine under the guise of a vapid stare (Berenstein, 1996: 98–100). Moreover, the looks exchanged between the monster and the heroine may signify not only her victimization, but also her shared status with the monster as an outsider to patriarchy, partly because the monster uses the gaze as a form of non-phallic potency (Berenstein, 1996: 104; Williams, 1984: 90). Moreover, the heroines are depicted breaking the bounds of convention in ways they may enjoy and reap benefits such as renewed vitality (Berenstein, 1996: 107–9). Describing the scene where Ardeth Bey (the persona of the Mummy/Imhotep) first meets with Helen Grosvenor (Princess Anck-es-en-Amon) Berenstein (1996: 110) explains that Helen is asleep on a couch until his stare awakens her and they are found by Sir Joseph Whemple, Frank Whemple (her suitor) and Dr Mueller, still mutually gazing. Helen announces that she has 'never felt so alive before'. 'Like a revived Sleeping Beauty, Helen's prior melancholy and exhaustion evaporate as she stares into Bey's eyes.' Furthermore, his pursuit of her seems to take the form of hypnosis in a later scene where Helen, having promised Frank she will not go out, is drawn into walking through the Cairo market to Bey's home after a shot of Bey's eyes glowing (Berenstein, 1996: 110).

While it is reasonable to assume that audiences infer hypnotism or mesmerism in these scenes, it is worth noting that the film does not use either of these terms. Instead, there is talk of spells, curses and protective amulets, such as one of Isis that Dr Mueller gives to Frank, insisting that he needs the charm because his life is in danger. Moreover, while Bey's gaze and chanting is sometimes used coercively, such as when he controls a servant in his bid to obtain the scroll, there is a sense in which coercion is only part of the story with Helen, as their mutual gazing appears to be more about recognition and attraction.

Considering the issue from another angle, I would like to suggest that the fears and attractions of hypnotism and mesmerism explored in classic horror films are related to the idea that these devices appear to bring about some kind of fusion between the fiend and those they control. As Berenstein has argued, although the heroines in these films are in once sense victims, in another, their time under the creature's thrall appears to be much more fun than their relationship with the hero. Taking this a step further, the renewed vitality the heroines refer to could be rooted in immersion in *collective consciousness* with the monster. Helen, for example, asserts her individual modern self at the end of *The Mummy*, but only after exploring a shared identity as lovers with Imhotep and exploring their past life experiences in mutual visions. Moreover, although the efficacy of mesmerism was originally explored by Mesmer (1734–1815) using a theory of invisible fluids that existed in and around humans and animals that could be manipulated with magnets, part of Mesmer's treatments included staring into a patient's eyes in order to project fluids emanating from his own eyes into the patient (Bartlett, 2020: 111–12). A later practitioner, Puységur, asserted that the cures effected by mesmerism were not due to the superfine fluid but were a result of the influence of the practitioner's will, an idea that Mesmer himself also considered (Bartlett, 2020: 113; Ellenberger, 1981: 72). This emphasis on the relationship between the practitioner and the patient may have been part of the reason why the other name for mesmerism, animal magnetism, has taken on connotations of charismatic influence in common parlance in the present day. Mesmerism, together with a related trance state, artificial somnambulism, were the subjects of intense debates in the nineteenth century that included postulations of divine or demonic agencies (Bartlett, 2020: 115–16).

The idea of demonic agency is also evoked by Barrett (2006: 13) in her analysis of films and television depicting hypnosis themes, who suggests that 'when a hypnotist appears on the screen, expect evil'. This is despite the fact that hypnosis played important roles in the early history of psychology and was utilized by Freud before he moved away from it in favour of the talking cure (Gabbard and Gabbard, 1999: 28). Hypnotherapy is, nonetheless, still an important clinical tool, and while Gabbard and Gabbard (1999: 29) suggest that the amount of hypnosis in films is over-represented and is often used to depict the 'cathartic cure' (a narrative device that oversimplifies the healing process) Barrett reminds readers of the considerable positive uses that hypnosis still has in a range of clinical settings and contrasts this with the inaccuracies in films and the frequency of its negative roles in their storylines, explaining that 'even when the depiction of hypnosis is positive, the emphasis is virtually always on it as a means of influence or control of another person' (Barrett, 2006: 21).

The relationship between a negative view of mesmerism and vampire literature and film has a long history. Bartlett (2022: 429) explains that Polidori, the writer of *The Vampyre* (1819), one of the earliest vampire novels, is likely to have been influenced by negative debates about mesmerism that were common in the period, and that, moreover, his medical thesis studied somnambulism, suggesting an interest in trance states more broadly. Lord Ruthven, the villain of the novel, appears to manipulate his victims in subtle ways. His mesmerizing gaze and rhetoric do not command so much as facilitate others to project their fantasies onto him and his 'monstrosity is fluid and shifts according to those around him, becoming what they imagine him to be' (Bartlett, 2022: 430). Examining 'psychic vampire' works from the latter part of the nineteenth century, Dear (2014: 97) places them in a context of fears of loss of control centred around debates about hypnosis, dreams and other altered states of consciousness, together with wider social and cultural anxieties around social change in the period affecting gender and colonialism. Drawing from Winter (1998), she notes how the connection between two people, that constitutes the basis for healing in many mesmeric and hypnosis practices, was a focus for concern about relinquishing control. Susceptibility to these states could be read as a 'primitive' weakness of persons who were thereby potentially prey to charismatic charlatans (Dear, 2014: 99–100).

While fears around loss of control to charismatic characters are certainly important in gothic writing and film, I suggest that their explorations of these themes have also contributed to the pleasures of the genre. Charisma can be a locus for concerns about revolutionary movements or the manipulations of individuals by unscrupulous persons, but as Lindholm (1992) explains, it has also been theorized more positively by sociologists such as Durkheim. Drawing from Durkheim's (1995 [1912]) *Elementary Forms of Religious Life*, Lindholm explains that self-loss experienced as a transcendent altered state of group consciousness can induce ecstatic vitality, because in this state the individual is immersed in the energies of the collective, otherwise known as *collective effervescence*. Moreover, although this state is primal and pre-logical, it is also the essence of the sacred; potentially volatile, it is also the foundation of morality, because individual concerns and appetites are subdued by the transformative participation in the social (Lindholm, 1992: 293–4).

This tension, between the dangers and attractions of charisma, can be seen to be played out even more acutely in gothic cinema, a form of mass media in which the actors who play charismatic fiends can become a focus of group adulation. Berenstein (1996: 88) illustrates this idea in quotations from Bela Lugosi in publicity material released by Universal Pictures just prior to the release of *Dracula* (1931) in which he claims that women love and feed on horror, are nourished by it and come back for more. Moreover, he is said to have received numerous love letters expressing their desires for horror and their hopes that he might drink their blood (Berenstein, 1996: 89).

Dracula (1931) has in common with *The Mummy* the fact that although neither hypnosis nor mesmerism are mentioned explicitly, they are heavily implied through close-ups on Dracula's eyes and the way people around him are compelled to do his bidding. In one example, a woman who works at the theatre is told that she will forget Dracula's instructions as soon as she has done what he had asked. Where Dracula drinks his victim's blood, this is not shown directly, but is implied by his arms spreading in a bat-like gesture as he bends over his victims. With Mina, the sharing of blood is depicted as being important to their connection and it is described as being key to his influence over her, so that, for example, she can understand what Dracula is saying to her when he is in his bat form. The link between Mina drinking Dracula's blood and her connection to him in consciousness can be illuminated by Durkheim's analysis of blood symbolism. Child argues that, for Durkheim, blood and 'a vital principle animating the group are not simply used as analogies for one another, but are felt to constitute the same substance. Another way to describe the same point is to suggest that blood is a collective representation of collective consciousness itself' (Child, 2007: 152; Durkheim, 1968 [1897]: 88) (see also Fields, 2013). Durkheim (1995 [1912]: 334) also explains how blood can be used to revitalize the sacred principle in religious objects, because it is, in itself, a sacred life principle, an idea echoed by Renfield's ravings suggesting that blood is life. The idea that drinking Dracula's blood has amplified his hypnotic effect on her, so that they share a consciousness is shown when Mina appears to be in a trance and walks like a sleep-walker in the last scenes of the film when Dracula takes her to his resting place in order to try to complete the transformation and make her a vampire. When he is staked, we see Mina clutching at her heart as if she is suffering the blows (Berenstein, 1996: 118).

Dracula's Daughter (1936) offers more explicit discussion of hypnosis. The film appears to begin where *Dracula* ended, with the discovery of Renfield's body (with a broken neck) and Dracula with a stake through his heart by two policemen who arrest Von Helsing. Von Helsing admits to the killings but explains to Scotland Yard that Dracula was a vampire and enlists his friend Jeffrey Garth, a psychiatrist, to help him with the legal case. Jeffrey is sceptical of the vampire story and asserts he is a man of science, not superstition, but Von Helsing points out that hypnosis used to be looked upon as black magic, but is now a tool used in medicine and asks Jeffrey to admit that the workings of the subconscious were little understood until relatively recently, but Jeffrey is uncomfortable with a defence based on folklore. A tension between psychiatry and vampiric powers is a theme that continues in the film, with Jeffrey using a machine to hypnotize Lili, a girl who arrives at the hospital where he works with amnesia and loss of blood after having been attacked by the vampire Countess Marya Zaleska (Dracula's daughter). Diagnosing a post-hypnotic state, Jeffrey uses the machine to help Lili remember what had happened to her. In the closing stages of the film, Jeffrey goes to Transylvania to rescue his assistant, Janet, who has been kidnapped by The Countess. Finding her lying prone in a trance, the doctor guesses that The Countess has used hypnosis, but she asserts that it is something older and much more powerful, a spell that cannot be broken by anyone but The Countess herself.

Burns (1995) analyses in some detail the use of the gaze in *Dracula's Daughter*. The film both does, and does not, offer a mutual lesbian gaze between The Countess and Lili, and this implication is countered by Jeffrey's hypnosis machine, which, according to Burns (1995: 207) acts in the film to signify the return of the cinematic apparatus as disciplinary technology. On one level the film offers an example of the trope of the sympathetic vampire. The Countess, having burnt the body of Dracula, hopes to be free of his curse. However, she remains subject to compulsions and desires to drink blood and instead pins her hopes on Jeffrey to effect a cure and offer her release through psychiatry. It is only when this endeavour fails that The Countess kidnaps Janet in an attempt to lure Jeffrey to Transylvania where she can make him a vampire. On one level therefore, the film explores tensions between psychiatry's attempts to understand and discipline desires, and the powerful forces of magic and spells that aid the villainess to fulfil them, even against her own wish to disavow them. However, I suggest that on further examination, the powers of the vampire and other monsters in these films evoke both religion and *collective consciousness*.

Vampire gods

Hallab (2009) explores the appeal of the vampire in a range of social and historical contexts, including religion, suggesting that the vampire stories raise questions about the nature of existence because of their combination of human and supernatural being (Hallab, 2009: 91). She suggests also how evil characters in stories are an important part of cultural definitions of religious beliefs and moral behaviours (Hallab, 2009: 92–3). Moreover, vampires can carry mythological associations with pagan deities, particularly those concerned with death and the renewal of life (Hallab, 2009: 71).

The film *Bram Stoker's Dracula* uses a backstory not found in the original novel to locate the source of Dracula's powers in sacrilege, born from his rage at the suicide of his wife that turns him away from his mission as a Christian warrior. Coppola uses this idea to juxtapose Christianity with Dracula's monstrous rage, for example in the scene where Mina and Jonathan are married and the wedding ceremony is intercut with scenes of Dracula 'killing' Lucy in order to make her a vampire with 'an eternal hunger for living blood'. As we see Mina and Jonathan drink from a cup of communion wine, its association with the blood of Christ is emphasized by the blood soaked scene of Lucy's murder and Dracula asserts that 'your impotent men with their foolish spells cannot protect you from my power' Rites of communion are central to Durkheim's theories of the sacred and collective consciousness. He uses examples from Aboriginal Australia to suggest that rituals in which normally sacred beings (totems) are eaten simultaneously re-vitalize the participants' relationships with their deities and renew the collective energies of the group. Because something normally forbidden is eaten in these ceremonies, the difference between sacred and sacrilegious is subtle and contextual (Durkheim, 1995 [1912]: 342–3). Communion wine, being thought of as the blood of Christ, carries these sacrificial connotations and therefore while on the one hand Coppola juxtaposes this with Dracula's murderous blood-letting, he also draws our attention to the ways in which both rites excite social energies.

Dracula's god-like powers also manipulate how Mina will see him, using magic to command Mina not to see him as a beast having sex with Lucy but allowing her to see him as an elegant young man on the street. Dracula can conjure up winds and storms, an idea depicted with relish in the film but which is also referred to in the novel when Professor Van Helsing explains the characteristics of vampires (Stoker, 2003 [1897]: 252). This power is also found in various mythologies, such as ancient Greek myths relating to the god Zeus controlling the weather (Dowden, 2006: 54–64). Sometimes Zeus *is* a storm; he rains, does lightning, thunders or throws thunderbolts (Dowden, 2006: 54–6). Dracula's ability to transform into or control animals and his transformations into natural phenomena such as mist are also found in the mythology of Zeus. Zeus disguises himself as a swan in order to seduce Leda (a married mortal woman) (Dowden, 2006: 43), and as a bull in his seduction of Europa (Dowden, 2006: 46). Danae is locked up in a bronze tower by her father, Akrisios, who fears the prophesy of an oracle that if she has a son (Perseus) that son will kill Akrisios, but 'there is no escaping Zeus, who descends in the form of fertilising golden rain' (Dowden, 2006: 47). Zeus also carries off a young man, Ganymede. Some sources state that Zeus turns into an eagle to do this while *The Homeric Hymn to Aphrodite* refers to Zeus as a whirlwind (Morford, Lenardon and Sham, 2011: 120).

At least in some accounts, Zeus assumes animal form because it is less intimidating than his true nature. Leftkowitz (2007: 67–8) for example, summarizes a section of a second-century BCE poem by Moschus that describes Europa's seduction by Zeus. When she goes out to pick flowers in a meadow, 'Europa encounters a remarkably beautiful bull – it is of course Zeus in disguise, hoping both to avoid Hera's jealous anger and to fool Europa … [who] does not run away. The bull is mild and gentle; there is a scent of ambrosia and the sound of music; he kneels before her and she climbs on his back' (Leftkowitz, 2007: 68). While Dracula is at pains to hide his bestial nature until he is ready to confess all, Zeus chooses to appear as an animal in many of his seductions and it is his true form as a god that must be hidden to protect his human lovers. This idea is illustrated in the story of the mother of Dionysus, Semele. Her affair with Zeus was discovered by Hera, who appeared to Semele, 'disguised as an old woman and convinced her rival that she should ask her lover to appear in the full magnificence of his divinity. Semele first persuaded Zeus to swear that he would grant whatever she might ask of him, and then revealed her demand. Zeus was unwilling but was obliged to comply, and Semele was burned to a cinder by the splendour of his person and the fire of his lightning flash' (Morford, Lenardon and Sham, 2011: 297).

The ideas animating these myths are complex. On the one hand, they could suggest that animal sexuality is less fearful for the women than seduction by a god. On the other, Zeus could be disguising or softening a *mysterium tremendum* the power of which is made up of sacred and phallic elements. As Dowden argues, 'the transformations and disguises doubtless each have their own origins, but they have in common that Zeus is an unseen force of incalculable power. Only Semele seeks to see that power as it really is and her mortal frame cannot withstand the thunderbolt that *is* Zeus' (Dowden, 2006: 48). The myths would thereby be evocative of spiritual emotions in human sexuality and simultaneously resonate with other means of accessing the divine, such as possession trance. Possession is certainly suggested in Dracula's relationship with Lucy. Shortly after Mina does not see the 'beast' copulating with Lucy, Mina leads her away, while Lucy raves, speaking of an agonizing feeling that pulls her and lures her, as if possessed by the vampire and simultaneously awakening to her own sexuality.

Nonetheless, while certain features of vampirism echo the powers and behaviours of gods, there is also a particular ambiguity in the vampire's gendered identity. Creed (2005) examines this idea in *Bram Stoker's Dracula* with particular reference to an analysis of Freud's conceptualization of 'the uncanny', arguing that he is 'a quintessentially uncanny figure, undermining all rational signification' who embodies 'death, doubling, blood, metamorphosis, intra-uterine phantasies, the feminine and animal worlds, as well as vampiric motifs associated with the compulsion to repeat, and the collapse of boundaries between imaginary and real, male and female, living and dead' (Creed, 2005: 68). This uncanny blurring of boundaries disrupts stable identities essential for the maintenance of patriarchy and the forms of masculinity that embody it (Creed, 2005: 70). Encompassing all desire, he is a 'consummate sexual initiator' whose 'monstrous oral sexuality threatens the very basis of phallic patriarchal civilization' (Creed, 2005: 72). A complex mixture of symbolisms related to maternity and to death makes him a bestial moon monster who can transform into a werewolf. Being fed by blood and sleeping in a coffin filled with earth from the 'mother-land' suggest a return to a womb that is also linked to decay and death 'the marked reversal of its natural function renders it uncanny in the extreme' (Creed, 2005: 80).

Using as an example the scene in which Mina and Dracula's love is 'consummated' Creed's analysis suggests that 'Mina drinks from his bosom as if he were a nursing mother. Some critics argue that the scene is a metaphor for oral sex; it also serves to feminise Dracula, to represent his breasts as erogenous zones, to transform him into a strange maternal figure' (Creed, 2005: 75). However, she also extends her analysis beyond that of Moretti's (2005 [1983]) breast theory to suggest that 'this scene evokes an even more archaic relationship ... that is the embryo *in utero* feeding on it's mother's blood, and hence parallels are drawn between the vampire and the nursing mother and blood-sucking foetus' (Creed, 2005: 90). Moreover, as she drinks from his chest, 'in an unusual reversal, the camera focuses on his pleasure. He is filmed in a way a woman is so often represented, the camera focusing on his face, head thrown back, an expression of ecstasy – of feminine *jouissance* – lighting his features' (Creed, 2005; 91).

This merging of boundaries that Creed identifies can also be explored using Durkheim's ideas about collective consciousness, in this case the telepathic connection between Dracula and Mina. When Mina begins to remember their marriage in the scene in the absinthe bar, her altered state of consciousness not only unlocks memories of a past life, but also awakens her to listen to an 'inner voice' that she feels is always with her, and that 'comforts me when I am alone'. Yet this inner voice is not depicted as an aspect of her own psyche, it is his voice expressing a telepathic connection between them.

Interestingly, although Stoker's book does not have the romantic storyline of Coppola's film, it does suggest a telepathic connection between Dracula and Mina. This is something initiated by Dracula in the scene where Mina is found drinking from his bosom, but instead of a consummation of the more tender emotions of the film, Dracula in the book is punishing Mina for using her intelligence to join in the hunt and targeting her because of her importance to the group as a whole. He goes on to say to Mina:

'You, their best beloved one, are now to me, flesh of my flesh; blood of my blood; kin of my kin; my bountiful wine-press for a while; and shall be later on my companion and my helper. You shall be avenged in turn; for not one of them but shall minister to your needs. But as yet you are to be punished for what you have done. You have aided in thwarting me; now you shall come to my call. When my brain says "Come!" to you, you shall cross land or sea to do my bidding; and to that end this', whereupon he opens a vein in his breast with his nails and forces her to drink his blood. (Stoker, 2003 [1897]: 306–7)

On the one hand, this speech suggests a kind of military strategy – to capture (or perhaps captivate) Mina because of her contributions to the vampire hunting group. Abbott (2007: 29), for example highlights the exploration of modernity in the novel, including the skills Mina utilizes such as memorizing train timetables and collating records. Dracula also plans to deplete the feminine heart of the group and thereby demoralize them. Interestingly, this strategy turns out to be a double-edged sword, as under hypnosis Mina's telepathic connection to Dracula can be used to help the vampire hunters identify his whereabouts while simultaneously the connection may also reveal the vampire hunter's plans (Stoker, 2003 [1897]: 344). There is also a religious or sacrilegious tone to the speech. The idea that Dracula is a kind of god is most prominent in the testimony of the madman Renfield who has succumbed to Dracula's powers and who explains to the group that Dracula had displayed some of his powers to Renfield and had promised him lives of creatures such as rats if Renfield would fall down and worship him (Stoker, 2003 [1897]: 298). Moreover, Van Helsing refers to the incident in which Mina is compelled to drink Dracula's blood as the 'vampire's baptism of blood' enabling a poison to enter her body that can, over time, corrupt her soul (Stoker, 2003 [1897]: 343, 351). In Stoker's (2003 [1897]: 300) account, Dracula's power is key. He not only forces Mina to drink his blood by holding her head against his breast but also exerts mind control over her husband Jonathan, who is in the room but paralysed by Dracula's will and therefore unable to do anything but witness the scene. Even here, however, the idea of a sacrament, albeit an unholy one remains, and the Eucharistic symbolism is reminiscent of both fantasies and images of medieval Christians, especially women.

Bynum in *Fragmentation and Redemption* (2012 [1991]: 80) draws attention to some interesting ways in which Christ's flesh was sometimes seen as female, as lactating and giving birth. Of particular relevance here is the image of Christ feeding people from the wound in his side (which was pierced during the Crucifixion). Christ both bleeds and feeds, squirting blood from his side just as his mother Mary feeds her baby in multiple Christian images (Bynum, 2012 [1991]: 103–8). In one particularly resonant example, Angela of Foligno writes about a vision in which she 'saw him place the heads of her spiritual sons in his wound to drink' (Bynum, 2012 [1991]: 162). This example suggests the possibility that the feminization of Dracula in this scene is not entirely inconsistent with images and ideas evidenced from medieval religious imaginations, although she does not propose that for early Christians the image was associated particularly with sexuality but rather with food, suffering and spiritual cleansing (Bynum, 2012 [1991]: 86–7).

The perils of thrall versus the kinship networks of past lives

In Chapter 4 I explored the first and second seasons of the television series *Buffy the Vampire Slayer* (1997–2003) and how The Master, an evil vampire renowned for his age, was the first vampire in the series to nearly defeat Buffy, using hypnosis to draw her to him and submit to his bite, which temporarily kills her and leaves her traumatized. While vampires such as Angel and Spike do not appear to use hypnosis, there is nonetheless an ambivalence about both of them and while Buffy appears to trust Angel while eschewing Angelus, that trust is never absolute and the possibility that Angel also deceives and enthrals lurks in the subtext of the series.

This storyline, in which Buffy's relationship with Angel appears to conform to a kind of gothic suspicion, is important for feminist readings because it illustrates ways in which women negotiate the attractions of love with needs for autonomy and respect. The theme re-emerges in the fifth season (*Buffy vs Dracula*, 5001), with an encounter with a mesmeric vampire who calls himself Dracula and appears to be a combination of Bela Lugosi's in *Dracula* (1931), The Count in *Sesame Street* (1969–2015), and Gary Oldfield's performance in *Bram Stoker's Dracula* (1992). The episode also contains scenes that suggest a humorous homage to previous vampire films such as when Giles falls prey to the three vampire women in an exuberant scene in which he is clearly ambivalent about escaping their embraces and Riley has to pull him away telling him 'no more chick pit for you'. When Buffy wears a scar to cover her bite marks (a device also used by Lucy in *Dracula* (1931)), Riley exclaims that she is under the thrall of the Dark Prince (5001) and thrall is also referred to in the episode when Dracula is described as having 'hypno eyes', and at the end when Dracula, who has pursued Buffy not because of a past life connection, but because he believes her powers are rooted in darkness, persuades her to drink from him. Far from succumbing to his power, Buffy uses this experience to realize her own dark power and its purpose, declaring that 'the thrall's gone out of our relationship'. The impact of this episode appears to have less to do with the dangers Dracula presents than with his triggering of a desire in Buffy to explore her own powers more fully and acknowledge the idea that they are rooted in darkness. However, there are echoes of the conflicts that she had encountered earlier in the series around the perils of thrall that appear to reflect the tropes in cinema that link hypnosis and mesmerism with evil.

As the dilemmas so well portrayed in *Buffy the Vampire Slayer* suggest, mad love and hypnotic seduction can, indeed, be dangerous, but a deeper examination of the structure of Angel's curse and Angelus's cruelty suggests that it is rooted in his fear of dissolving the self in sexual union, a fear that I have argued is rooted in patriarchy. Nevertheless, the predominance of extreme examples in Western film and television bears further consideration. If understood with Durkheim's theoretical framework as forms of *collective consciousness*, then the energies depicted are certainly volatile, contagious and less subject to the disciplines of the rational mind, but they are also deeply entwined with the emotional energies that ultimately make us social beings and are therefore also at the root of the impulses that form social morality and ethics. Their volatility is channelled and contained within social structures such as taboos and the forms and customs of ritual contexts, for example. Yet we rarely see that balance in film, and I suggest that this is because, although tensions between individual and social consciousness are common to all societies and persons, there appears to be a cult of individualism in the modern West that renders the collective deeply problematic, subject to the most wild of its fantasies, desires and fears simultaneously. In contrast, I have explored in this book many examples observed by anthropologists of societies with more animist perspectives, with modes of personhood that engage with and are at times penetrated by the social world in a wide sense that includes spirits, deities and ancestors through dreams and trance-states. Moreover, these engagements are often associated with helping to preserve balance, social order and practical assistance. Goulet's (2012) ethnography with the Dene Tha peoples of North-western Alberta in Canada, for example, led him to have significant dream and visionary experiences, that were nonetheless very down to earth such as a dream in which the elders appeared and woke him in time to catch a plane when his alarm clock failed and a vision that showed him how to fan a ritual fire properly (Goulet, 2012: 29–30). In another article, Goulet (1994) explores how Dene Tha may develop a relationship with certain animals, often as children. Animals are regarded as a material form of spirit animal beings and a special relationship with an animal can be understood as a bond with a spirit helper as well, giving the person visions and other assistance. Such relationships are subject to a range of prohibitions, lest the animal become offended and the exchange relationship disturbed. One is not supposed to speak about one's animal helpers, or eat their kind, for example (Goulet, 1994: 159–61). While these kinds of relationships, dreams and visions are worthy of extreme respect, they are also a 'fact of life' for the Dene Tha, who similarly regard reincarnation as a normal event (Goulet, 1994: 165). Often occurring in the same family or that of a close friend, reincarnation is one way in which indigenous culture maintains continuity in the face of challenges and privations of Canadian colonialist policies, and there are interesting ways in which an identified reincarnation is socialized into that role over time. However, the initial recognition of a reincarnated individual often occurs through dreams and visions (Goulet, 1994: 161–4).

Such examples offer a different perspective through which to observe potent dreams, shared visions and past life stories in film and television. They challenge us to question rigid distinctions between natural and supernatural worlds and to re-examine the models and tools we use to explore how fictional accounts reflect, explore and interpret selfhood and society. Certainly ghost stories and visionary worlds offer powerful metaphors that nuance accounts of race, gender, sexuality and class, but I contest that they may also encourage viewers to consider important but mysterious aspects of communicative personhood that are also illuminated by ethnographers who lived in different social worlds and listen to accounts of what it means to be a person within them.

Bibliography

Abbott, S. (2007) *Celluloid Vampires: Life after Death in the Modern World.*
    Austin: University of Texas.
Barrett, D. (2006) 'Hypnosis in film and television', *American Journal of Clinical Hypnosis*, vol. 49, no. 1, pp. 13–30.
Bartlett, M. (2020) ' "A power invisible": How somnambulists' blindness reflected debate on the existence of the soul', in L. Child and A. Rosen (eds) *Religion and Sight.* Sheffield: Equinox, pp. 106–21.

Bartlett, M. (2022) 'John Polidori's mesmerizing vampire', in C. Bloom (ed.), *The Palgrave Handbook of Gothic Origins*. Cham, Switzerland: Palgrave Macmillan, pp. 427–44.

Bender, C. (2007) 'American reincarnation: What the many lives of past lives tell us about contemporary spiritual practice', *Journal of the American Academy of Religion*, vol. 75, no. 3, pp. 589–614.

Berenstein, R. J. (1996) *Attack of the Leading Ladies: Gender, Sexuality, and Spectatorship in Classic Horror Cinema*. New York: Columbia University Press.

Bevan, G. (2014) 'Lesbian vampires and the Medusa'. Dissertation submitted for the award of MA in Religious Studies, Cardiff University.

Botting, F. (1996) *Gothic*. London: Routledge.

Botting, F. (2008) *Gothic Romanced: Consumption, Gender and Technology in Contemporary Fictions*. London: Routledge.

Boyle, K. (2002) '"Not all angels are innocent" – violence, sexuality, and the teen psychodyke', in H. Karriker (ed.), *Film Studies: Women in Contemporary Cinema*. New York: Peter Lang, pp. 35–49.

Burns, B. (1995) '*Dracula's Daughter*: Cinema, hypnosis, and the erotics of lesbianism', in K. Jay (ed.) *Lesbian Erotics*. New York: New York University Press, pp. 196–211.

Bynum, C. W. (2012 [1991]) *Fragmentation and Redemption: Essays on Gender and the Human Body in Medieval Religion*. New York: Zone Books.

Child, L. (2007) *Tantric Buddhism and Altered States of Consciousness: Durkheim, Emotional Energy and Visions of the Consort*. Aldershot: Ashgate.

Child, L. (2013) '*Elementary Forms* versus psychology in contemporary cinema', in S. L. Hausner (ed.) *Durkheim in Dialogue: A Centenary Celebration of The Elementary Forms of Religious Life*. New York: Berghahn, pp. 86–105.

Child, L. (2020) 'Sensing reelism: Portals to multiple realities and relationships in world, indigenous, and documentary cinema', in L. Child and A. Rosen (eds), *Religion and Sight*. Sheffield: Equinox, pp. 69–86.

Creed, B. (1993) *The Monstrous Feminine: Film, Feminism, Psychoanalysis*. London: Routledge.

Creed, B. (2005) *Phallic Panic: Film, Horror and the Primal Uncanny*. Melbourne: Melbourne University Press.

Clements, S. (2011) *The Vampire Defanged: How the Embodiment of Evil became a Romantic Hero*. Grand Rapids, MI: Brazos Press.

Coppola, F., and Hart, J. V. (1992) Bram Stoker's Dracula: *The Film and the Legend*. New York: Newmarket Press.

Dear, B. (2014) 'All in the mind: Fin de Siècle psychological vampire fiction, powers of mind control and mesmerism', in S. A. Dauber (ed.) *Monsters in Society: An Interdisciplinary Perspective*. Oxford: Interdisciplinary Press, pp. 98–107.

Dowden, K. (2006) *Zeus*. London: Routledge.

Durkheim, E. (1968 [1897]) *Incest: The Nature and Origins of the Taboo* (translated with an introduction by E. Sagarin). New York: Lyle Stuart.

Durkheim, E. (1995 [1912]) *The Elementary Forms of Religious Life* (translated with an introduction by Karen E. Fields). New York: Free Press.

Ellenberger, H. (1981 [1970]) *The Discovery of the Unconscious: The History and Evolution of Dynamic Psychiatry*. New York: Basic Books.

Fields, K. E. (2013) 'The notion of soul and *science positive*: A retrieval of Durkheim's method', in S. L. Hausner (ed.) *Durkheim in Dialogue: A Centenary Celebration of The Elementary Forms of Religious Life*. New York: Berghahn, pp. 19–44.

Fox, A., Grant, B. K., and Radner, H. (eds) *New Zealand Cinema: Interpreting the Past*. Bristol: Intellect.

Freeland, C. A (2000) *The Naked and the Undead: Evil and the Appeal of Horror*. Colorado: Westview Press.

Fuss, D. (1991) 'Introduction', in D. Fuss (ed.), *Inside/Out: Lesbian Theories, Gay Theories*. New York: Routledge.

Gabbard, G. O., and Gabbard, K. (1999) *Psychiatry and the Cinema* (2nd edn). Washington, DC: American Psychiatric Press.

Gelder, K. (1994) *Reading the Vampire*. London: Routledge.

Graham, P. (2013 [2011]) *Anne Perry and the Murder of the Century*. New York: Skyhorse.

Goulet, J. (1994) 'Reincarnation as a fact of life among contemporary Dene Tha', in A. Mills and R. Slobodin (eds), *Amerindian Rebirth: Reincarnation Belief among North American Indians and Inuit*. Toronto: University of Toronto Press, pp. 156–76.

Goulet, J. (2012) 'Dreams and visions in other lifeworlds', in D. E. Young and J. Goulet (eds) *Being Changed by Cross-Cultural Encounters: The Anthropology of Extraordinary Experience*. Toronto: University of Toronto Press, pp. 16–38.

Hallab, M. Y. (2009) *Vampire God: The Allure of the Undead in Western Culture*. Albany: State University of New York Press.

Hart, L. (1994) *Fatal Women: Lesbian sexuality and the Mark of Aggression*. London: Routledge.

Heller-Nicholas, A. (2017) 'Seductive kindness: Power, space and "lesbian" vampires', in D. Baker, S. Green and A. Stasiewicz-Bieńkowska (eds), *Hospitality, Rape and Consent in Vampire Popular Culture*. Cham, Switzerland: Palgrave Macmillan, pp. 201–18.

Karriker, A. H. (ed.) (2002) *Film Studies: Women in Contemporary Cinema*. New York: Peter Lang.

Krimmer, E., and Raval, S. (2002) ' "Digging the undead": Death and desire in *Buffy*', in R. V. Wilcox (ed.), *Fighting the Forces: What's at Stake in Buffy the Vampire Slayer*. Lanham, MD: Rowman and Littlefield, pp. 153–64.

Lacan, J. (1975) *On Feminine Sexuality: The Limits of Love and Knowledge, 1972–1973* (ed. J. A. Miller and trans. B. Fink). New York: Norton.

Leftkowitz, M. R. (2007 [1986]) *Women in Greek Myth*. London: Duckworth.

Lindholm, C. (1992) 'Charisma, crowd psychology, and altered states of consciousness', *Culture, Medicine and Psychiatry*, vol. 16, no. 3, pp. 287–310.

Meintel, D. (2014) 'Spirits in the city: Examples from Montreal', in J. Hunter and D. Luke (eds), *Talking with the Spirits: Ethnographies from between the Worlds*. Brisbane: David Grail, pp. 73–97.

Mellor, P. A. (2002) 'Sacred love: Religion, marriage and *l'amour fou*', in A. Thacher (ed.), *Celebrating Christian Marriage: New Hopes, New Agendas*. London: T & T Clark, pp. 119–41.

Mills, A., and Slobodin, R. (eds) (1994) *Amerindian Rebirth: Reincarnation Belief among North American Indians and Inuit*. Toronto: University of Toronto Press.

Moretti, F. (2005 [1983]) *Signs Taken for Wonders: On the Sociology of Literary Forms*. London: Verso.

Morford, M. P. O., Lenardon, R. J. and Sham, M. (2011) *Classical Mythology* (International 9th edn). Oxford: Oxford University Press.

Mulvey, L. (1999 [1975]) 'Visual pleasure and narrative cinema', in S. Thornham (ed.), *Feminist Film Theory: A Reader*. Edinburgh: Edinburgh University Press, pp. 58–69.

Obeyesekere, G. (2002) *Imagining Karma: Ethical Transformation in Amerindian, Buddhist, and Greek Rebirth*. Berkeley: University of California Press.

Plate, S. B. (ed.) (2003) *Representing Religion in World Cinema: Filmmaking, Mythmaking, Culture Making*. New York: Palgrave Macmillan.

Polidori, J. W. (1998 [1819]) 'The Vampyre', in R. Morrison and C. Baldick (eds), *The Vampyre and Other Tales of the Macabre*. Oxford: Oxford University Press, pp. 1–24.

Rueschmann, E. (2000) *Sisters on Screen: Siblings in Contemporary Cinema*. Philadelphia, PA: Temple University Press.

Saler, B. (1977) 'Supernatural as a western category', *Ethos*, vol. 5, no. 1, pp. 31–53.

Schüttpelz, E. (2015) 'Trance mediums and new media: The heritage of a European term', in H. Behrend, A. Dreschke and M. Zillinger (eds), *Trance Mediums and New Media: Spirit Possession in the Age of Technical Reproduction*. New York: Fordham University Press, pp. 56–76.

Stoker, B. (2003 [1897]) *Dracula*. London: Penguin.

Thornley, D. (2002) 'Executing the commoners: Examining class in *Heavenly Creatures*', in H. Karriker (ed.), *Film Studies: Women in Contemporary Cinema*. New York: Peter Lang, pp. 51–68.

Verhoeven, D. (1993) 'Biting the hand that breeds: The trials of Tracey Wigginton', in H. Birch (ed.), *Moving Targets: Women, Murder and Representation*. London: Virago Press, pp. 95–126.

Waterhouse, H. (1999) 'Reincarnation belief in Britain: New age orientation or mainstream option?', *Journal of Contemporary Religion*, vol. 14, no. 2, pp. 97–109.

Weinstock, J. (2012) *The Vampire Film: Undead Cinema*. London: Wallflower.

Williams, L. (1984) 'When the woman looks', in M. A. Doane, P. Mellencamp and L. Williams (eds), *Re-Vision: Essays in Feminist Film Criticism*. Los Angeles, CA: American Film Institute, pp. 83–99.

Wilson, D. G. (2013) *Redefining Shamanisms: Spiritualist Mediums and other Traditional Shamans as Apprenticeship Outcomes*. London: Bloomsbury.

Wilson, J. (2003) 'Pathologies of violence: Religion and postcolonial identity in New Zealand cinema', in S. B. Plate (ed.) (2003) *Representing Religion in World Cinema: Filmmaking, Mythmaking, Culture Making*. New York: Palgrave Macmillan, pp. 197–217.

Winter, A. (1998) *Mesmerized: Powers of Mind in Victorian Britain*. Chicago: University of Chicago Press.

Wilts, A. (2009) 'Evil, skanky and kinda gay: Lesbian images and issues', in L Y. Edwards, E. L. Rambo and J. B. South (eds), *Buffy Goes Dark: Essays on the Final Two Seasons of Buffy the Vampire Slayer on Television*. Jefferson, NC: McFarland, pp. 41–56.

Filmography

Bram Stoker's Dracula (1992) Directed by Francis Ford Coppola: Columbia Pictures.

Buffy the Vampire Slayer (1997–2003) Created by Joss Whedon: Mutant Enemy Productions and 20th Century Fox Television. Seasons 1–5, Warner Bro, Seasons 6 and 7, United Paramount Network: 10 March.

Dracula (1931) Directed by Tod Browning: Universal Pictures.

Dracula's Daughter (1936) Directed by Lambert Hillyer: Universal Pictures.

Dreamkeeper (2003) Directed by Steve Barron: Hallmark Entertainment.

Heavenly Creatures (1994) Directed by Peter Jackson: Miramax Films.

The Mummy (1932) Directed by Karl Freund: Universal Pictures.

Sesame Street (1969–2015) Created by Joan Ganz Cooney, Lloyd Morrissett and Jim Henson: PBS 10 November.

7

Conclusion

In this book I have suggested that although the predominant methods of scholarly film analysis are psychoanalytic theories derived from Freud, alternative perspectives have much to offer. In particular, the anthropology of religion has fresh perspectives on dreams, ghosts and spirits, because many of the people who inform anthropologists about their worlds engage with these phenomena and beings in ways that break the bounds of psychological understandings and suggest, instead, expanded social worlds that include deities, spirits, ghosts, animals and personified aspects of the natural environment.

Conceptions of personhood are key here, because although the group of scholars who contribute to the broad category contemporary animism is diverse and wide-ranging in the societies that they study and the perspectives they employ, they nonetheless have in common a desire to investigate personhood as a socially constructed category and thereby uncover a myriad of ways that different societies imagine and use it in their day-to-day and religious ways of relating to persons in their social worlds (Harvey, 2013a). Their findings suggest that personhood is often more complex and porous than tends to be assumed in scholarship grounded in theories of Freudian interiority. Key examples are when some part of a person (often translated as soul) can leave the body during sleep and communicate with human, spirit or animal persons or, when the inverse happens and individuals are visited by others in their dreams. Similarly, shamanistic or possession trances enable communication with deities and spirits so that communities can engage with spirits in ways often deemed as healing. What is perhaps even more startling is that an examination of popular Western film and television suggests that these modes of personhood are not lost in the wake of modernity, but rather that, multiple media narratives continue to explore them with relish.

In *Twin Peaks*, for example, Waldo the Bird, The Log Lady's Log and to some extent the woods are all given personhood, and Agent Cooper breaks the bounds of typical film noir storylines by including magic, visions and telepathic dreaming as key investigative tools. Vampire programs such as *Buffy the Vampire Slayer* explore the ethical dimensions of the soul and suggest that this is displaced in vampires in a form of demonic possession. Romantic ghost films explore other aspects of spirit or soul as an aspect of persons that can survive death and reaffirm connections with loved ones, and this idea helps to shape the revisions and re-imaginings of the relationship between Dracula and Mina in *Bram Stoker's Dracula*, a film that infuses vampirism with rage against Christianity and explores past life romantic connections. Moreover, vampire and other horror films of the 1920s and 1930s appear to explore a kind of *collective consciousness* between their heroines and fiends, highlighting both shared blood and trance as ways of breaking the boundaries of the interiorized individual.

Nonetheless, there are important differences between the manifestations in these films and accounts collected by anthropologists from indigenous persons. Firstly, it must be borne in mind that there are numerous differences between First Nations, even when they are found in geographical proximity. Secondly, there is no evidence that any of the media creation teams of the films and television shows discussed used indigenous consultation or anthropological research. A key example, *Twin Peaks*, is set in the Pacific Northwest of America. Although there is one indigenous character, Hawk, who talks of his belief that there are many souls, indigenous experts were not consulted in the making of the programme. Moreover, the character of BOB, a personification of evil, fits poorly into an animist paradigm and I have therefore used ideas from Jung, including collective consciousness and the shadow, to examine BOB instead. Secondly, the most positive representations of ghosts and spirits tend to be found in the ghostly romance and focus on spirit communications between the dead and their loved ones. This perhaps reflects the cultural and religious landscapes that generate Hollywood movies in which Spiritualists and ghost stories are more familiar. Family spirits are certainly a part of many spirit traditions globally, but there are also many traditions that include beings that have wider significance such as deities, and communication with these beings through possession trance often helps communities. Such spirits are much less in evidence in Western film and television and while part of the reason for this may be a lack of awareness, dynamics of racism and colonialism also contribute to the shaping of depictions of Africa and its diaspora, so that, for example, the term 'Vodou' may be mentioned but the actual tradition is barely engaged with and instead, tropes familiar to horror and witchcraft films abound.

There are also more subtle phenomena that can also be attributed to the power dynamics of twentieth and twenty-first-century political and social frameworks, including colonialism, late capitalism and patriarchy. One useful way to think through these is to consider the question of boundaries. For example, there are media characters depicted who experience love relationships that transcend boundaries through participation in mutual past lives, telepathy or visions, but these depictions tend to portray them in terms of excess, monstrosity and criminality, whereas past lives in indigenous North America are more likely to be associated with the affirmation of kinship networks and tradition and in South Asia with ethical questions. Nonetheless, these examples do not suggest the erasure of either animism or collective consciousness in modern life, but rather that, while still present, they are a source of fear and suspicion in societies that define themselves through Western individualism. Drawing from Durkheim's (1995 [1912]) insights, tensions between the individual and social modes of being and consciousness can be found in both indigenous societies and those of Europe and America, but those tensions express themselves differently in different cultures. Moreover, extending beyond Durkheim's own work, this book suggests that although animism and other social modes of being have not been erased by the power dynamics inherent in late capitalist societies, such dynamics have contributed to an exaggerated elevation of the individual Self and a corresponding anxiety concerning animist storylines that threaten both the Self's boundaries and by extension the specific structures that hold in place patriarchy, colonial powers and late capitalism.

This finding is important because scholars such as Tylor (2010 [1871]) and Freud (2001 [1919]) were influenced by the power structures of their place and time, and in many ways accepted and propagated, rather than investigated, erroneous evolutionary assumptions about society and religion that were prevalent in Europe in the late nineteenth and early twentieth centuries. Both of them assumed, firstly, that indigenous societies were relics that could be studied to make assertions about Western modernity's primitive past, and secondly, that they would evolve in ways that exactly resembled the structures of that modernity, and that this evolution was a positive progress. Moreover, animism, and the ideas and ways of relating connected to it, including spirits, souls and communicative dreaming, were examples of erroneous thinking that were dying out in Europe and that its vestiges were relics of a primitive past that would be superseded completely by forms of interiorized individualism that they associated with science and rational modernity.

Writing over one hundred years later, I contend that they were wrong on both counts. Anthropologists have documented change in indigenous societies, including engagements with new technologies. Nonetheless, far from simply conforming to the ways of thinking that scholars such as Tylor understood as progress, indigenous peoples have found their own ways of moving forward that challenge evolutionary paradigms and open, rather than close, doors to alternative ways of relating to the world and building futures. Scholars such as Watts (2013: 21) are reasserting indigenous histories emphasizing their importance in recognizing common intersections of, and interactions between, animals, the spirit world, and mineral and plant worlds in a cosmological system that includes, but de-centres, human beings. Such projects offer contemporary creative explorations of the 'pre-colonial mind' (Watts, 2013: 22). Indigenous peoples continue to critique the present and imagine futures with creative endeavours inspired by their own cultures (Dillon, 2012; Estrada, 2014; Garuba, 2003) and I have written about indigenous film elsewhere (Child, 2015, 2020). Here, however, the focus has been on thinking and relating with roots in social dimensions of being that are also present in popular film and television, mediums which at first glance seem to be the epitome of the modern Western project. I have explored multiple examples that offer complex, permeable and relational forms of personhood and in that sense this work is aligned with Haraway (2016: 30) who cogently argues that Modernity neither accurately describes the world we live in nor offers visions of the future that are good to think with.

This is not to deny the influence of modernity on genres such as the gothic, but to emphasize the ways in which its products are also the result of creative engagements with, and sometimes challenges to, conceptions of personhood embedded into the ages in which they appeared. In suggesting this I am positing that something like Garuba's (2003: 265) 'animist unconscious, which operates through a process that involves what I describe as a continual re-enchantment of the world'. In doing so, it is important to note that Garuba does not use psychoanalytic works to define unconscious and that he is speaking about the subtle ways in which an animist orientation to the world influences literature in West Africa. His work has been important to a number of scholars of indigenous literatures globally (Harvey, 2013b) and the particular characteristics of each will influence the ways an animist unconscious might operate, but here I use the idea to suggest counter forces in the narratives of popular film and television, creative processes that pull in different directions to, for example, the 'patriarchal unconscious' that Mulvey (1999 [1975]: 58) describes. Rather than dismissing them as a 'suspension of disbelief' or as relics of a bygone age, I want to assert that they can tell us much more about the depth and complexity of the age in which we live and the very real possibilities for our collective futures.

Bibliography

Child, L. (2015) 'Māori arts as film art: An analysis of ritual and myth in *Whale Rider, Once Were Warriors,* and *Te Rua*', *Diskus: The Journal of the British Association for the Study of Religions,* vol. 17, no. 3, pp. 1–17.

Child, L. (2020) 'Sensing Reelism: Portals to multiple realities and relationships in world, indigenous and documentary cinema', in L. Child and A. Rosen (eds), *Religion and Sight.* Sheffield: Equinox, pp. 69–86.

Dillon, G. L. (2012) *Walking the Clouds: An Anthology of Indigenous Science Fiction.* Yucson: University of Arizona Press.

Durkheim, E. (1995 [1912]) *The Elementary Forms of Religious Life* (trans. Karen E. Fields). New York: Free Press.

Estrada, G. (2014) 'Navajo sci-fi film: Matriarchal visual sovereignty in Nanobah Becker's *The 6th World*', *Journal of the American Academy of Religion,* vol. 82, no. 2, pp. 521–30.

Freud, S. (2001 [1919]) 'The Uncanny', in J. Strachey (trans.), *The Standard Edition of the Complete Works of Sigmund Freud,* vol. 17 (1917–19). London: Vintage, pp. 217–56.

Garuba, H. (2003) 'Explorations in Animist materialism: Notes on reading/writing African literature, culture, and society', *Public Culture,* vol. 15, no. 2, pp. 261–85.

Haraway, D. J. (2016) *Staying with the Trouble: Making Kin in the Chthulucene.* Durham, NC: Duke University Press.

Harvey, G. (ed.) (2013a) *The Handbook of Contemporary Animism.* Durham, NC: Acumen.

Harvey, G. (2013b) 'Animist realism in indigenous novels and other literature', in G. Harvey (ed.), *The Handbook of Contemporary Animism.* Durham, NC: Acumen, pp. 454–67.

Modleski, T. (2016 [1988]) *The Women Who Knew Too Much: Hitchcock and Feminist Theory* (3rd edn). New York: Routledge.

Mulvey, L. (1999 [1975]) 'Visual pleasure and narrative cinema', in S. Thornham (ed.), *Feminist Film Theory: A Reader.* Edinburgh: Edinburgh University Press, 58–9.

Tylor, E. B. (2010 [1871]) *Primitive Culture: Researches into the Development of Mythology, Philosophy, Art and Custom.* Vols. 1 and 2. Cambridge & London: Cambridge University Press.

Watts, V. (2013) 'Indigenous place-thought and agency amongst humans and non-humans (First Woman and Sky Woman go on a European world tour!)', *Decolonization: Indigeneity, Education & Society,* vol. 2, no. 1, pp. 20–34.

Index